T0330231

The New Consumer Online

The New Consumer Online

A Sociology of Taste, Audience, and Publics

Edward F. McQuarrie

Professor of Marketing, Santa Clara University, in California's Silicon Valley, USA

Edward Elgar
PUBLISHING

Cheltenham, UK • Northampton, MA, USA

© Edward F. McQuarrie 2015

All rights reserved. No part of this publication may be reproduced, stored in a retrieval system or transmitted in any form or by any means, electronic, mechanical or photocopying, recording, or otherwise without the prior permission of the publisher.

Published by
Edward Elgar Publishing Limited
The Lypiatts
15 Lansdown Road
Cheltenham
Glos GL50 2JA
UK

Edward Elgar Publishing, Inc.
William Pratt House
9 Dewey Court
Northampton
Massachusetts 01060
USA

A catalogue record for this book
is available from the British Library

Library of Congress Control Number: 2015950506

This book is available electronically in the **Elgar**online
Business subject collection
DOI 10.4337/9781784716004

ISBN 978 1 78471 599 1 (cased)
ISBN 978 1 78471 600 4 (eBook)

Typeset by Servis Filmsetting Ltd, Stockport, Cheshire
Printed and bound in Great Britain by TJ International Ltd, Padstow

Contents

Figures

Tables

Boxes

Acknowledgments

Each essay began life as a research project, aimed at journal publication, as expected of tenure-track academics in the social sciences. Each of those research projects was conceived and conducted jointly with long-time colleagues, either Barbara J. Phillips, or Shelby McIntyre and Ravi Shanmugam, as noted on the title page for each essay. Placing their names on these title pages acknowledges my debt to them. None of these essays started with me alone. But by using the "with" formula to describe authorship, I absolve my colleagues of such howlers, pretention, or ignorance as may remain. They had no say over the versions of our ideas presented here, and cannot be blamed for whatever has gone awry.

I'd also like to acknowledge my editor at Edward Elgar Publishing, Alan Sturmer, for taking a chance on me. And finally, I'd like to acknowledge Santa Clara University for its generous retirement policies, which helped in making the career transition from journal publishing to book authorship. Santa Clara was a wonderful place to have spent 30 years in academia.

Introduction

Consumers do new things online. But this novelty has been obscured. This book applies a sociological lens, to lift the curtain and shine a light on the exercise of taste, the consequence of audience, and the pleasures of a public.

It is hard to overstate the distaste that scholars feel toward claims that something is new. Experience shows such claims to be either hyped, or ignorant of history, both of which are distasteful to people whose lives center on knowledge. In the rare case where a claim of newness seems credible, it creates even more difficulties, as it suggests that what the scholar thought was settled knowledge may no longer be so. A truly new thing would call into question existing theories and threaten to obsolesce a conceptual toolkit that the scholar had spent decades refining. Oscillation and development are fine, but a claim that something is new will be fiercely resisted.

Nonetheless, the Web has produced new forms of social being, which this book explores. I focus on new forms of consumer behavior online, but define this behavior more narrowly than some colleagues. I mean actions toward products and services that are bought and sold, as viewed from the perspective of the buyer, rather than that of the seller, as in marketing. This may not sound very restrictive—uncounted items across many life domains are bought and sold here in Late Capitalist America—but it is. My more imperialistic colleagues are wont to expand consuming to every part of life. In the expanded definition I eschew, the company of relatives would be consumed at family holidays, the flag would be consumed in patriotic ceremonies, ideas of God would be consumed at church, yada yada.

My restrictive definition excludes from this book Facebook, Twitter, Instagram and all similar social media sites. On Facebook people socialize, much more than consume. Yes, a great deal of selling, and more of it all the time, occurs on Facebook, and the challenge of promoting brands by means of social media is one of the great new challenges in marketing; but this is a book about consuming, not friendship, and about buyers, not sellers. If you picked it up to learn about selling to the unsuspecting, as they mingle online, put it down.

Conversely, Yelp has to be part of the book. Yelp is a site where ordinary consumers write reviews of goods and services that other consumers can buy or patronize. Yes, writing and reading reviews is a form of social interaction, but the social experience revolves around items that can be purchased. That puts online reviews within my declared sphere.

Blogs are a more complicated case. Like Facebook and Yelp, blogging is new. But whole categories of blogs lie outside my sphere. For instance, a vibrant category, present from the beginning, consists of political blogs. Several of these have become a staple of my media usage. And just there I could almost as readily have spoken of my media consumption without doing too much violence to the verb consume. After all, I do purchase a subscription to the *Wall Street Journal*, the *New York Times*, and sundry other publications. But I am reluctant to subsume leisure reading, voting or citizenship under consuming. When it comes to political blogs, I think that media usage remains the better term, and that communication, which is a separate discipline, has scholars better placed than me to discuss political blogs, reality television, and sundry other new things I ignore (see Turner 2010 for an entry to this literature).

Other kinds of blogs do fit, as when a blogger writes about some category of good for sale. A study of fashion blogs was the genesis of this book (McQuarrie et al. 2013), and the first essay delves into this new consumer behavior. Fashion, insofar as it involves tastes, is central to any account of modern consumers, as Campbell (1987) knew.

Pinterest provides a liminal case. This site, described as an online scrapbook, could have been devoted to pictures of pets, babies, and other personal mementos, meant to be shared with family and friends, as happens on Instagram. Instead, my colleagues and I found that many pinboards displayed commercial goods rather than personal photos, placing Pinterest within my sphere (Phillips et al. 2014). But Instagram, by this same metric, falls outside it.

People do many new things online. But my ambit is restricted to some blogs, Yelp reviews, and Pinterest boards. I must leave Facebook, Instagram, Twitter, Tumblr, Youtube and the rest to other scholars better placed.

I trust a few of you stumbled over that loaded term, Late Capitalist America. I'm not a Marxist (as far as I know), and don't subscribe to the worldview seen in a Jameson (1991). But this book has to be historically aware. To claim "new" is to make a historical assertion. Why locate these new consumer actions in a historical epoch termed Late Capitalist America?

By Late Capitalist I mean an era in which the market has perfused nearly all aspects of life. Late Capitalist means a period when an author has to take space, up front in his book, to assert that not everything is consuming;

an era where economists claim with a straight face that economic theory can explain any element of human behavior (Levitt and Dubner 2011). So much of contemporary life in America does revolve around the purchase of goods for sale. Only a few centuries ago, most people spent most of their day not spending money or consuming purchased goods. People used to grow their own food, sew their own clothes, and make their own images. Now these activities are so vanishingly rare as to have cultish aspects when performed. Most of what we need for everyday life, and much else that we don't need but happen to want, we obtain in the market. The late in Late Capitalist means a society where the penetration of the market, into every corner of life, is far along (Sandel 2012).

Although the market had begun to penetrate more and more elements of daily life in the West even by centuries ago (McCloskey 2010; Mokyr 2009; Muller 2007), in Late Capitalism, necessities account for less and less of what we buy. Four hundred years ago, residents of Amsterdam were already buying most of their food and clothing in a market, but mostly what they purchased were necessities like food and clothing. There wasn't yet the discretionary income, or distance from necessity, so characteristic of a wealthy developed nation like the USA in 2015. Campbell (1987) gives a deeply illuminating account of the early years of this transition, on which I will draw, and the phrase "distance from necessity" is Bourdieu's (1984), whom I'll discuss at length.

The new in online consumer behavior is newness piled on newness; because the perfusion of the market into daily life, and the spread of consuming beyond necessities, is a new development in human history, on which online behavior is a still more recent overlay. To take the perspective of Big History, the Agricultural Revolution was exactly that: the defining event in human history for 10 000 years (Morris 2010). The Industrial or Scientific or Technological Revolution (which is the better descriptor remains heavily contested) was every bit as revolutionary as the advent of agriculture (Landes 1999; Shapin 1996), and transformed the daily life of peasants as much as farming had transformed the life ways of hunter gatherers (Morris 2010). But the I/S/T Revolution, and the associated perfusion of the market—it might even be called the Capitalist Revolution—is still very recent (McCloskey 2010). The conversion of daily life into market activity is still new. The opportunity to go online, which is difficult to conceive, absent a substrate of market-based wealth with its incestuous relationship to technological development (Mokyr 2009), is a newness laid on top of that newness.

Consumer being is new, gathering steam only a century or two ago, and consumer being online is very new, emerging in the last decade. The new actions to be discussed are new forms of consuming, departures from what occurred during the post-World War II American economy. The benchmark for new, then, will be the life ways and institutions that were established from the 1950s through about 1995 in the USA, even though these old life ways and institutions were themselves new, or at least late, when viewed within the history of modernity in the West.

Finally, as the phrase Late Capitalist America suggests, I will offer a sociological view of consumers online. The label sociological might sound like a neutral descriptor—sociology is most commonly grouped with either psychology or economics or both, within a broader grouping called the social sciences—but, among scholars who write about the consumer, to adopt a sociological stance is to make a radical departure. Most consumer researchers are either psychologists or economists by training. For instance, I have a social psychology PhD, and most of my research has a psychological cast. I spent my scholarly career in a business school where economic perspectives dominated. Journals where I published or reviewed have titles like the *Journal of Consumer Psychology*, the *Journal of Consumer Research*, the *Journal of Economic Psychology*, or *Psychology and Marketing*. Neither my past work, nor most of what is published in these journals, has much to do with sociology.[1]

There currently exists no *Journal of Consumer Sociology*, and I see little prospect of one any time soon. The widening beyond psychology that did occur within consumer research in the 1980s and 1990s can be seen in new titles such as the *Journal of Consumer Culture* or *Consumption, Markets and Culture*: it was an opening toward anthropology and ethnography, not sociology. Unlike sociology, consumer ethnography, as seen in work by Eric Arnould, Rob Kozinets, John Sherry, and Melanie Wallendorf, is thriving, although still dwarfed by consumer psychology.

What distinguishes a sociological perspective on consumers from a psychological or economic stance in the first instance, and an anthropological view in the second? Today, within consumer research, sociology is so eclipsed, so obscure, so remote, as to require this clarification.

To do psychology is to explain things by properties of individual human beings. Individual agents are primary and all else is secondary. These individual psyches may be more governed by situational factors than they suspect (Kahneman 2011), but it is individual behavior that is explained by situational factors. In the consumer sphere, economic theory merges seamlessly with psychological perspectives: individual decision-makers seek to maximize utility, and the actions of autochthonous buyers and sellers make up market activity.

At the neuropsychological extreme, the focus is individuals conceived as organisms, which is to say, on events in brains and bodies. At the other, social psychological extreme, a second individual enters the picture, so that the behavioral equation contains two variables, me and you, individual and social object. In social psychology, what people do is a joint function of the properties of the individual and the properties of the social object, which may be another person, or an inanimate object such as a brand. Social psychology is about as social as most consumer research gets, and this perspective dominates the study of consumers. That makes it important to grasp the gap that separates social psychology from sociology proper.

In psychology, there is always me, and maybe you, but never us. We only become visible when a sociological or anthropological lens is applied. Sociology studies collectivity, rather than individual actions or dyadic interactions. A further clarification: biologists often find it useful to analyze phenomena at the level of the population rather than the organism. But population exists only as an analytic device; a population is nothing but the individual organisms of which it is composed. By contrast, in sociology collectives are real and have a reality apart from the individuals that participate. For instance, an organization, such as a corporation, consists of more than the employees who work for it. Its reality is more than an aggregate of the behavior of these employees. To get the reality of collectivity accepted, and to mark out a space for its study, was the foundational struggle in sociology (Nisbet 1966). I take the separately subsisting reality of collectivity to be the central sociological idea, and the one most alien to a scholar trained in psychology.

As noted, anthropology also admits of supra-individual entities, but here the preferred term is culture, and the tacit context that of an intact culture in isolation, as in the hunter-gatherer tribes and small farming villages which provided fodder for the pioneers of anthropology. The "culture of the tribe" sums up the anthropological lens on human affairs. Sociology, by contrast, begins with the death of the tribal community and the destruction of intact cultures, as occurs in any urban, mass society, and as executed most thoroughly in Late Capitalist society. Anthropology can be and has been applied to modern mass societies, but in my view it is a force fit. One can call a habit a ritual, and a group a tribe, but naming them thus does not make them so (Cova and Cova 2002; McCracken 1986).

Sociology didn't make much sense, perhaps could not even exist, prior to the 19th century, in the developed and cosmopolitan West, after the alienation consequent to a market economy had gone farther than ever before. Mass and stranger are to sociology what tribe and identity are to anthropology. Sociology was made possible, and became necessary, following the Industrial/Scientific/Technological/Capitalist Revolutions that were at full bore after about 1820. Sociology is best placed to describe what is new in consuming online, because sociology is so bound up with the earlier newness of the I/S/T/C Revolutions that constructed modernity.

A sociology of consumers online will examine new ways of being a consumer, itself a new way of being that flowered over the last century or two, as the I/S/T/C Revolutions shaped life in the West, and in America most of all. Some have been tempted to apply a cyclic interpretation to the advent of the Web, and approach online consuming as a return or reversion to older tribal forms of being. This anthropological take, which uses the language of community and authenticity, did shape initial narratives about what was happening online (Muniz and O'Guinn 2001; Rheingold 2000; Schau et al. 2009). I will argue against this tendency to celebrate community online. The new online world is not about recapturing community and reforming into tribes. Those are category errors in this context. Something new occurs instead.

Under a sociological lens, the new possibilities created by the Web consist of new opportunities to relate to masses of strangers, new connections among people not joined by community, and new routes along which collective phenomena, such as taste, develop. This isn't a book about blogs or Yelp or Pinterest, so much as a reflection on sociological ideas central to consuming. These ideas will sometimes be accepted, and used to illuminate online behavior; and sometimes challenged and extended, by confronting the new reality of consuming online. As a work of scholarship, the focus is more on these ideas, some very difficult, and less on descriptive facts about blogs, Yelp or Pinterest.

Those impatient may now proceed to the Prelude and Essay One. The remainder of this Introduction consists of what Pinker (2014) disparages as meta-discourse, or writing about writing. It addresses readers who prefer to get more context, before wading into a book.

AUDIENCE

I target young scholars and PhD students whose research direction is not frozen in place. Probably these persons have or will earn a PhD in one of the social sciences. The goal of the book is to unfreeze you from the individualistic perspective that dominated your graduate training, and open your eyes toward a sociological take on consumers and what they do online.

A NOTE ON STYLE AND APPROACH

This book does not summarize a lifetime of research; I came to study consumers online late in my career. Nor does it advance a grand theory of consumer behavior, or try to summarize the state of the art in a subdiscipline, as in a handbook. And neither does it offer a sampling of current work by like-minded colleagues on the topics in the title. Most scholarly books fit one of these models, but my effort is closer in spirit to Billig (2013), Campbell (1987), Gronow (1997), Lanham (2006a) or Turner (2010). I offer explorations intended to advance a point of view, a sociological perspective on what consumers do online.

Mea culpa: it is arrogant to think that anyone cares about a contest that pits sociology against economic, psychological and anthropological perspectives. I couldn't pursue this contest in a scholarly journal. Sociologists don't care what economists think, and the feeling is mutual. Academics stay in their silo, taking for granted that other disciplines are remote and inapt. It is also arrogant to assume that I know enough, about disciplines in which I was not trained, to identify shortcomings in the economic explanation for online reviews, or the ethnographic account of blogging. The risk: that you only wander through a field of straw men set ablaze. And it is arrogant to suppose that there is anything new online not explained by existing theory. I shall be astonished if some reviewer of the book, unimpressed, does not crack wise: "what is new in the book is not sound, and what is sound in this book is not new."[2]

Yet more arrogance: I position sociology as the nemesis of economics and of the individualistic psychology on which it rests. I mean exactly Nemesis, in the usage of Greek myth; this word is not some synonym for opponent, plucked off the thesaurus page. A nemesis is a corrective, brought into being by hubris and over-reaching, an inevitable snapback that restores order. The operation of nemesis is not commutative. Economics cannot be the nemesis of sociology in America today, because sociology is too minor and obscure and weakly established. Economics, by contrast, especially in business academia where I spent my career, can invoke a nemesis, because it has waxed so full during Late Capitalist times.[3]

In this book I violate the scholarly style expected of a social scientist. The language is too literary and too relaxed; metaphor replaces math. I have two reasons for transgressing. The first is simply because I can, here in a book; I grew so pained by the Procrustean bed of journal style! My second motive is to guide consumer sociology—a discipline that does not yet exist—down one path not another. Traditional sociologists are infamous for writing badly. To fish out a quote from Talcott Parsons has been the easy way to win a Bad Writing contest (although postmodernists now vie for the honor). English translations of Simmel's German don't read much better. And when Lanham (2006b, p. 47) needed a passage so darkly twisted that it could not be resuscitated, even by his Paramedic Method, a sociologist was there for him. The new consumer sociology must not repeat the mistakes of the old sociology. It is no accident that sociology has been eclipsed within the social sciences.

The pitfalls that dogged past sociological writing are not incidental. The risk of writing badly in sociology is not just an instance of a widely shared affliction, as Billig (2013) or Lanham (2006b) or Pinker (2014) might argue. The risk is specific to the topics that comprise sociology. It is hard to write well about its subject: collectivity. In physical science we write about tangible things, and formulate matter in math. In psychology, although the subject is intangible, we all have a reference psyche to use as a touchstone. In sociology, there is neither tangible anchor nor immediate referent: none of us is a collectivity, nor can collectivity be touched or prodded. So we start using words like collectivity, which must wrinkle the reader's brow; and from there to the metastasized prose of a Talcott Parsons is but a short step.

Physics has math, and psychology has me and you. Sociology has got nothing, and verbiage flows like lava from that rent, a hot stifling congealment that petrifies even the willing reader. The problem is endemic, and has to be confronted if consumer sociology is to flourish. My solution is to play with language, to channel off the magma of abstraction. On occasion I use set-piece metaphors, as in this paragraph. That may be the worst of my scholarly sins. Since the dawn of modern science and the banishment of rhetoric (Bender and Wellbery 1990; Lanham 2006a), metaphor has been illegitimate, bastard knowledge perverted at its root, the Benedict Arnold of social science, Aaron Burr under the scholarly saddle, murderous and larcenous of truth, to be scorned and shunned. However, if we want to glimpse what is proper to sociology, and speak about it clearly, there is no escape from metaphor. I'll return to these matters in a short Epilogue on assimilating Foucault.

OUTLINE OF THE BOOK

The first essay discusses fashion blogs, and uses ideas from Pierre Bourdieu to illuminate the success enjoyed by some bloggers. The key concept is cultural capital—now a familiar term in some circles, but an enduring puzzle elsewhere. I tie cultural capital back to longstanding debates about taste, and forward to blogging, where fashion blogs reveal a megaphone effect. With the Web as megaphone, ordinary people can reach a mass audience, one instance of what Turner (2010) calls the demotic turn in mass media.

The second essay examines online reviews. To keep the topic tractable I focus on restaurant reviews on Yelp, a leading hosting site. Here the antagonistic, sociology-as-nemesis positioning is strong. Economists think they have a perfectly good explanation for why online reviews exploded. Psychologists have a plethora of theories to explain the motivation of reviewers. Neither of these disciplines lays a glove on it, because restaurants are taste goods—as are reviews themselves. I hark back to an old distinction introduced by the German sociologist Tonnies: the difference between *Gemeinschaft* and *Gesellschaft*, sometimes translated as the difference between a community of intimates and loose association among strangers (and a wonderful example of the obfuscatory tropism that bedevils sociology). Of course, there are more than two basic types of social formations, to use Simmel's term (Gronow 1997). The essay develops a typology of social formations, and situates Yelp as an instance of a new social formation: the Web-based public (Warner 2002). Later I consider the institutional logics needed for the smooth functioning of a corporate-hosted, Web-based public. Trust is a big problem there.

The third essay looks at Pinterest: a digital scrapbooking site where millions of ordinary consumers are busy acquiring and possessing images from around the Web. I draw on Walter Benjamin to set the scene, and argue that Pinterest enables the demotic consumption of immaterial goods. With a nod to Matthew Arnold, I describe how Pinterest became a site for taste discovery, and consider the implications of assuming that ordinary consumers do not know their own taste.

In a more traditional and less promotional era, before keyword search ran riot, this book could have been titled *Three Essays on Consumer Taste*. Ideas about taste provide the unifying theme. Consumers online navigate new vicissitudes of taste. Taste can pry the consumer loose from the clutches of economists, psychologists, and anthropologists, and clear a space for sociology.

The parts are called essays because historically, this is the most free-form of non-fiction genres, and elements of this book are very freeform. Because each essay covers a great deal of ground, the risk is real that the reader may get bewildered, and lose the thread. To forestall confusion, I've resorted to two formatting devices. I make liberal use of subheadings, and all the subheadings in an essay are listed at its beginning, so the reader knows where the essay will go. Second, to keep the main narrative moving forward, while taking a multifaceted approach, I've exported some topics to boxed text. If interested, you can depart from the main narrative and read a gloss, or an aside, or a brief description of method, data, and even a bibliographical essay; or you can just skip these boxes, and maybe come back later. I got this template from Bourdieu's (1984) *Distinction*.[4]

I avoid scare quotes. The first draft of this introduction was full of them, out of an urgent need to make the reader focus on the words I use and just what I mean by them. Pinker (2014) talked me off that ledge; quote marks that remain were re-inserted by the copy editor. Sometimes you may trip over a word because of the frustrated expectation of seeing scare quotes. That momentary pause will serve the purpose just as well. So be careful, dear reader: this isn't a podcast, but a repeatedly revised written work, by a scholar who made his reputation in rhetoric (McQuarrie and Mick 1996), and isn't chary to wield what he learned there. If you haven't read Richard Lanham, you have idea not, that which I.[5]

Another feature of the style, which I learned from Billig (2013), is an excess of commas, some of them oddly placed, their usage not wrong exactly, even in Sister Bernadette's class, but not right either, so that those who misremember Strunk and White's dictum as "omit needless commas," will surely balk. I do it for clarity and for rhythm, so that you can breathe what I wrote, the better to understand.

Last, I was reading Pinker (2014) and Billig (2013) while writing, and then went back to Williams (1990), and on to Lanham (2006b).[6] Their cautions were liberating, loosening the grip of hoary conventions, but also a rap on the knuckles, a spur to use short words and choose verbs over nouns. Although I will disagree with Billig (2013) on one big point (see the Epilogue), his book was like the slap of a master, to wake the dozing acolyte. I grew ashamed of my tendency, when younger, to seek the sonorous orotundity of the polysyllabulary. I see now how it gets in the way. Then Lanham and Williams beat me up. If I healed well, you will never glimpse the tiresome verbosity of early drafts. Apologies, if attempts to be crisp come across as abrupt.

The book was enormously engaging for me to write. I hope it works for you in the reading.

NOTES

1. There are exceptions, of course, prominent among whom are Douglas Holt and Craig Thompson, who have published copiously in the *Journal of Consumer Research*. Although I follow in their footsteps temporally, I think you will find that, for better or worse, I do not follow them conceptually. The situation is better in Britain, where Colin Campbell and Alan Warde, among others, have contributed to a consumer sociology. Nonetheless, most journal papers that address the consumer do so from within psychology.
2. This has to be one of the oldest slams used to reject the scholarship of others, dating back at least to Lewis Mumford, seen recently in Goldthorpe's (2007) takedown of Bourdieu, and if my own experience on the receiving end is representative, remains a staple of journal reviewing. It nicely captures that distaste for the new so characteristic of scholars every when.
3. Although after reading McCloskey (2010), perhaps I flatter myself, with this talk of nemesis. In this assault on economic theory, I am rallying bowmen at Agincourt, while she hits the beaches at Normandy. The disproportion in rhetorical force is about that large.

4. I've also inserted a couple of dozen endnotes. I could not see writing an essay on Web behavior without simulating the hyperlinked aspect of Web text. Consider the boxed text to be like an on-page bookmark, and these notes to be mouse-triggered pop-ups. My promise: an endnote never just gives a bibliographic citation; these are inserted parenthetically in the main text. An endnote offers an aside for the interested, to motivate the labor of paging to the back.

5. This note confirms that wasn't a typo. Interesting, I thought, that my copy of Word put no squiggly green line under this aberrant sentence.

6. Thomas and Turner (2011) had an even more salutary effect, in weeding out metadiscourse and like verbiage. I mention them only in a note, because the ideology behind their classic style troubles me. Is anyone else bothered, that the acme of classic style is said to be a field guide for identifying birds? Can the visual metaphor that underwrites classic style work for gustatory explorations? And why ignore Lanham's work on style?

Prelude: The Borg

The Borg Collective is a literary fiction, created as part of the *Star Trek* movie franchise. The Borg are a collective of beings who maraud around the galaxy, attempting to assimilate new species and technologies. An individual human, when assimilated, receives cybernetic implants and maybe genetic manipulation, and becomes a drone, lacking autonomy. The Borg Collective has been built up through thousands of years of marauding.

The Borg appear in the movie, *Star Trek: First Contact*, and in several episodes of the associated TV series. A documentary is available here: http://www.startrek.com/watch_video/vid-borg-doc-full, which will tell you more than you need to know, after a slow start; alternatively, a quick exposure to the recently assimilated Captain Picard can be obtained from this clip: https://www.youtube.com/watch?v=JIQmfwe3YAM. Also, you can search images.google.com using the single term "Borg," and find many pictures of assimilated individuals that showcase the cybernetic implants.

I'll return to the Borg from time to time in the book, and make this central to the Epilogue. The question raised by the Borg is whether a metaphor or other literary device can be knowledge. Of course, the Borg, like any metaphor, can be used to aid in conveying an idea, to make a concept more vivid or concrete, easier to grasp. All writers, even physicists, use metaphor for this purpose (see the extended example in Pinker 2014, pp. 31ff.).

It is far more radical to claim that a metaphor can hold an idea that can't be known any other way, can offer or directly provide knowledge. No practicing social scientist believes this to be true today; the mainstream position is that a metaphor may serve as a helpful stylistic device, but cannot carry knowledge otherwise unavailable. The idea that metaphor could be anything else, anything more than a stylistic device, does not intrude.

But a sociologist cannot avoid this question, of what metaphor can know, and of whether collectivity can be grasped, except through metaphor.

Essay One: Blogs and the megaphone effect

with Barbara J. Phillips[1]

THE MEGAPHONE—CULTURAL CAPITAL—A Point of Beginning—Class Tastes Versus Cultural Capital—The Vicissitudes of Cultural Capital—Beyond Habitus—THE FORMS OF CAPITAL—Metaphor or Theory?—How many Capitals?—Metaphor Run Amok—Another Rival: Human Capital—What is Cultural Capital?—TASTE AND CULTURAL CAPITAL—What is Taste?—Taste Goods—Two Meanings of Taste—Consumer Taste Levels—Goffman on Audiences—EMPIRICAL EVIDENCE—Method in Consumer Sociology—Findings: Blogger Trajectory—Findings: Blogger Outcomes—Findings: Maintaining an Audience—DISCUSSION OF FINDINGS—Bourdieu on the Web—Ideology of Giftedness—LIMITATIONS—Not All Goods Are Taste Goods—Consumer Culture, Consumer Sociology

The Web allows ordinary consumers to reach a mass audience, to grab hold of the megaphone. More consumers have more opportunities to reach thousands of other consumers than ever before. I draw on Turner's (2010) idea of a demotic turn, to situate fashion blogs as one way in which ordinary consumers get a megaphone. I then delve into Bourdieu's idea of cultural capital to explore how a few consumers succeeded in realizing the potential for a mass audience. Fashion blogs yield new insight into the meaning of cultural capital, one of Bourdieu's most original and subtle ideas, and a gateway to viewing consumers through a sociological lens.

THE MEGAPHONE

Among the first fashion bloggers to grab the megaphone was a 13-year-old girl (Rosman 2009); by 2010 this blogger had been profiled in the *Wall Street Journal*, the *Guardian*, and other publications, and her blog posts were read by tens of thousands. This blogger got hold of the megaphone by means of her actions, not by birth or through institutional position.

The megaphone is not bound to the fashion context. *Chocolate and Zucchini* is a food blog whose author was not trained as a chef and did not work for a food magazine before starting the blog. Her posts may receive more than 100 000 views. *Tight Ass Little Apartment* is a blog about interior design and home decor. This blogger was not trained in design or employed as a designer before she started the blog.

The megaphone effect occurs when ordinary consumers, defined as people lacking professional experience and not holding an institutional or family position, post to the Web about consuming, with the potential to acquire a mass audience. The blog posts of interest deal with consumer goods: fashion, food, home décor. Consumer bloggers achieve an audience that in the past was only available to institutionally located professionals (McCracken 1986). Consumers achieve this audience by means of publicly consuming: choosing, evaluating, and engaging with clothing (in the focal example for this essay), and posting accounts that may be read by a large audience of strangers.

This new consumer action, made possible by the Web, has not been explained. By 2010, anyone who wished to share their thoughts with others could do so on Facebook. When someone chooses instead to reach for a mass audience of strangers, this action can't readily be labeled as sharing (Belk 2010; Giesler 2006). The fashion bloggers studied mostly don't display clothes they sewed by hand, but mass-marketed, branded goods; likewise, food bloggers do not only show meals cooked from scratch, and online reviewers do not only write about craft breweries and artisan bakeries. Hence, consumer blogging can't readily be understood as prosuming (Campbell 2005). You could label it electronic word of mouth and call these bloggers opinion leaders or market mavens (Kozinets et al. 2010; Feick and Price 1987), but this obscures what is new and different: ongoing posts, by ordinary consumers, directed at a mass audience of strangers. Box 1.1 develops in detail what fashion blogs are not.

Turner (2010) provides a conceptual framework that can locate the megaphone effect. He points to a larger cultural movement, the demotic turn, which embraces talk radio and reality television, as well as online behavior. The demotic turn occurs when ordinary people get more opportunities to appear in the media, relative to some baseline, which I will locate in about the 1959–1995 period.[2] That baseline period, as argued in my Introduction to this book, represents the full flowering of consumer society in the United States. During this period, conventional mass media flourished: it was the age of broadcast and then cable television, before the advent of the Web shattered the dominance of television and opened up the mass media. The 1959–1995 period can also be described as the apex of the movement toward a consumer society, which dates back to the Industrial / Scientific /

BOX 1.1   WHAT FASHION BLOGS ARE NOT

Blogs marked one of the first instances of Turner's (2010) demotic turn, taking off early in the 2000s, well before Yelp or Pinterest. In early accounts, blogging allowed consumers to become producers, or prosumers (Beer and Burrows 2010; Campbell 2005; Reed 2009). Digital prosumers were thought to share information with the aim of building online communities (Firat and Dholakia 2006; Hodkinson 2007; Jarrett 2003; Schau et al. 2009). This viewpoint, that blogs acted as personal diaries online (Hodkinson 2007), connects with Belk's (2010) ideas about sharing. Blogging may be approached as "sharing out," intended to expand one's community of intimates, in contrast to "sharing in," where the motive is to tighten existing bonds.

In the early 2000s, blogging was also seen as a hallmark of Web 2.0, proposed as a more democratized and participatory phase in the evolution of the Internet. With Web 2.0, it was prophesied, user-generated content, experienced as more authentic and personal, would overwhelm content generated by traditional power centers such as marketers and publishers (van Dijck 2009). Bloggers, as consumers, could now co-create the meanings of the brands, rather than passively absorb meanings engineered by established, authoritative culture makers (Holt 2002; cf. McCracken 1986; Zwass 2010). The Web was on the frontier of co-creation, as individuals devoted long hours to creating content without pay (Ritzer and Jurgenson 2010). Yet, prosumption and co-creation were also criticized as doubly exploiting consumers through the capitalist system (Cova and Dalli 2009; Zwick et al. 2008), because prosumers are not paid, yet create value for a company or brand.

Some studies based on interviews found that bloggers posted to express their own identity and point of view (Hodkinson 2007); they write for themselves, as an archive of their own thoughts and feelings for later reconsumption (Reed 2009). This matched findings from interviews with non-digital prosumers (for example, craft consumers such as amateur carpenters, chefs, and quilters) who desire to engage in creative acts of self-expression (Campbell 2005). Craft consumers are concerned with the possible alienating and homogenizing effects of mass market goods; in a postmodern vein, they focus on authenticity and resistance to mass culture (Campbell 2005). Likewise, digital prosumers were thought to pursue empowerment and emancipation (Firat and Dholakia 2006; Jarrett 2003; Schau et al. 2009). To synthesize early ideas: blogging consists of personal disclosures made in the pursuit of an identity project, aimed at forging community bonds between blogger and followers, with the hope of emancipating from the market.

These views of blogging, which dominated consumer research when I started thinking about consumers online, yield predictions about fashion blog content. First, if blogging is about authenticity and emancipation, accepting free goods and flogging them on one's blog should be controversial, and liable to stress both the blogger's self-concept and community bonds with readers. Kozinets et al. (2010) found this type of stress among bloggers given a free cell phone and invited to blog about it. Second, because blogging is about emancipation from the marketplace via prosuming, you would expect branded goods to be de-emphasized in blog posts, especially popular mainstream brands. In fashion blogs, you would expect thrift store chic to be mandatory, store-bought clothing rare, and conventional designer brands absent. Third, because blogging empowers, then in addition to avoidance of mass-market brands, you also would expect active resistance to and criticism of commercial goods, advertising messages, and marketing efforts (Shankar et al. 2006). Fourth, because blogging is sharing (Belk 2010) and sharing involves reciprocity, comments on blog posts by readers should often take the form of sharing back, in which readers reciprocate by sharing details of their own personal lives, so that bloggers and readers together build community. Finally, because blogging is fundamentally about creating online community, the relation between blog posts and reader comments should be dialogic, akin to what is seen in peer-to-peer networks and discussion forums (Mathwick et al. 2007; Schau et al. 2009).

None of these predictions were borne out. What fashion bloggers do is new and different.

Technological / Capitalist Revolutions (Campbell 1987; Gronow 1997; McCloskey 2010; Muller 2007).

Continuing with Turner's (2010) thesis, during the baseline period only media professionals, other occupants of powerful institutional positions (for example, government officials or business leaders), and designated celebrities could appear on television or otherwise gain a mass audience. Moreover, celebrities became that way by successful performances in credentialed institutional settings (entertainment, sports, and so on). Until very recently, ordinary people lacked access to the mass media and could only gain that access by successful performance in some institutional setting, however extraordinary their motivation or skill. From this perspective, an ordinary person is defined precisely by the absence of institutional credentials.

These restrictions began to loosen with the spread of reality television. Here the media began to create celebrities, rather than mediate between existing celebrities and the mass audience. Turner (2010) notes, however, that the celebrity gained by reality television participants is not gained by their actions nor even owned by them (his discussion of exploitative contract terms is bracing). Reality television celebrity remains an institutionally mediated outcome in which the owners of mass media select the citizens who are to be granted a mass audience.

The megaphone effect is distinctive within the larger context of Turner's demotic turn, because in the consumer sphere, people are now able to grab the megaphone for themselves, without institutional certification. Unlike reality television participants, who must satisfy a casting call controlled by professionals, a successful blogger gains her audience directly: she blogs in such a way that many other consumers begin to follow her posts. Once a consumer gains a mass following, this audience can be converted into institutional access, and further leveraged. But institutional mediation is no longer required to gain a mass audience. That is new.

However, most bloggers never gain a big audience (Lovink 2008). How did a few fashion bloggers succeed in realizing the newfound possibility to build a mass audience? What's special about them? This essay offers a sociological explanation centered on taste judgments and the accumulation of cultural capital (Bourdieu 1984, 1986 [1983]). To explore the meaning of cultural capital takes me on a lengthy detour away from fashion blogging. But as noted in the Introduction, this book is not primarily about blogging, Yelp or Pinterest. It aims to launch a consumer sociology. Cultural capital is central to that enterprise.

CULTURAL CAPITAL

Bourdieu's signature idea is refractory and elusive. What makes it difficult is, first, that Bourdieu designed his prose to be difficult (see Box 1.2). Cultural capital is difficult, second, because Bourdieu's thinking is supple and innovative; and third, because his thinking on this topic did not stand still. What Bourdieu meant by cultural capital early in the 1960s is not the same as what he meant by it later in the 1980s; and by his death in 2001, the term had almost disappeared, scarcely present in his posthumously published "not an autobiography" (Bourdieu 2008). It was not in Bourdieu's interest to admit that cultural capital ever meant anything other than what he meant by it that day, for the occasion at hand. Its mutations and divagations have been left tacit, even as it has accreted unhelpful meanings in the hands of later scholars.

A novel take is made even more difficult, because cultural capital has become an encyclopedia entry, a highlighted phrase in a textbook, a commonplace in the rhetorical sense. Bourdieu's most famous book, *Distinction* (1984), has been cited more than 30 000 times as this is written, and based on my haphazard checks since 2010, its citation count continues to mount by thousands per year. Everybody already knows what cultural capital means, and the term can be tossed off by historians and social scientists across diverse fields in confidence that the audience will get it (see, e.g., Lanham 2006a; Muller 2007; Wickham 2005). As I will try to show, that confidence is misplaced; often what the audience gets is not what Bourdieu meant, but just some fragment of conventional wisdom, of the sort Bourdieu spent his life inveighing against.

And yet, despite the thousands of muddied citations and its diffusion through literate circles, cultural capital remains the glittering, oddly shaped shell that draws the eye on the beach because nothing like it was there yesterday. Cultural capital continues to be an unfamiliar and unconventional idea, if only because it is a sociological term of art, and sociology remains *terra incognita* for scholars in the behavioral and social sciences. You could

BOX 1.2   BOURDIEU'S PROLIX PROSE

Bourdieu wrote in a style alien to behavioral science journals in the Anglo-Saxon world. Here is a pertinent example from *Distinction* (1984, p. 256), describing practices of those high in socio-economic position:

> Verbal virtuosities or the gratuitous expense of time or money that is presupposed by material or symbolic appropriation of works of art, or even, at the second power, the self-imposed constraints and restrictions which make up the "asceticism of the privileged" (as Marx said of Seneca) and the refusal of the facile which is the basis of all "pure" aesthetics, are so many repetitions of the master–slave dialectic through which the possessors affirm their possession of their possessions. In so doing, they distance themselves still further from the dispossessed, who, not content to being slaves to necessity in all its forms, are suspected of being possessed by the desire for possession, and so potentially possessed by the possessions they do not, or do not yet, possess.

This sentence is representative of Bourdieu's writing style in length, syntactical complexity, and embedded historical allusions (that is, to the Stoics, Kant, Hegel, and Marx). The sentence ends in a complex rhetorical figure, in this case antanaclasis, the repetition of the same word in multiple senses ("business is business" would be a familiar example in English). This antanaclasis to the ninth degree is typical of *Distinction*: it is full of rhetorical figures.

To hear Bourdieu tell it, he wrote in this rhetorically stylized way because cultural sociology, to advance, had to "make the familiar strange" (1984, pp. xiv, 227; Bourdieu and Wacquant 1992, p. 169). Bourdieu believed that sociological facts were systematically misrecognized, and his rhetoricized prose attempts to slow down the reader, to provoke her, to make her engage the motivated misrecognition of social facts.

Billig (2013) provides an alternative, and less supportive account, of why Bourdieu wrote as he did. Either way, the passage quoted should place the reader new to Bourdieu on alert. His ideas, such as cultural capital, are difficult, and his prose style doesn't help.

Finally, this passage highlights a common misunderstanding of cultural capital. It is a deadly error to mistake knowledge or education for capital. For example, not all readers will have recognized the tacit references to Kant and Hegel in the quoted passage. Does that mean you lack cultural capital, relative to Bourdieu? In parallel, Kingston (2001, p. 97, n. 2), confronted with the unknown word "glissando" in the title of Lamont and Lareau (1988), laments how his incomprehension exposes his own lack of cultural capital, relative to theirs.

But this usage of cultural capital is not correct. Whether you recognize glissando depends on how much education in music you had. Whether you linked "master and slave dialectic" to Hegel and "pure" to Kant depends on your knowledge of 18th and 19th century Continental philosophy. Knowledge of cultural products is not cultural capital. Education means education, not cultural capital, and certainly not educational capital, a lapse to which Bourdieu was all too prone.

Later I'll show how fatal this confusion can be to Bourdieu's project. To use cultural capital as a catchphrase for knowledge or education throws away victory to Becker (1993), in his contest with Bourdieu.

go through an entire PhD program in psychology in the 1980s, and never encounter the term (I did).

The challenge is how to convey the idea of cultural capital to those unfamiliar with it, so that it can be applied to fashion blogging, while simultaneously setting up a critique, both of misunderstandings and of outmoded senses of it, so that it can be renewed to illuminate new things consumers do online. By the time I am finished, it may not be Bourdieu's idea any more, but only my own concoction. Nonetheless, he will remain at least its father, and I think it fit to acknowledge that paternity, even if I may not lay claim to his patrimony.

Not everyone working in sociology is so enamored of cultural capital (e.g., Lamont 1992, 2010). Younger scholars do well to remember that cultural capital remains a controversial idea, a bold conjecture worth considering, as Sir Karl Popper might have said, but possibly, one already found to be scientifically wanting, and ossifying into cant. Not everyone thinks it provides a correct or even useful take on social success (Goldthorpe 2007; Hennion 2010).

To anticipate what follows, I will first point to a misunderstanding of cultural capital, that has to be bracketed and set aside, and then discuss two legitimate but quite different senses of cultural capital, now in circulation, only one of which is helpful for studying new things consumers do online. To further complicate the picture, I will introduce two rival ideas which vie with cultural capital, and which, if accepted, would make it unnecessary to ever speak of cultural capital any more. I will hammer cultural capital, using these rivals, to temper it and sharpen the cutting edge.

The misunderstanding is to collapse Bourdieu into Veblen, and mistake social position, and behaviors that come with it, for cultural capital. The two legitimate senses correspond to the static and dynamic operation of cultural capital; in metaphorical terms, to its rentier and capitalist aspects. Only the dynamic meaning is suitable for exploring what consumers do online. And the two rivals that must be let into the ring are boundary drawing, per Lamont (1992), and the human capital beloved of Becker (1993), and still prominent in rational choice theory (Ratchford 2001).

The goal of these next sections is clarification and purification, achieved through a trial by fire. Cultural capital risks a slow death from conceptual arteriosclerosis, but is worth the effort to beat into shape.

A Point of Beginning

Bourdieu's thinking about cultural capital evolved. This evolution is best grasped by returning to one of his early accounts of cultural capital, given in Bourdieu and Wacquant (1992, p. 160), and then, articulating

---

BOX 1.3 BOURDIEU THE POLEMICIST

Bourdieu became a skilled polemicist, not bound by the politeness conventions of American academia, and not constrained by journal peer review and its narrow culling to a hedged and pallid norm. Here is an example:

> I was reacting no less against the microphrenic empiricism of Lazarsfeld and his European epigones, whose false technological perfection concealed an absence of any real theoretical problematic . . . One needs to take into account the whole effect of domination by American science . . . [and its] inadequacies and technical mistakes . . . in which segments of experience aping experimental rigour conceal the total absence of a real sociologically constructed object. (1990, pp. 19–20)

These are not the fiery words of a young Turk: Bourdieu was well into his fifties. The quote is not an isolated instance, nor did Bourdieu mellow with age. See Bourdieu (2008, pp. 72ff.) for another assault on Lazarsfeld, and Bourdieu (2005, p. 2) for a reference to the "flabby" ideas of Becker (1993).

There was no coming to terms with Bourdieu's work while he was alive; he was tenacious in defending his turf. Only now can we sort through it, to find the seed and discard the chaff. But what a garden of delights, despite its rank wildness!

---

the criticisms that led Bourdieu to move on. Wacquant was chosen by Bourdieu to receive his mantle and carry forward his legacy (if I have read Lamont 2010 correctly). Their book takes the form of a sympathetic interview, a format that allowed Bourdieu to speak in a more accessible style about his ideas. As Box 1.2 shows, Bourdieu's own writings were not always so accessible.

However, we cannot take what is written in Bourdieu and Wacquant (1992) as an accurate transcription of what Bourdieu actually thought decades earlier. Rather, the 1992 account shows how Bourdieu wanted us to think about his thinking, with an eye to securing his legacy. We must approach Bourdieu's remarks as rhetorically structured comments, designed more to draw the reader to his side, than to provide historical insight (see Box 1.3).

Bourdieu writes that he developed the idea of cultural capital "in the early sixties to account for the fact that, *after controlling for economic position and social origin*, students from more cultured families not only have higher rates of academic success but exhibit different modes and patterns of cultural consumption and expression in a wide gamut of domains" (emphasis added). Now put this formulation in context: Parisian society, 50 years ago. To illustrate, let Alain and Jean attend the same preparatory school. Set their family income and fathers' level of education to be the same, and assume each grows up in a large apartment in a good Parisian neighborhood. In terms of conventional indicators, we've told a story that places Alain and Jean on a par with respect to socio-economic position.

Bourdieu's contribution was to assert the potential significance of one difference that might still separate these two youths. Suppose further that Alain grew up surrounded by paintings and sculpture, and had a piano in the house, on which he learned to play classical pieces; while in Jean's case, money was spent on furnishings and high-end appliances, and the music heard was popular songs on a phonograph.

Bourdieu's thesis was that because they differed in the cultural goods consumed (a wonderful black box of a term, which will later need to be unpacked), Alain would grow up endowed with a greater amount of cultural capital, and that this endowment would give Alain an advantage over Jean in multiple social contexts. Because of the centrality of aesthetic judgment in the French elite schools of that era (Bourdieu 1996), Alain's endowment would lead to better performance in prep school, and a head start in acquiring a high socio-economic position. Specifically, Alain's capacity to exercise taste in cultural activities, of the sort expected and respected among fellow Parisians who already held a high socio-economic position, would enhance Alain's own life trajectory.

This definition of cultural capital is an early formulation, or at least, is distinct from others found in Bourdieu's work. It nonetheless illuminates how Bourdieu's thinking differed from that of Theodore Veblen and other sociologists. It provides a prophylactic against the key misunderstanding of cultural capital: to mistake it for an afflatus of social position. The second phrase in the quote lays it out: that "after controlling for economic and social position" there was still a difference between Alain and Jean. That is, after equating the socio-economic position of two families at a high level, in the Paris of that era, you could find yet a further systematic way to separate families, which would predict how their offspring would follow different social trajectories. One set of families possessed a form of wealth not present in the other: a wealth of culture.

Class Tastes Versus Cultural Capital

This first quote makes cultural capital sound straightforward enough. Nonetheless, the selected quote provides a radical perspective on Bourdieu's thinking, given the frequency with which this definition has been ignored in empirical efforts to study cultural capital. Holt's (1998) study—and let me first acknowledge that Holt did more than anyone else to recapture Bourdieu for consumer research—is illustrative. In a small college town,

Holt interviewed two polarized samples, comparing the top quintile, in terms of father's education and occupation, to the bottom quintile, also in terms of father's education and occupation. In short, he compared the scions of college graduates to those of manual laborers.

Holt's sampling strategy, based on selecting polarized social positions, was subsequently applied in consumer research by Berger and Ward (2010), Bernthal et al. (2005), Henry (2005), and Üstüner and Holt (2010), and I believe, has been frequently applied elsewhere in the social sciences. Schematized, you first pick two groups of people who occupy very different social positions, one high and one low. Second, you survey broadly their habits and preferences, to find where the two groups differ. Last, you take the preferences and habits that distinguish the high group, and label these as signs of an abundance or deficit of cultural capital. Done.

Now suppose Bourdieu had executed a similar sampling strategy back in Paris. He would have compared a sample of Alains and Jeans from the wealthy 16th Arrondissement, to a sample of Mohammeds and Sachas from a poor *banlieue* out in the sticks. He did not do that. Such a sampling strategy would conflate cultural capital with, rather than control for, economic and social position (and ethnic and urban versus rural differences). Any sample that draws from polarized social and economic positions, and then attributes cultural capital to the high group, is going to submerge cultural capital proper—Bourdieu's innovative take on how social position reproduces across the generations—into the more conventional sociological idea nicely captured in Goffman's (1951, p. 301) term, "restrictive practices." And that merged (nay, mongrel) idea will no longer capture Bourdieu's unique insight.

Goffman's (1951) earlier account emphasized the potential for faking, and the need to police wishful or fraudulent claims to a high status. A restrictive practice is a defensive maneuver, designed to prevent entry by the undeserving and ineligible. Bourdieu recognized, I believe, that taste judgments in the realm of art and music, in the Paris of that era, provided the urban, educated upper middle class with such a restrictive practice. (One can find friendly comments about Goffman scattered through Bourdieu's work.) Only persons surrounded by objects of high culture from birth, and engaged early in mandated forms of cultural production, such as playing classical piano music, were likely to succeed in making, reflexively and without effort, the aesthetic judgments required to be accepted among others holding high social position. In this telling, cultural capital is an endowment obtained from the family, manifest in tastes for one type of cultural product over others.

To update Goffman's account, and tease his notion apart from Bourdieu's, note that restrictive practices can be used, not only to rebuff claims to high social status, but also to test and check claims to in-group status, for any group, whether high or low in social position. And restrictive practices need not involve cultural products, or even tastes. The underlying sociological insight has been developed most fully by Michele Lamont (1992): members of social groups must draw boundaries. External boundaries control membership in the group, and hence are most salient in the case of voluntary associations, subcultures, and similar groups scattered through the vast middle of a developed society like the United States. If you want to be accepted by Harley-Davidson owners, you may have to speak a certain way, wear particular clothing, and kit your bike one way not another. To be accepted as a hipster, rather than a wannabe, likewise requires visible practices (Arsel and Thompson 2011).

Oftentimes, taste judgments are the restrictive practice that controls group membership. You won't be accepted by other members of the group if you don't give signs that you share their tastes. Holt (1998) gives numerous examples of consumer taste practice; Arsel and Thompson (2011) and Thornton (1996) describe ridicule, by in-group members, directed at failed attempts by out-group members to display the proper taste; and Berger and Ward (2010) and Elliott and Davies (2006) discuss articles of clothing that signal shared tastes.

However, boundary-drawing, as studied by Lamont (1992), and taken as an extension of Goffman's (1951) ideas about how groups police membership, has little to do with cultural capital, defined in shorthand as that new idea Bourdieu had. Lamont (2010) is firm that her thinking about group boundaries does not build on or require Bourdieu's idea of cultural capital. Group boundaries, and the use of taste as a practice to control group acceptance, are bona fide sociological ideas, which are not alien to the broader corpus of Bourdieu's thinking. But the meaning of cultural capital—that new idea—has to be sought elsewhere.

Re-reading Bourdieu (1984) may not help in this quest. Bourdieu deliberately plays on the two meanings of distinction throughout *Distinction*, making this word refer sometimes to difference and boundary, while at others to elevation and prestige. To keep the two meanings straight, I will refer to distinction-between versus distinction-over. Distinction-between draws boundaries, creates groups, and fosters solidarity. It operates locally and acts to cluster like-minded individuals and sequester them from others with different tastes. Distinction-over asserts preferment, sustains hierarchy, and elevates one above others. It operates at the societal level and can raise select individuals to prominence. Rather than grouping peers together into an Us apart from a Them, taste, when it underwrites distinction-over, acts to elevate a few relative to the many.

Prior accounts in consumer research have successfully imported Bourdieu's account of taste aimed at distinction-between, and developed how taste can be pressed into service as a boundary marker between groups, to promote affiliation and community (Holt 1998; Arsel and Thompson 2011). Put another way, much past consumer research on taste has followed Lamont (1992), while trying to lay claim to the patrimony of Bourdieu by means of incessant references to capital. After all, Bourdieu (1984) has been cited 20 times as often as Lamont (1992), which counts for a lot, in the scholarly search for authority. But the gap that separates Lamont from Bourdieu is huge, and blurring the difference can only obscure what we seek to study.

What separates the distinction-between of Lamont, from the distinction-over implied by references to capital, is the democratic character of drawing boundaries. No elite position, and no unusual heap of resources, is required to draw boundaries. People at all levels of society draw boundaries that include espoused others and exclude shunned others. It's just what people do, every day and automatically. Groups low in the pecking order mark out their boundaries just as enthusiastically, and with the same deadly seriousness, as highly ranked groups. Groups not ranked, as with so many voluntary groups in the United States, are just as concerned to draw the line as an English nobleman. Boundaries construct identity and promote affiliation with like-minded others, which reinforces identity, which makes it easier to see with whom one might affiliate. No capital of any type—no wealth—is required.

To summarize: cultural capital must have something to do with distinction-over, but must not be conflated with socio-economic level. It is hard to keep this straight. Individuals who amass cultural capital get elevated, and people endowed with cultural capital tend to stay elevated; but sampling from a group of people who already have elevated socio-economic status, defined in conventional terms as falling at the high end of the income, wealth, occupation, and education distributions, does not secure insight into cultural capital. If Bourdieu's initial definition is correct, as embodied in my Alain and Jean example, some people with high income and good position possess lots of cultural capital, while others do not. Sampling on socio-economic level does give insight into the restrictive practices used by the elite of that time and place. Sometimes these restrictive practices rely on cultural products, but they need not. In Paris in the 1960s, art and music served that goal; for the senatorial elite in the late Roman Empire, the ability to compose fine Latin verse served that purpose (see Wickham's 2005 discussion of Sidonius Apollinaris). For the American elite of the early 2000s—hedge fund honchos perhaps—neither art, music, nor verse need be central to the restrictive practices in use. Sheer gobs of money, or gigantic homes nobody else can afford, may do the trick. Restrictive practices and cultural capital are separate sociological ideas, which are sometimes found intertwined and sometimes separate.

In metaphor: low social position is a sink filled from many a slough, gutter, swale, and pipe. You cannot dip a cup and say, "this bit came down that pipe." High social position is a forest canopy, reached by vine and trunk, monkey and moth. Running a scoop across the canopy is no sure way to collect blooms, or fur, or wings. You cannot pick out cultural capital by sampling something else. You can't face cultural capital from behind.

The heart of the tangle: cultural capital must be associated with distinction-over; it must involve elevation and prestige and advantage. But starting with some empirical distinction-over defined in some other terms—a high level of income or education, say—cannot yield any sure grasp of what separates cultural capital from other routes to distinction. Conversely, abandoning distinction-over, in favor of analyses based on distinction-between, is to abandon Bourdieu for the quite different ideas captured by Lamont in her work on boundary-drawing.

This tangle forced Bourdieu to revise, or better, remodel his idea of cultural capital.

The Vicissitudes of Cultural Capital

An objection, raised early in the diffusion of Bourdieu's ideas, was that cultural capital might only be meaningful within a rare milieu, such as Parisian society of that era. Evidence was not long in coming that American schools did not reward familiarity with high culture or art objects in the same way, nor did cultural knowledge appear to be so crucial to social preferment in American or British contexts (Halle 1993; Lamont 1992; see Goldthorpe 2007 and Silva and Warde 2010 for British accounts).

In consumer research, Holt (1998) checked this critique of cultural capital as insular. Holt detached cultural capital from high culture and art objects. He focused not on differences in what objects were owned, but on how consumers from different social backgrounds consumed the same product categories differently. So far, so good. Holt then attributed differences, across social positions, to differences in the amount of cultural capital possessed. From that point in consumer research, high cultural capital (HCC) consumers became those people who had the tastes that Holt discovered among the people in his sample who held a high social position. In concrete terms, these were college town residents whose education and occupation, as also their fathers', fell at the high end of the sample. By this maneuver, very specific taste preferences—and anyone who spent time during the later 1990s on the gown side of the town–gown divide can guess what these were, per Lander (2008)—got anointed as markers of high cultural capital.

But I repeat: you cannot get to cultural capital by starting from a sample polarized in terms of social position; especially when all the sampled positions are circumscribed within a small college town in the US east of the Mississippi River. Yes, per Goffman (1951), individuals holding high social position will engage in restrictive practices; and yes, some of these practices will take the form of taste judgments applied to consumer goods; and yes, failure to internalize these taste judgments and make the correct displays will be grounds for marking out the offender as not one of us, that is, as someone holding an inferior social position. But these acts represent boundary drawing, not the deployment of cultural capital.

And yet, it is still not quite fair to categorize the use of samples polarized in social position as a mistaken view of Bourdieu, or as a misunderstanding of his ideas—because Bourdieu himself was not always true to the unique insight behind cultural capital (or, if you prefer, didn't always hew to my confection of his ideas about cultural capital). Bourdieu can be read, especially in some of his earlier accounts of cultural capital, as not saying anything different than what Goffman and Lamont say. And while Bourdieu did evolve his thinking, it was not in his interest to acknowledge that his ideas had changed. Nonetheless, to make cultural capital useful, in an online context, requires that these divagations in his thinking be untangled and pulled apart.

Bourdieu's early ideas about cultural capital were tied up with habitus, another central term in his system. Habitus consists of dispositions instilled from birth, and perfected while growing up in this kind of family occupying that social position. Habitus explains not so much different levels of cultural capital, as the word capital is conventionally used, but differences in cultural endowment. To return to my Parisian example, Alain obtains his cultural resources through his family, while Jean is sunk from the start: he was born into the wrong family. Conceived as an endowment, cultural capital does become difficult to distinguish from "to the manner born":[3] a summary label for all the differences in habit and preference that flow from high versus low social position. The endowment definition implies that a woman who did not grow up surrounded by high fashion— who did not grow up wealthy, with access to haute couture, runway shows, designer brand clothing, and occasions to wear it—would lack the proper habitus to succeed as a fashion blogger. Conceived in terms of habitus, no ordinary consumer could possess or even acquire cultural capital, inasmuch as ordinary, consistent with Turner (2010), means not endowed with pre-existing social position.

To conceive cultural capital as an endowment received from the family, a habitus acquired over the years as a person matures, makes it a static notion. But to portray cultural capital as static violates the underlying metaphor: capital—economic capital—is inherently dynamic. Capital builds, disrupts, changes things. Per Gronow (1997), an endowment conception of cultural capital is unsustainable in the modern world, because it presumes a static social arrangement (Lamont 1992). As an endowment, cultural capital can explain reproduction (Bourdieu and Passeron 1977): how social position is maintained, newcomers denied, and upward social mobility thwarted. But static ideas like endowment can't explain modernity following the I/S/T/C Revolutions. And no static idea can explain fashion—where change is of the essence (Davis 1992).

To personify and make vivid the difference between a static and a dynamic perspective on cultural capital, compare a rentier to a capitalist. Both are wealthy, but the rentier's wealth is not active; he simply collects his rents, and spends them freely. He may not have any less wealth than the capitalist, but he is not engaged in amassing wealth through enterprise; he already has more than enough, and need not be productive. Conceived as an endowment received from birth, perfected within the bosom of the family, cultural capital reduces to habitual display. Alain displays the tastes inculcated by his family. Because the cultural rentier's family already holds a high social position, these tastes will match the tastes of others whose families also hold high positions. Shared habitual tastes cement his membership in the elite, in the time-honored way of restrictive practices everywhere. In its rentier manifestation, cultural capital is a restrictive practice that excludes parvenus even as it identifies those who do belong. It is the exercise of designated tastes as a matter of habit. If not acquired from birth, it is almost impossible to display these tastes reflexively, without effort, naturally and automatically. This makes it easy to identify parvenus by the effort seen in their struggles to display proper taste.

A capitalist, by contrast, in its root financial and economic meaning, is a dynamic individual who amasses capital, who has a trajectory, so that she ends up in a different place than she started. A capitalist invests capital to earn a return of even more capital. Her capital produces. She makes the effort. She gains.

Now you can see the problem Bourdieu faced: a habitus-based concept of cultural capital both denies the root metaphor, and implies almost perfect reproduction of pre-existing social position. An utterly static society, with zero social mobility, is the predicted result. Doubtless there have been such societies, but as Gronow (1997), following Simmel (1957 [1904]), hammers home, this is not a good description of Western Europe following the I/S/T/C Revolutions, and still less a good description of the contemporary United States (although Clark 2014 might be used to counter-argue this point). Bourdieu wished to be, and be seen as, an empirical sociologist, making this disjuncture, between static prediction and the observed dynamism of real societies in the West, a vexing problem.

Bourdieu faced a further difficulty: his own life trajectory contradicted any static conception of cultural capital, and made a mockery of the idea that habitus was all-determinative. As Box 1.4 develops at more length, Bourdieu came from modest circumstances in the extreme southwest of France. He did not grow up speaking Parisian French at home. Yet his personal trajectory raised him to an endowed chair at the most illustrious academic institution in France. Bourdieu was the French equivalent of hillbilly goes to Harvard, or the don from Donnybrook. His trajectory is inconceivable in a truly static society where family-inculcated habitus acts as a restrictive practice to control access to high social position. Bourdieu, the scholar of global renown, was the grandson of a peasant from a marginalized rural group, among the Appalachians of France.

Beyond Habitus

In response to critiques of its static character (Schatzki 1996), Bourdieu's thinking evolved away from a reliance on the concept of habitus toward a reliance on field. He began to speak of field-specific capital (Swartz 1997). He focused less on social position within society as a whole, and more on how people maintained or advanced their position within a field. Bourdieu gradually ceased to speak of cultural capital, or of any type of capital, replacing these with either "specific capital" or "[name of field] capital" (Bourdieu 1998, 1999, 2008).

The more dynamic concept of field-specific capital emerges in this alternative account, also given in Bourdieu and Wacquant (1992):

> A capital does not exist and function except in relation to a field . . . We can . . . compare a field to a game . . . [and] picture each player having in front of her a pile of tokens . . . players can play to increase or conserve their capital . . . A species of capital is what is efficacious in a given field, both as a weapon and as a stake of struggle, that which allows its possessors to wield a power, an influence, and thus to exist . . . instead of being considered a negligible quantity. (pp. 98–101)

Here there emerges a view of capital that could explain why some bloggers are able to grab the megaphone and acquire a mass audience. In the later Bourdieu, a consumer can put her tokens at risk to amass more. Capital can be invested and further accumulated, just as money can.

Field-specific capital can act as both input and output: "as a weapon and as a stake of struggle." This evolution rejuvenates the money metaphor that underlies references to capital. Money is distinct, relative to most resources: it can be invested to generate more of itself, with the amount of money returned a function of the risks taken. Cultural capital emerges as a resource, for cultural matters and within the aesthetic domain, which can

BOX 1.4 BIOGRAPHICAL NOTES ON BOURDIEU

When Bourdieu's ideas began to diffuse in the Anglo-Saxon world, in the 1980s, facts about his life, of the sort found in Bourdieu (2008), were not well known among scholars. Even today, scholars outside the sociological core might find it difficult to distinguish Bourdieu from, say, a Foucault, Derrida, or Lacan. Aren't they all Parisian intellectuals, members of the French avant-garde of the 1960s? No. Bourdieu's origins differ from what the image of a Parisian intellectual suggests.

Bourdieu grew up in a remote region of southwest France speaking a scorned provincial dialect, grandson of a peasant farmer, and son of the village postman. His youthful experience of the French school system seared him. After a Dickensian boarding school experience, his scholastic ability was such, that despite more than 300 detentions, he advanced through competitive examinations to an elite École, where he received a degree in philosophy. Drafted into the army, having refused officer's training, he was sent to the Algerian front in a unit "made up of all the illiterates of Mayenne and Normandy and a few recalcitrants . . . second class soldiers, illiterates from the whole of western France" (2008, pp. 38, 95). There he turned to the study of sociology and anthropology, and on his return to France, advanced to a series of professorships, and ultimately to the pinnacle of French academe, a Chair at the College de France. He never submitted his Doctoral thesis.

As mentioned, Bourdieu studied philosophy before turning to sociology. But this sentence misleads. The American reader assumes it means something like: Bourdieu majored in philosophy as an undergraduate, or perhaps, Bourdieu switched programs in grad school. Actually Bourdieu passed an entrance exam to study philosophy at the École Normale Superieur (ENS). This is an elite school, whose entrance exam Jean Paul Sartre and Michel Foucault failed on the first try, one that Jacques Derrida failed twice, and that the philosopher Gilles Deleuze never did pass (Gutting 2011). Deleuze had to go to the Sorbonne as his safety school, to use another American term. After ENS, Bourdieu got his teaching credential in philosophy (Fr. *aggregation*). But that's another woefully misleading statement in an American context, where teaching credential, in elite circles, does not cue positive inferences. In France, however, to obtain the *aggregation* required a written and oral exam, which at the time, may have exceeded in stringency the combination of the comprehensive exam and oral dissertation defense required to earn a PhD from an American university. It took Foucault and Derrida two tries to pass the aggregation; in Foucault's year, 94 percent of those who took the *aggregation*, all presumably graduates of the ENS and other Grande Écoles, who had survived the earlier culling, nonetheless failed it. This gives some perspective on "Bourdieu studied philosophy."

Bourdieu was very bright. Yet he was an outsider to the establishment, and always remained conscious of that fact. He owed everything to school but nourished a lifelong desire for revenge against the tyranny of academic categories (Swartz 1997). He could be the academic equivalent of a street brawler, a junkyard dog loosed on the genteel precincts of the Parisian salon. He was a villager in the metropolis, a peasant among lords, a scientist against the philosophes, even as he was a Humanist against the Positivists.

be wielded as a weapon, to win a struggle for position, and also awarded as stakes, to those winning that struggle. This formula isn't found in Veblen, Goffman, Lamont, or anywhere else; it is unique to Bourdieu. This later definition redeems the root metaphor of capital. This thing called capital is not only manifest as money, as economic capital, but also occurs, and can be accumulated, in other spheres as well.

This dynamic sense of cultural capital can be linked back to taste, and taste judgments will take us forward to fashion blogging. But before making that return, there is more to be said about Bourdieusian capital, cultural and otherwise. These next few pages are offered as janitorial work, clean-up, to help the dynamic sense of cultural capital emerge more clearly from the matrix of neighboring ideas, superficially similar but unrelated ideas, and misunderstood relationships with yet other ideas.

Once the Bourdieusian idea broadens out to field-specific capital—one capital, many fields—we have to confront a new rival, the human capital of Becker (1993). To grasp the challenge posed by Becker, let me ask you a rhetorical question. If you were new to these matters, which phrasing would you select, as the more plain and lucid: field-specific capital, with its many substitutions—academic capital, educational capital, social capital, political capital, bodily capital, as many as there are fields—or just, plain, human capital?

THE FORMS OF CAPITAL

Another problem dogs attempts to apply Bourdieu's idea of cultural capital. Bourdieu didn't only refer to cultural capital, but discussed many other forms of capital as well. And his occasional attempts to corral his usage of capital, most notably Bourdieu (1986 [1983]), sometimes create as many new difficulties as they remove. I am reminded of a feature that used to run in the *New Yorker* magazine, called "Block that metaphor," which offered snippets of writing where the metaphors tumbled over one another, or were really a stretch. Bourdieu's writing on capital recalls that *New Yorker* feature. The question that emerges, from the welter of Bourdieu's usage, is whether cultural capital, and the other forms of capital found in Bourdieu's writing, is only a metaphor, and not a theoretical idea;[4] that is, does not refer to a real cause. DiMaggio (1979, pp. 1468–69) put this criticism well, and notably, could offer it as early as the 1970s, when Bourdieu still had thousands of pages yet to write, and countless metaphors to unleash:

> capitals proliferate: in addition to economic, cultural, and symbolic capital, we have linguistic capital, social capital, academic capital, scholastic capital,

credentialed cultural capital, capitals of authority and consecration, university, scientific and artistic capital . . . As the number of capitals increases, the metaphorical currency undergoes inflation and its value declines accordingly.

Metaphor or Theory?

To anchor this discussion, let's focus on economic capital. Many people accept economic capital as real, and not synonymous with either currency or money. Real or not, economic capital is a very intangible entity, and not easy to understand or simple to explain (for instance, try sometime, to explain money to a preteen, without defining it as currency or coin). And although capital is a real entity in economic theory, this reality, embodied in equations, is not necessarily the same reality as that of capital in the world, as seen in the daily operation of business (ideally, the two are not alien). And, the theoretical capital visible in a Keynes is not the same real thing as the capital visible in Marx, or that seen in a contemporary textbook of macroeconomics, even as the reality of any and all of these formulations remains open to scientific questioning. Note finally that the reality of capital in a textbook on microeconomics won't be the same as that of the capital discussed in a macroeconomics textbook. And it bears emphasis that economic capital, whatever it is, is not the same thing as money, wealth, or assets.

This brief excursion bodes well for the reality of cultural capital: it suggests that very difficult and subtle ideas, having an uncertain relationship to similar concepts, can nonetheless refer to real causes, as economic capital does. The question becomes, are all the forms of capital of which Bourdieu spoke real, or as real as cultural capital might well be? Any of several answers is possible. Cultural capital might enjoy a special place in the pantheon of non-economic capitals. Or, per Bourdieu's (1986 [1983]) attempted summary, there may be a master triumvirate of capitals: economic, cultural, and social. Or, per the later Bourdieu (2008), there may be only one non-economic capital, whose count of manifestations equals the number of fields where the phrase "both as a weapon and as a stake of struggle" applies.

This question cannot be resolved by reading Bourdieu, especially not in the English to which I am confined. In any case, I don't care what Bourdieu's final word was, or what he really thought. I care about what can be done with his ideas to illuminate my subject, the new things consumers do online. The test is whether my take on Bourdieu stimulates other scholars to build on this account. I acknowledge this to be a very American attitude, not so much disrespectful of authority as oblivious (Reed-Danahay 2005). It would be inappropriate, if my task were intellectual history or biography, where I would need to nail down the elements in Bourdieu's thinking shared with Foucault and with early French structuralists, what was new in Bourdieu versus what was repurposed from Weber, and so forth. But that is not my task.

I need to break you free of the conviction that cultural capital has a settled meaning, like a good encyclopedia entry should; or that Bourdieu's (1986 [1983]) book chapter represents a reliable summary of his mature thinking about capital; or that terms like social capital, educational capital, academic capital, and the many other usages scattered through Bourdieu's work are unproblematic instances of some basic, underlying idea of capital. Bourdieu was not a straightforward thinker. He wasn't a hedgehog, to use a contemporary metaphor, who had one big idea. Not to put it too bluntly, his work is a mess; or rather, a mash, a great yeasty mass of intellectual ferment, in the end very nutritious, even intoxicating, if you have the intellectual enzymes needed to digest it, which it is the purpose of this essay to provide.

To start, let's plant this stake in the ground: the capital metaphor is theoretically fruitful. Social settings do exist where resources can function as "both a weapon and a stake of struggle." And any such resource is aptly metaphorized by using an economic vehicle such as capital, because money is one of the very few inputs identical in form to its output. Most inputs are transformed into a dissimilar output. Food exemplifies the normal case: tasty morsels are transformed into useful heat and repellent waste. Money is different: as the saying goes, "It takes money to make money." Money itself—more money—is the output of inputting money to an investment process.

How Many Capitals?

Capital can be an apt metaphor in any social domain where performing an activity produces a greater capacity to perform it. Unfortunately, after some years of reflection, and good-faith attempts to adopt Bourdieu's (1986 [1983]) position, I have had to conclude that in most domains, to refer to this or that capital is to give only a metaphor, and to fall short of theory. Mere metaphor occurs whenever we can offer an equally good and more straightforward, if less literary, description.

A case in point is social capital, as Bourdieu (1986 [1983]) defined it: the number of social connections. The capital metaphor at first appears apt. It is easy to see how effort invested in making social connections might make these connections produce even more connections, in the same way that investing money produces even more money. If you already have many social connections, this makes it easier to gain new social connections, just as it is easier to make a million more dollars, if you already have half a million, than if you have only a few thousand dollars in savings. And it is the social connections themselves that produce additional social connections, just as it is money that makes money.

But, however applicable, what is gained by applying the metaphor of social capital to the count of social connections?[5] Such locutions might help hitch a ride on the coattails of Economics, Queen of the Social Sciences. It might even be necessary to flog the capital metaphor, if you wrote for an audience that had a Vince Lombardi view of Marx: "capital isn't the most important thing in human affairs—it's the only thing!" Perhaps that view of Marx was widespread in Paris, when Bourdieu began his career. And Karl Marx's work continues to resonate for young Americans on the Left. The fascination, with calling everything a capital, perhaps comes from the sense of having grasped through Marx a revelation: everything comes back to money. Those not grounded in the Marxist intellectual tradition do well to recognize that calling everything a capital rests ultimately on a fascination with Marx's thought. The degree of fascination depends on how appealing you find his materialistic take on the human condition. But invocations of Marx do not a theory make, and no number of allusions to Marxist theory can turn a metaphor into a theoretical concept.

In the end, Bourdieu wanted to be a scientist, a scientific sociologist, and however powerful metaphor may be as a literary or even a teaching device, an enormous gulf separates metaphor from scientific theory (or at least, today almost every scholar in the social sciences believes this to be the case; see the Epilogue for further reflections inspired by Foucault). Social connections can be counted and measured in the normal scientific way; social capital suggests something more. The insight that social connections lead to more of the same is easily grasped. What is gained by adding a metaphorical gloss, and speaking of social capital?

Taking social capital as an exemplary case, might cultural capital also be naught but a metaphor, having an equally effective and more straightforward counterpart, one that can be readily quantified? This challenge must be confronted if Bourdieu's legacy is to bear fruit. We cannot assume that cultural capital has potential as a scientific idea, just because Bourdieu was a great thinker, or because he is a frequently cited authority, or because it's listed in encyclopedias. If we are to be scientists, then tradition counts for little; it doesn't matter that cultural capital has been accepted as an informative notion for several decades. To try another metaphor, think of Bourdieu's oeuvre as a large and elaborate vegetable garden, containing unique sub-races produced over many years of cross-breeding, unfortunately abandoned by the gardener some time ago, and now in a sorry, tangled state. The garden remains verdant, and still contains valuable and rare plants, but it is choked with weeds and gone to seed.

Metaphor Run Amok

As I was writing this section, the October 2014 issue of the *Journal of Consumer Research* (*JCR*) arrived, containing a paper that illuminates the consequences of not weeding the garden of Bourdieu's ideas about capital (McAlexander et al. 2014). I won't be discussing this paper's primary aim, which is to delve into the experience of leaving a major Church, Mormon in this case, under Late Capitalist conditions where everything is marketized. And I want to apologize in advance to the authors if the verbiage I criticize was added at the behest of reviewers, as sometimes occurs at this journal. Keep in mind that *JCR* is the finest and most prestigious journal in consumer research, one that rejects 90 percent of papers submitted. McAlexander et al. had to run a gauntlet which few survive, where reviewers took whacks with a stone ax, slashed with an obsidian blade, threw mud in its authors' faces, tried to trip them up, before it could be published in the *JCR*, and come in for criticism here.

The value of quoting from the paper lies in showing what happens when all of Bourdieu's ideas about capital are accepted as is, everything harvested and put in the pot, weed and seed. The authors state:

> The most important form of symbolic capital in Mormonism, indeed the distillation of all other forms of capital, is . . . worthiness . . . Like all symbolic capital, worthiness is interpreted, discerned, and judged by members of the field who have the cultural capital to do so . . . [what others] call spiritual capital is simply symbolic capital derived from field-specific cultural capital and social capital. (McAlexander et al. 2014, p. 866)

> the fear of losing field-dependent symbolic, social, and economic capital can also make leaving a field very difficult . . . field-specific symbolic capital (status) predictably loses its value outside its field of origin . . . [but we found that] field-specific cultural capital can be migrated to an oppositional field. (ibid., p. 872)

To see the difficulty posed by this barrage of references to capital, imagine that these passages had appeared in a college admission SAT test, followed by multiple choice questions designed to measure reading comprehension. Like this:

In the passage, symbolic capital refers to:

1. Status
2. A master capital that integrates other forms of capital

3. One of several types of field-specific capital
4. One of several types of capital present across multiple fields
5. In the religious sphere, a more apt term than spiritual capital.

It would be a very difficult SAT question, inasmuch as all the answers are supportable, but each one denies the correctness of the other. This style of thinking, which multiplies capitals without end, does Bourdieu no favors.

For instance, given the second definition from Bourdieu and Wacquant (1992) quoted earlier in this essay ("A capital does not exist and function except in relation to a field"), the term field-dependent seems redundant with field-specific: how could a resource specific to a field not depend for its efficacy on remaining within that field? And once there is field-specific capital, how can there be field-specific cultural capital, field-specific social capital, and so forth, since naming them separately, and applying them across multiple fields, requires precisely that they be field-independent types of capital? And what can it mean for your symbolic capital to be dependent on the cultural capital of others? Or to parenthesize symbolic capital, using the everyday word status? Readers not already initiated into the cult are going to get stuck on this verbiage, and find it more an obstacle to understanding than a route to it.

My point is not to criticize these authors. It's easy enough to pull quotes from the vast corpus of Bourdieu's own work to create the same jumbled impression (see Box 1.5). Here is a flagrant example from the later part of *Distinction*, the book that made Bourdieu's international reputation:

> engineers have the monopoly of the means of symbolic appropriation of the cultural capital objectified in the form of instruments, machines and so forth . . . [but] the profits accruing from their cultural capital are at least partially appropriated by those who have power over this capital, that is, those who possess the economic capital (1984, pp. 301–302)

This passage cues the same critical response as the one by McAlexander et al. (2014): if cultural capital is an autonomous resource, how can economic capital dominate it? How can cultural capital be both objectified in an instrument, and possessed by a person? Why would cultural capital have first to be symbolically appropriated, when it is "efficacious in a given field," per Bourdieu and Wacquant (1992)?

No single term can stretch to include both the exercise of taste displayed in fashion blogging, and the knowledge incorporated into machinery and instruments. The elastic snaps, and the idea fails.

We must show great discipline in applying modifiers to capital, if Bourdieu's legacy is not slowly to be dismissed, as just another piece of dated obscurantism erupted out of Paris. At Bourdieu's worst and most

BOX 1.5   THE MANY CAPITALS OF BOURDIEU

Below, I've tabled some of the different ways Bourdieu used the term capital. My purpose is not to catch out Bourdieu, but to show how loosely and metaphorically he approached the notion of non-monetary capital, in contrast to the seemingly tight definitions found in Bourdieu (1986 [1983]). Too many people think that essay wraps Bourdieusian capital into a neat package, as clear and structured as Aquinas.

Quotation and source	Comments
"capital can present itself in three fundamental guises: as *economic capital*, which is immediately and directly convertible into money ... as *cultural capital*, which is convertible, on certain conditions, into economic capital ... and as *social capital*, made up of social obligations ('connections')" (1986 [1983])	This is the conventional tripartite definition, adopted by those who view cultural capital as straightforward. The tripartite division postdates *Distinction*, where the key graphics have only the two dimensions: cultural and economic capital.
"Cultural capital can exist in three forms: in the *embodied* state, i.e., in the form of long-lasting dispositions of the mind and body; in the *objectified* state, in the form of cultural goods ... and in the *institutionalized* state ... in the case of educational qualifications" (1986 [1983], p. 47)	The definition of embodied cultural capital in terms of dispositions sets up a confusion with habitus. To speak of educational qualifications raises the question of how Bourdieu's cultural capital differs, if at all, from Becker's human capital.
"cultural capital, which we should in fact call *informational capital* to give the notion its full generality" (BW 1992, p. 119)	If cultural capital is information, how does it differ from knowledge, i.e., the human capital of Becker?
"*capital presents itself under three fundamental species* ... to these we must add symbolic capital, which is the form that one or another of these species takes when it is grasped through categories of perception that *recognize* its specific logic" (BW 1992, p. 119)	How can cultural capital be defined apart from the symbolic realm? In some later work, symbolic capital tends to supplant the others, suggesting again a generalized metaphor of (non-monetary) capital. But for these purposes, Bourdieu ultimately settled on "specific capital."
"symbolic capital, commonly called prestige, reputation, fame ... is the form assumed by these different kinds of capital when they are perceived and recognized as legitimate" (1991, p. 230)	Here Bourdieu appears to conflate the outcome of the capitals—distinction— with another species of capital.

Quotation and source	Comments
"The state [concentrates] different species of capital: capital of physical force or instruments of coercion (army, police), economic capital, cultural (or better) informational capital, and symbolic capital . . . [leading to] the emergence of a specific, properly statist capital . . . [and] the concentration of juridical capital, an objectified and codified form of symbolic capital" (1998, pp. 41, 47)	Note the disappearance of social capital. To call the army a capital shows how far Bourdieu was willing to stretch the metaphor. This essay, which postdates "The Forms of Capital" by a decade, makes it difficult to maintain that Bourdieu defined exactly three types of capital, neatly separated and organized in accordance with the first quote.
"have to be able to consider the society activities of the aristocrat, or the religious activities of the priest or rabbi, as . . . oriented towards preserving or increasing specific forms of capital" (1990, p. 88)	Aristocratic capital? Rabbinical capital? Is there no limit on how far the metaphor can stretch?
"science . . . must endeavor to grasp capital and profit in all their forms and to establish the laws whereby the different types of capital (or power, which amounts to the same thing) . . ." (1986 [1983], p. 47)	Power and capital can only be the same thing in a loose metaphorical usage of each.

Note: The year given links to the quotation to citations in the references section. If there are no initials, the citation is to a sole-authored work by Bourdieu; initials indicate a co-authored article, i.e., BW for Bourdieu and Wacquant (1992).

ineffective, references to capital become a tic, a label to be slapped on just about any trait, resource, or item of value, many of which already have a good everyday referent (for example, bodily capital in place of good looks, or educational capital for education). Absent an urge to draw the mantle of Marx around oneself, and to enforce a reading of social being in terms of "it's all about money," this reflexive labeling of everything, as some type of capital, is pointless, and cannot help us to explain social reality.

If cultural capital is not taken as unique, then either there is one type of non-economic capital, a core metaphor of money manifest across all fields; or, there are many types of capital, which each have to be justified and carefully distinguished, and not said to be both field-specific and manifest across fields. Under the first branch we can accept, as a handy abbreviation, when the underlying money metaphor is applied within a field, references to academic capital, spiritual capital, political capital and any other name-of-field capital; but our usage must be strict, and be limited to academic capital and no other, when we are working within the academic field. That way we preserve the fruitfulness of the underlying money metaphor, while harvesting that metaphor in a wide variety of fields. But as soon as we slip, and refer to the social capital gained in academia, by having a degree from an elite university, or the cultural capital obtained in academia, from publishing in top journals, while elsewhere reverting to academic capital, then Babel ensues.

I do not believe there can be many types of non-economic capital. Money isn't everything, everywhere. The metaphor isn't that fruitful. And there's no stopping rule, which is why Bourdieu continued to proliferate references to fill-in-the-blank capital for decades after declaring in Bourdieu (1986 [1983]) that there are but three (Box 1.5). And to introduce symbolic capital as "one ring to rule them all," while tying it back to the old term status, scrapes the nail across the chalkboard. Bourdieu's beautiful idea, grown over-ripe, rots into jargon.

Another Rival: Human Capital

Unfortunately, when we try to protect Bourdieu, by abstaining from needlessly proliferating forms of capital, we open him up to a new avenue of attack. If there is only one underlying capital metaphor, that likens resources across many fields to money, why not refer, as the economists do (Becker 1993), to human capital? It's a simpler term than field-specific capital, and the reference to human, because it is so encompassing, doesn't feed the temptation to proliferate labels across fields. In English, we refer to human when we want to invoke universality, some property or capacity, shared by all, across every human context—every field. One underlying metaphor yields one overt label. And who better to apply an everything-is-money metaphor than economists, who know the most about the real vehicle for the capital metaphor? Bourdieu was alert to the danger posed by rational choice economics, and the risk of having his metaphor hijacked. He repeatedly inveighed against Becker (see Box 1.3).

You may never have seen my gambit here before. To challenge the utility and legitimacy of Bourdieu's thinking, by substituting human capital for the unending mentions of fill-in-the-blank capital—it just isn't done in polite company. An Us-versus-Them mindset has developed among those favorably inclined toward Bourdieu's work.[6] Not many English-speaking business academics read Bourdieu, and nobody finds him an easy read. If one has invested—I was about to say intellectual capital, but trust you can see its redundancy, courtesy of this aside—in grappling with Bourdieu, he becomes the home team and the underdog. Mainstream economists like

Becker and psychologists like Kahneman dominate English-speaking business academia; the sociologically inclined and invested are a marginalized minority. No one so inclined wants to be relegated to the periphery of the all-conquering Economics discipline. Besides, if you have an overarching personal commitment to the political Left, as sociologists often do, Becker and the other rational choice economists can never be forgiven for their dismissal of Marx. Human capital comes out of the wrong economics tradition.

But the challenge posed by human capital, as an alternative formulation of what Bourdieu came to call field-specific capital, will not go away. In most applications, human capital refers to skills and knowledge. Interestingly, skills and knowledge are input factors akin to money, inasmuch as the input looks very like the output. Practicing a skill yields more skill. The more you know, the more you can know. Human capital is also attractive ideologically: it substitutes for the Marxian maxim, "it all comes down to money," a replacement of the form, "it all comes back to learning." Knowledge is wealth. Knowledge is the master resource. And if it is true that we now live in a knowledge economy, with the diffusion of the Web a case in point, then human capital might yield a more fruitful metaphor, relative to any Marx-derived metaphor dating to the metal-bending manufacturing age.

Ideas about human capital have shortcomings. Any reference to the pan-human denies group differences (Box 1.6), and carries ideological water for one philosophy of science versus others, privileging psychology and biology over sociology and anthropology. But human capital has to be taken seriously as a well-founded rival, most threatening when the field-specific capital formulation is adopted and flogged (one capital, under heaven, manifest in many fields, hallowed be thy name). Human capital would not so threaten, if Bourdieu had been able to confine himself to one or a few types of non-economic capital; but he never had that discipline, or not for very long.

What Is Cultural Capital?

The chain of reasoning thus far: (1) Cultural capital doesn't have a settled meaning, not even in Bourdieu's own work. (2) Some interpretations of cultural capital blur it with other sociological notions, such as the restrictive practices of Goffman or the boundary drawing of Lamont, so that whatever innovation Bourdieu made is lost. (3) Sampling across polarized social positions and attributing differences to the presence of cultural capital is a dead end. (4) Some readings of cultural capital can only apply to a highly static society with little mobility, and hence, are not

---

BOX 1.6   NATURAL HUMAN

An acquaintance with sociology, or anthropology, produces a deep-set skepticism toward claims of the kind, "It is human nature to . . . ." For a sociologist, the baseline is never the human, but rather, "People in this social group characteristically . . . ," while for anthropologists, the baseline is "Members of this culture are wont to . . . ."

For sociologists and anthropologists, the epistemic value of labeling an action as human, universal across all groups, now and forever, is inherently suspect. Not much in the social, cultural, or political spheres is universal. Hunter gatherers differ from peasants, who differ from city dwellers, who differ again from Late Capitalist consumers. They are all *Homo sapiens*, and that's important, for understanding the shared physiology that unites us. But the sociologist must resist the notion that our social being is a fixed concomitant of our biology, no less universal than the ability to convert sugars into cell energy. No. There are countless differences across groups.

In a sociological frame, to claim that something is human nature is to make a rhetorical move, to sneak in a claim that some viewpoint is uncontestable, correct beyond any questioning, because it is natural, as plain as the nose on your face. Or it is a reductive move, an assertion that the differences across collectivities and cultures are superficial, in comparison to the shared biological substrate, which actually drives behavior.

The sociologist believes in difference, in variation at a fundamental level, over groups and across time, within his proper sphere of the social and collective. If you want to be a consumer sociologist, you must learn to highlight every mention of human nature, in any text you read; to stop in your tracks, pause, and reflect: "Wait a minute; what claim has been slipped in here, and on what grounds?" Else, you may succumb to biologism.

---

useful to describe a modern consumer society, and especially not fashion categories within it. (4) The meaning of cultural capital must tie back to the underlying metaphor of money. (5) Unfortunately, this metaphor runs riot in Bourdieu's work and in many of those who claim him as a source. (6) Run riot, the metaphor risks losing its potency, and becoming mere metaphor, a literary embellishment of ideas that could be expressed in more familiar, straightforward and illuminating ways, which would be more productive from a scientific standpoint. (7) A defensible solution to the problem of proliferating capitals is to speak strictly of field-specific capital, a capital that always ties back directly to the money metaphor, expressed differently as needed to accommodate each field. (8) However, a single underlying non-economic capital, independent of field, might more simply be labeled human capital, tying the root metaphor to skill or knowledge, and returning ownership of the metaphor to non-Marxist economists. (9) Leaving Bourdieu and sociology with nothing.

The most fruitful path forward is to retain the idea of cultural capital, but ditch the other capitals: social, symbolic, field-specific, fill-in-the-blank capitals, every one. In terms of intellectual history, this is to acknowledge Bourdieu for a great insight, which got diluted through overgeneralization, into the coils of which later authors have become entangled, to the exclusion of the genuine insight with which Bourdieu started, and to which he often returned, without ever having the discipline to stick with it. Cultural capital, flexibly interpreted across the fields to which it pertains—which are far fewer than all fields—can be defended as not mere metaphor, and as not the same thing as restrictive practice, and as more illuminating than other contending ideas, such as human capital. Cultural capital is real, with a theory behind it; all other references to non-economic capital may be dismissed as metaphor, confusion, or ideology.

In sum, to understand fashion blogs, we first had to preserve and replenish the insight underlying cultural capital, by pruning back the overgrowth and tearing out the weeds. Stripped back to its essentials: (1) A few people possess a wealth that is not money wealth. (2) Some people, whom we might call cultural capitalists, can amass this non-financial wealth, and even reinvest, to earn more. (3) This investing and accumulating only occurs in the domain of cultural goods. (4) Some but not all consumer goods are shaped by what Bourdieu called "the cultural arbitrary." (5) Therefore, some consumers, of some types of goods, can amass and deploy cultural capital.

TASTE AND CULTURAL CAPITAL

To accomplish this pruning, so that Bourdieu's ideas may once again bear fruit, the discussion of cultural capital has to be recentered on the idea of taste. At first glance, this may not seem to help much. The term taste is subject to as many conflicting definitions as cultural capital. Explaining the one in terms of the other is like having to solve a single equation with two unknowns. But cultural capital can't be rescued from rivals, such as human capital or restrictive practices, and made useful for studying consumers online, without linking it to taste. We gamble that taste and cultural capital participate in enough sentences, in enough different contexts, to not leave us with two unknowns in a single equation. Rather, we gain two places from which to view our subject, which is the megaphone effect manifest in fashion blogging, seen now in stereo vision.

What Is Taste?

Taste is contested (Gans 1999; Gronow 1997; Holt 1998; Johnston and Baumann 2010; Lynes 1980 [1955]). As Bayley (1991, p.xviii) puts it, "an academic history of taste is not so much difficult as impossible." The meaning of taste in the West has been controversial since at least the 18th century (Gronow 1997). A fact that complicates discussion, and promotes confusion: taste is owned by at least three, and possibly four or five disciplines, each of which claims, as Bourdieu was wont to say when in a Weberian mood, a monopoly on the legitimate use of taste. It will clarify matters if I first name these disciplines and state their claims on taste.

The oldest claim belongs to the field of aesthetics, as when critics evaluate individual works of art, music, and literature. Here taste is the capacity that enables a person to act as a literary or art critic. Good taste in literature means the ability to discriminate the sentimental from the sublime, the schlock from the genuine, the merely pretty from the truly beautiful. Taste in an artistic context has elements of a habitus. The very tasteful critic is unable to enjoy pulp or kitsch—mere exposure makes him retch—but responds readily to the great or sublime, at which he swoons. The dullard who lacks taste simply cannot enjoy a Proust or a Joyce, a Stravinsky or a Schoenberg, a Duchamp or a Pollock; the capacity to appreciate the art in these more challenging works is missing. The clod has not got the habitus to see the art.

The critic appreciates true art, and beauty provides one of several anchors for existence, once God is Dead. Within an artistic context, to possess good taste signals character and establishes worth. Bad taste comes from bad character, and lack of taste shows lack of worth. The elision from aesthetics to ethics is quick and easy, causing ethicists also to dispute about taste, as Campbell (1987) notes. Taste balloons out from art to encompass conduct, as in the phrase "[not] in good taste." With this elision from Beauty to the Good, the stage is set for the conflation of sociological and artistic claims on taste, as described next.

Not as old, but in the 20th century rivaling aesthetic claims for prominence, is the claim laid by sociology on taste, advanced by Bourdieu, Goffman, and others. Classically, sociologists study the connections between taste and the elite, or taste and social class more broadly. Goffman's (1951) notion of restrictive practices captures this meaning of taste. Sociologists look at taste as a class marker and as a device for policing the boundaries that fence off and protect the higher strata. Here terms of art include parvenu, nouveau, and arriviste,[7] or snob, sophisticate, and swell, versus boor, rube, and hick. Good taste and bad taste line up with high versus low, subtle versus coarse, and refined versus vulgar. When in the grip of a structuralist fantasy, Bourdieu would natter on about such homologies.

But confusion spreads, once literary and artistic meanings of taste get mixed up with class. Bourdieu rose to prominence because he had a keen eye for class masquerading as taste, and loved to expose the pretensions of professed aesthetes, who only acted as jealous guardians of class interests. Unfortunately, some confusion of (artistic) taste with social class is almost inevitable in European societies and their descendants such as the United States. For centuries, European art that entered the canon of the great was first produced for, and primarily consumed by, a small group of the aristocratic elite. When that aristocracy ebbed, as it did at different rates in different nations in the 19th century, matters of taste became confused. Sometimes this cropped up in disputes about the quality of art in this work versus another, and sometimes in arguments about who could claim to be elite, based on what art they liked. You have probably encountered discussions of taste that did not recognize the separate claims of aesthetics and sociology, or the great danger of conflating the two.

I hope to inoculate you, so that when the term taste is encountered in neutral territory, such as a book review or newspaper article, you will immediately grow vigilant, and hesitant. Literary types know little of sociology; social scientists are too often ignorant of aesthetics and its philosophical heritage, including the link to ethics. Taste is a dangerous term; be careful out there. What masquerades as a simple metric for development of character, or fitness for elevated position, can often be unmasked as a restrictive practice, designed to defend and exclude, group identity burlesqued as good judgment and refinement.

The third claim to ownership of taste comes from ethnography, which sometimes makes its academic home in sociology departments, but more commonly in anthropology departments. Lamont's (1992) ideas about symbolic boundary drawing reflect the meaning of taste within contemporary ethnography. Ethnography comes into it because taste as boundary is taste as (group) identity, and from this scholarly apercu group identity means culture. Tastes identify a person as a member of this or that subculture, this or that voluntary association, and often, this or that marginalized, ostracized, and scorned group (Arsel and Thompson 2011; Holt 1998; Thornton 1996).

Under an ethnographic take on taste, there can no longer be good or bad taste in the literary, artistic, or ethical sense. Goffman's (1951) idea of restrictive practices becomes less apropos here. These practices restrict entry to the small elite at the apex of society, which others clamor to enter, and who emerge thereby as the right people, who presumably have the right taste, that is, good taste.[8] Ethnographers tend to be radical levelers, scornful of the idea of an upper class, and protective of The People (best said out loud in a deep, gruff, male voice). Ethnographically, in a post-Boaz world, there cannot be good taste or better taste; there are only in-group and out-group tastes. Accordingly, the role of (taste) boundaries is to include as much as to restrict or exclude. Shared tastes bring us together and make our common interests, our community, visible and real to each and all. The emphasis in ethnography is on taste practices, viewed as socially visible choices and preferences that confirm membership and confer identity.

The ethnographic take on taste has dominated discussions in my home field of consumer research, as part of work in consumer culture theory (Arnould and Thompson 2005). Works by Arsel and Bean (2013), Arsel and Thompson (2011), Holt (1998), and Thornton (1996) emphasize non-hierarchical taste preferences as the foundation of taste communities. Participants in Arsel and Thompson (2011) used taste preferences to protect their identity investments in the alternative music field, when under a devaluing assault from a commercialized mythology of the hipster. These consumers strove to know the right music to like, and the more centrally placed did tend to like the right music, the music that the most authentic among their fellows liked. Thornton (1996) similarly sees subcultural capital as a resource for authentication, which young club-goers achieve by differentiating their taste preferences from those of a despised (and fictive) mainstream. For these authors, tastes serve as a resource for drawing identity boundaries that include desired people and objects and exclude scorned others (Lamont 1992). Under an ethnographic lens, there can be no good or bad taste, but only my taste, which I discover is our taste, which shows that we belong together, and are different from them, who have no taste, because they do not share our tastes, which is how I learn they do not belong.

The ethnographic view on taste is sometimes undergirded by an explicit ideology: that there is no social hierarchy, that no one is elevated above anyone else, and hence no one can have better taste than anyone else. There are only different tastes, corresponding to different (group) identities, which group members, of course, put on a pedestal as the right taste. Here all claims to better taste are only assertions of identity, the claims of group members and wannabes. The underlying ideology may be explicit or implicit; where explicit, it may be glossed as postmodernism, the idea that during the baseline period, by about the 1990s, society had fragmented, causing hierarchy to lapse and putting legitimacy up for grabs, so that tribal identities, new and old, become the only refuge (Firat and Dholakia 2006).[9]

Young scholars need to recognize that there is a well-developed point of view, more common among ethnographically educated scholars than else-where, which denies the idea that there can be levels of taste. Since levels of taste are central to my analysis, I mean to alert you to these differences in ideology. For some scholars, to speak of levels of taste is bad politics, which is to say, bad taste, the taste of a foreign ideology. As a younger scholar you will need to take a stance on this matter.

A fourth claim to ownership of the term taste comes from scholars— I lack a handy label—who study food perceptions and customs (call it gastronomy? home economics? perceptual psychology?). These are scholars who study taste in the most literal and concrete sense of the term, the taste of bringing food into the mouth and onto the tongue. Gronow (1997) has an historically informed discussion, and Warde (1997), Fantasia (2010), Johnston and Baumann (2010), Gopnik (2012), and McQuaid (2015) also provide entry points. If tasting food is the metaphorical root, per Lakoff and Johnson (2008), of all usages of taste beyond eating food, then grasping literal taste, taste for food, and the extent to which even literal taste is culturally shaped, rather than natural or necessary or automatic, may repay the effort.

A consumer sociology, which does not yet exist, might someday assert a fifth claim over the meaning of taste. This claim would bear two distin-guishing marks. First, it would confine itself to taste in the context of con-sumer goods, narrowly defined as items bought or sold in a mass market. That definition excludes art, music and literature, as outside the consumer sociologist's area of expertise. Yes, you can buy a copy of *Ulysses* on Amazon, but that purchase is peripheral to the experience of this work of literature, and to its cultural import, and also unnecessary, since you could check it out of a library. And most people's experience of Rembrandt does not come about through a purchase, again dismissing as peripheral the need to sometimes pay admission to a museum. Conversely, you can't check a crème brulee out of a library; either it or its ingredients must be purchased, and to experience it is literally to consume it. Neither can you get a couch from a concert hall, or take a skirt out of an art museum; it or its components must be purchased. A consumer sociology will study taste in purchased items, consumer goods for short: items mostly experienced via purchase and use, and that get used up in that experiencing, as seen most clearly with food, and so very differently in works of literature and art, which are not used up, no matter how often experienced, or by how many.

A consumer sociology has nothing to say about literature or art. It will not try to wrest the topic of taste away from literary critics. It will warily but avidly observe discussions of taste in other disciplines, with an eye to what might be learned, in humble recognition that the boundaries drawn around consumer sociology are imprecise. Artworks may be consumed, I suppose; this usage doesn't do violence to the ear in the way that the consumption of spirituality does. But consumer sociologists don't have the training to contribute to aesthetic philosophy, and will know better than to try.

Pop culture provides a liminal case. Pop culture can be defined as purchased entertainment. Music, film, and fiction account for the bulk. Taste is huge in popular culture. But I think it is the ethnographer who owns the concept of taste in these domains. Ethnography is primary because taste in popular culture revolves around affiliation and identity: in-group and out-group taste. The dominance of ethnography may be strongest in popular music (Arsel and Thompson 2011). For instance, I have a profound distaste for country music—how about you? But reggae, that's got a nice beach vibe. Quick: how many inferences can you draw about my group identities, and my personal history, from these two statements? If such inferences flowed readily, I rest my case, as to why taste in popular culture belongs to ethnography.

Taste Goods

The second element that marks out a consumer sociology of taste is its rigorous restriction, within the category of consumer goods, as to where taste pertains. Preferences are everywhere across consumer goods, but preference is not a synonym for taste. There are some product categories where it is meaningful to speak of taste, and many, many other categories where neither taste nor cultural capital apply.

To be concrete, food, clothing, and home furnishings are taste domains. There may be others, but interestingly, these three crop up as a triplet in Bourdieu (1984, p. 78). He groups such products under the heading of the cultural arbitrary. What might he mean by that evocative phrase? I will apply it to goods whose quality, in the usage of economists, is difficult to inspect or verify, but where people often have a visceral response, pro or con. This green couch looks putrid. A torte in this style melts in the mouth. That skirt on her makes me retch. Why call it the cultural arbitrary? Because the visceral responses, of different people, may starkly differ, and even be opposed—that sea green couch relaxes my eye. Although arbitrary, these visceral responses do cluster by group and by era; they are not purely idiosyncratic. Their shared character justifies the cultural half of the label. And yet, what makes taste responses visceral is the shock of recognition— this is my style, this is what I like. And this gut reaction is underwritten by a tacit conviction of universality: I only like good style, stylish goods.

Later, in the Pinterest essay (Essay Three), I will try to interrelate style, fashion, and taste in a more systematic way. The reader who needs that clarification now can flip ahead to pages 187–224. Here the focus must stay on identifying product categories where the terms taste, style, and fashion are apropos, which are categories where the cultural arbitrary is manifest.

By this criterion, paper towels and other everyday convenience items are not domains of taste, whether toothpaste for the teeth, detergent for the clothes, or mops for the floor. These are too minor to have much aesthetic potential, or to be culturally appropriated.[10] Vacuum cleaners, microwaves, desktop computers, and other machines are domains of knowledge, where consumers may differ in expertise, but not in taste. We can meaningfully say, "she has good taste in clothes," "he has good taste in restaurants," and "her apartment is tastefully decorated." But it is conceptually and linguistically awkward to say, "she has good taste in vacuums," "he has good taste in microwaves," or "her Windows file directory has been tastefully arranged."[11] These sentences contain category errors, in Gilbert Ryle's memorable phrase. We can speak of a preference for stainless steel appliances, or a liking for some brand of paper towels, or expertise in the case of computers, and we can also speak of good design in the case of a machine. But none of these requires or even allows use of the word taste, nor do we gain insight by substituting taste for preference or liking. Taste is different.

Based on these limits, cultural capital in a consumer goods context is most likely to be visible in the food, clothing, and home décor categories. Here, better is arbitrarily determined, but judgments of better are made, and shared, and felt as much as known. Here the concrete and literal meaning of taste, for food, provides a helpful anchor. If you don't like the taste of beets, you want to spit them out. Food that tastes bad, undeniably tastes bad; food that tastes good is immediately pleasurable. These are visceral not cognitive responses.

Two Meanings of Taste

To pull together the threads, consider the graph in Figure 1.1, which distinguishes a vertical from a horizontal operation of taste. In its horizontal operation taste distinguishes in from out, us versus them. The horizontal dimension captures the ethnographic take on taste. In its vertical operation, taste distinguishes better from worse, above from below, up versus down. This is the literary or artistic take. With one further assumption, it is also the classic sociological take on taste: that better artistic taste will be found to be the taste of the better sort of people; moreover, that people born to higher social positions readily like and respond to better art, in a manner difficult for people who are not to the manor born. As Bourdieu liked to say, the societal realm and the realm of art are homologous: similar

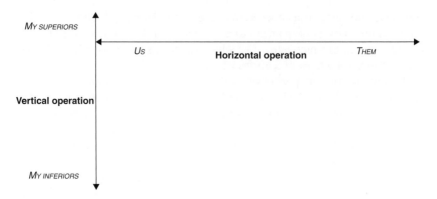

Figure 1.1   Two dimensions of taste

in structure. To which, those of us not bewitched by the structuralist fantasies of 1960s France can only respond: "Maybe." Whether truly homologous or accidentally similar, it is the shared use of taste in the vertical sense, by students of art and students of sociology, which promotes a fatal confusion of the two domains, and gives traction, especially here in America, to the ethnographic dismissal that it's all a crock; there is no better and we have no betters.

The next step, in founding a consumer sociology of taste, and retrieving cultural capital for use in the consumer sphere, is to retain the vertical operation of taste, inherited from the aesthetic realm, while leaving behind the automatic equation of better taste to endowment with better social position. Gronow (1997) provides the lock release. In the aesthetic realm, he speaks of judgment power. This is the power to discriminate better from worse in realms where there is no mechanical or standardized test; aesthetic realms, the domain of the cultural arbitrary. Better, in this domain, means more pleasing, to more of those people, who have more capacity, to take more pleasure, within the aesthetic realm at hand—net, net, net, net. Pleasure is central to this definition of aesthetic (Campbell 1987). It need not be central to other definitions of aesthetic, but again, we are focused on a few categories of discretionary consumer goods, items which provide pleasure, not the satisfaction of needs.

Aesthetic realms in the consumption sphere—domains of the cultural arbitrary—can be concisely defined as places where *Consumer Reports* magazine dare not go. A paper towel or a vacuum cleaner is an excellent candidate for a *Consumer Reports* article, which is why we can exclude these product categories from the domain of taste. The absorbency of the paper towel can be measured. The dirt removal capacity of the vacuum cleaner can be tested in a variety of standardized settings. Either it picks up > 80 percent of 2 grams of dog fur dropped from a height of 50 centimeters onto a 2 centimeter deep carpet pile, or it fails. There are better and worse products in these categories, but there is not better or worse consumer taste.

Now imagine a *Consumer Reports* article on fashion handbags. Imagine measurements of the amount of weight that can be carried before the strap tears, of the stitch count and the regularity of their spacing, of the thickness of the leather and its grade. It would all be beside the point. None of it would help the consumer decide whether the Michael Kors handbag, with these boots and this hat and scarf, would make a pleasing impression on the people who care about looking good, that she cares about. That fashion decision requires taste.

Taste is not skill. Taste is not knowledge, and this is how we can protect cultural capital from the charge of being just another form of human capital—which has to rest on knowledge. You can have knowledge of vacuum cleaners, and skill in cleaning a house with a knack for keeping it neat. But there is no knowledge of how to appear fashionable, no facts about what will look good together, and nice on me. There is no skill in handbag selection, but you can display better or worse taste in choosing a handbag to complement an outfit.[12]

Aesthetic realms in consumption, domains of the cultural arbitrary, are product categories where moderately shared judgments can be made about better or worse, and where better means more pleasing to more people who get pleasure from these products. Because discriminating judgments are made, and by individuals, we can speak of taste as an individual capacity, that may be possessed to a greater or less degree. Because the pleasure is the pleasure of other people, and these other people are uncounted but potentially very many, taste isn't entirely idiosyncratic and subjective, even though it can't be said to be objective either, as developed in the *Consumer Reports* example.[13] Because taste is not entirely subjective, it depends crucially on other people; not so much on certain individuals, but on all of us collectively, or some group of us. That is why consumer taste belongs to sociology.

Your taste has to be ratified by other people before it can be called good taste or better taste. These people can't only be part of your group, or limited to fellow travelers in your subculture; that would toss us back into the lap of ethnography, and its perspective on taste as shared in-group preferences. Consumer taste is ratified in the mass among strangers. Because it is ratified in the mass, it will tend to be mainstream taste. Studies of taste in consumer ethnography, which focus on marginalized or oppositional groups and subcultures (Arsel and Thompson 2012; Thornton

1996), must be set aside, not as wrong, but as unhelpful. Sociology studies strangers in the mass.

Consumer Taste Levels

The conclusion: in domains such as food, clothing, and home décor, consumers will be distributed throughout a range of taste capacity, with some consumers having little taste, most having some taste, and a few having high levels of taste capacity. It does not matter whether taste has exactly a normal distribution, but it does seem likely to be humped in the middle, with many consumers ranking neither high nor low. Next, it may be helpful to profile consumers at low, middle and high levels on the taste gradient for clothing, to show how better and worse consumer taste operates in that category. My argument does not require there be bad consumer taste (Box 1.7), only better and worse taste; a gradient from less to more.

A consumer low on the taste gradient for clothing need not make mistakes. We need not imagine these individuals dressed, Rodney Dangerfield style, in striped top with plaid bottom and polka dot coat. Rather, the consumer low on the taste gradient doesn't pay much attention to his own or others' dress (the male pronoun slipped in there). He may observe a few simple rules to avoid clashing colors and patterns. The clothing he buys is ordinary, probably neither expensive nor rare, and not much time is spent shopping. If female, accessories may be minimal, and little time will be spent in the morning deciding how to dress that day; if male, what to wear that day is only a matter of rotating through his stock. No one notices how this person is dressed; compliments are only rarely received, but also, are neither sought nor expected.

The consumer low in taste for clothes might seem also to lack what consumer psychologists call involvement with the product category. Dressing right is not important to the persons just described. And it's true: at low levels, taste lines up with involvement. No news. To grasp how taste differs from involvement, we have to move up to the middle of the taste gradient, and beyond. People with middling good taste will spend more money on clothes, and more time and effort on shopping and on dressing for an occasion. Wardrobes expand and broaden in range. Involvement is much greater. But taste will remain middling, to the extent that the following descriptions apply: (1) Not many compliments on dress are received, and these tend to be lukewarm or casual, and come mostly from people who are not themselves exemplary dressers, but who have personal or professional reasons to curry favor. (2) No one turns their head on the street when this person walks by (throughout these taste gradient examples, I hold constant a moderate personal attractiveness, by the local standard,

---

BOX 1.7   BIPOLAR AND UNIPOLAR CONCEPTS

Elsewhere in the social sciences, in the design of measurement scales and questionnaires, researchers have to stay alert to the difference between bipolar and unipolar responses. A familiar bipolar case is the survey item whose five response options range from "strongly agree" to "strongly disagree." These polar response categories work well, when you study statements of opinion, where there is no right or wrong. An example: "Nuclear power is a clean form of energy." It may be low in carbon omissions, but it is not low in radiation production, so is it clean? That is a matter of opinion, which hinges on whatever clean, in the context of energy, means to the respondent.

Now consider this very different statement, found perhaps on a student evaluation form: "The instructor is highly qualified to teach this course." You can apply an agree–disagree scale to such a question, but it is a force-fit. If a respondent disagrees, is it because she perceives the instructor to be only moderately qualified rather than highly qualified, or because the instructor is perceived as unqualified? Either could be the case. And what does it mean to strongly disagree with this statement? Does it mean you are highly confident that the instructor's qualifications are exactly moderate, not high?

Personal characteristics are often distributed on a gradient from absent to present, from zero to a lesser or greater degree. There is neither minus nor plus sign, just less versus more. That's my stance on consumer taste: best to approach it as a capacity that varies from mostly absent, to minimally present, to moderately present, to present to a high degree. This maneuver helps to avoid the trap of talking about bad taste, which so often drives off an ideological substrate, rooted in group identity or social position. To speak of the relative absence of taste, rather than bad taste, keeps discussion on a neutral plane.

Speaking to the PhD student: beware of bipolar concepts. Left brain versus right brain thinking is a familiar and pernicious example. Bipolar concepts tend to become all-embracing, and hence, empty. Bipolar concepts are magnetically attracted to one another; everything lines up: heaven and earth, male and female, yada yada. A silly and hollow structuralism threatens. Unipolar concepts cry out for supplements. Unipolar concepts never quite line up, preserving a rich diversity of intellectual content that has some hope of capturing the real.

---

when naked, unadorned, and without cosmetics). (3) This person does not believe herself to have excellent taste, and doesn't strive to make her clothing choices exemplary or outstanding. She's careful about how she dresses—she's involved—and would be appalled to be thought badly dressed. Dressing is important, but she's not greatly accomplished at it, or invested in becoming more accomplished.

At the high end of the taste gradient, involvement in the product category may not be any greater, nor need the expenditure of money, time and effort; but a different set of descriptors applies: (1) This person often gets compliments, these compliments are sometimes enthusiastic, and compliments come from a broad spectrum, not just people with strong ties or a need to curry favor. (2) Compliments come from people who themselves receive compliments on their dress. (2) People who don't know this person do turn their head to take a second look, when she walks by; and the glance of every one tends to linger, once she's been noticed, which she is more likely to be, than others in the room. (3) She's confident about her dress. Deciding what to wear in the morning, and having to decide what to wear for a novel occasion, are positive challenges, exciting and engaging. She'll take a risk in her dress, when in the mood, and wins that wager more often than not. She's got good taste in clothes.

I hope it has dawned on you why traditional analyses of cultural capital would not be helpful here, and why I had to spend so many pages unfreezing ideas about capital. Taste as just described could not easily be joined to any traditional definition. Under a habitus-based conception of cultural capital, the person portrayed as having good taste in clothes would have to have been born into a family that already had good taste in clothes, where her mother, her grandmother, and even her aunts, also had good taste. She would had to have been immersed, from birth, in dressing right. Otherwise she'd never quite figure out how to dress that certain way. From a restrictive practices point of view, these clothes would have to be expensive and rare and from exclusive outlets. But I did not need to go there; good taste in clothes, among ordinary consumers, requires some money, but not large amounts. From an ethnographic point of view, the account is radically incomplete; I did not say anything about the group she espoused or what her clothes signaled about her cultural identity. That expansion was neither necessary nor possible in this pleasure-based account of mainstream taste.

Finally, and this will be the bridge back to a refounded definition of cultural capital, I stayed ambiguous on one count. Were her taste displays static, showing the same good taste, year after year? Or, might her display have been dynamic, changing in style and extending in range, different this year than last? I didn't say.

In the account given, taste is a personal ability or gift, unevenly distributed in the population. Some people have high amounts of it, most don't. This taste may or may not be specific to a product category. Our exemplar of good taste in clothes may have a well-decorated home or may not; may be an adventurous chef or may not. In other words, we can allow for some people to have a taste gift that extends across categories, while letting others be gifted in only one domain. Cultural capital effective in one domain need not be effective in other cultural domains.

Here is the link that joins taste to capital: when an individual's good taste is dynamic, so that she takes chances, is adventurous, tries and often succeeds at new taste displays, she may be said to amass cultural capital within that domain. Her increasing stock of cultural capital fuels new adventures and more pleasing taste displays. A virtuous circle gets rolling, consistent with Bourdieu's later formulation, where capital serves as "both a weapon and the stakes at issue." Taste displays amass capital, and amassing capital fuels new more tasteful displays. By contrast, static taste probably reflects an endowment, which came from the family. Endowments need not be accumulated, or amassed further.

And now at last we come back to blogging. In describing low, medium, and high taste levels I did not mention the Web. I sketched only a vaguely urban setting, and did no more than assume a mass society with a large and prosperous middle class, as could have been found in many parts of the USA in 1990, or 1965; and probably in 1950, and maybe 1920; and in London or Paris, for a few decades further back. None of the clothing or dressing described required the Internet, but only a consumer society, our modern world, whose genesis is teased out in Campbell (1987). The argument in brief: because there was no Internet, not much cultural capital could be accumulated by ordinary people who dressed as described.

The Web alters this world. Now the taste displays of an ordinary person can gain a much bigger audience. The megaphone effect becomes possible. During the baseline period, an ordinary woman could never escape her immediate surroundings; her tasteful dress could never please, outside the circle of family, friends, associates, and workmates. Someone on the street who did turn their head for a second look might never see her again, and could not know her or take repeated pleasure from her tasteful dress. So bounded, the tastefully clothed person could not accumulate cultural capital from her displays of taste. Capital accumulation, before the Web, was a variable-speed motor getting only a trickle of current. It didn't turn over very fast. It could not power much.

With blogging, the motor of capital gets a jolt of electricity. Now the switch can throw to full on, and stay at max. A display of tasteful dress can be seen by thousands, instantly. This mass audience may send accolades and cheers to the blogger by posting comments. Thousands of followers turn the blogger into a taste leader. Exercising leadership, she gains and maintains an audience, and builds cultural capital. New and more adventurous taste displays result. These reinforce leadership, gain more audience, and build further cultural capital.

Remember, it makes no sense to speak of cultural capital except in a context of distinction. To be elevated within a small group of workmates does not provide much distinction; not enough people. But to be distinguished for one's tasteful dress on the World Wide Web, where an audience of thousands can be gained, produces capital.

The new definition of cultural capital highlights the connection between taste and aesthetic judgment: a person's capacity to discriminate the beautiful and graceful from the labored and unappealing. In this account, taste has levels, a vertical aspect, and individuals can be sorted by how good their taste is—on their ability to discriminate stylish, fashionable clothing from merely acceptable dress. Cultural capital in the fashion field means the capacity to exercise better taste, to have a higher level of aesthetic ability. But, consistent with the later Bourdieu's dynamic formulation, cultural capital also refers to the stakes that may be gained from that exercise of taste. Fashion bloggers are people who start with some capacity for taste, and proceed to accumulate cultural capital, by the repeated exercise and display of taste, which builds capital, which fuels more and better displays.

This definition of cultural capital, and this depiction of the role of taste in capital formation, differs from the established view in consumer research, which hews to the ethnographic model. Following Holt (1998), taste in contemporary American consumption has been treated as a means to affiliate with a group and to signal that identification. The focus: how taste communities are formed, rather than how an individual can exert taste leadership. As Arsel and Thompson (2011) put it, consumers learn to calibrate their tastes to a field, community, or group with which they identify, to join with others who share the same taste regime (Arsel and Bean 2013). Likewise in Holt (1998), members of the social elite find one another and recognize one another based on shared tastes (for example, for movie directors), even as non-elite and elite members are repelled from one another by differences in taste (regarding a $22 couch purchase). For scholars in consumer research, taste has meant group-based preference, and not judgment power exercised by individuals, per Gronow (1997). The one sees taste as a device for affiliation, while the other views taste as the capacity to discriminate the laudable from the pedestrian.

Why has past consumer research not teased apart the vertical and horizontal operation of taste? In part, because Bourdieu's own work encompasses both meanings, as seen in this oft-cited remark: "Taste classifies, and it classifies the classifier. Social subjects, classified by their classifications, distinguish themselves by the distinctions they make" (Bourdieu 1984, p. 6). The double meaning of distinction corresponds to the double meaning of taste. Taste can be used to draw boundaries (Arsel and Bean 2013), as in, "Do you like what I like?" But taste can also function as a claim of and a denial of worth, as in, "He has a lot of taste . . . all of it bad" (Bayley 1991, p. 77).

Prior accounts in consumer research have successfully imported Bourdieu's account of taste aimed at distinction-between, and developed how taste can be pressed into service as a boundary marker between groups, to provide a basis for affiliation and community. The new things consumers do online allow us to examine taste in the service of distinction—over, taste as an agent of social mobility, taste as a resource for clambering up the ladder. It is this kind of taste that enables some fashion bloggers to wield the megaphone.

Goffman on Audiences

If we had enjoyed clairvoyance, back in 1995, and intuited that fashion blogging would come into existence, what might we have predicted, about the role played by taste in these blogs? In principle, fashion bloggers could have deployed taste either horizontally or vertically. Clothing choice—taste as group preference—can identify the community or subculture to which the wearer belongs: hipsters or clubbers or indie rockers (Elliott and Davies 2006; Goulding et al. 2002). Fashion blogs might have drawn their audience from among consumers pursuing identity projects. The clothing displayed on the blog might have been selected to send a strong signal about the community or subculture to which the blogger belongs (Berger and Ward 2010), and to draw together the like-tasted.

Had fashion blogs fit this model, authenticity would be primary. Holt (1998) argued that consumers with a large stock of cultural capital preferred authentic products. Authenticity implies taste displays that reflect the central tendency of the group (Arsel and Thompson 2011). That is the problem with outsiders and wannabes: their taste displays come across as inauthentic, because deviant or inept. They fail to gain entry because they do not grasp the group taste. Their clothing choice is not judged authentic.

Stepping back, authenticity has been a central value in Late Capitalist times (Johnston and Baumann 2010). Back in 1995, our clairvoyant might have found it plausible, as an anchor to explain the new things consumers might do online, such as fashion blogging. Kozinets et al. (2010), in an early study of bloggers given free products, did find authenticity to be a leitmotif of the dialogue between bloggers and followers, concerning the free cell phone supplied, and the controversy it created.

However, authenticity is not the only core value held by consumers. Arnould and Price (2003) find two threads, woven together, to bind the domain of the cultural arbitrary: consumers care about authentic performances, but also authoritative performances. Authority suggests leadership. Leadership implies the vertical operation of taste, and a very different prediction, from back in 1995, about how fashion blogging might unfold.

Goffman's (1959) work on the presentation of self supports this different prediction. I read him to emphasize taste leadership rather than taste preference. Goffman applied a dramaturgical metaphor to everyday life, arguing that in social encounters, people could be parsed into actors and audience, with actors striving to put on a front and convey a persona, and audiences accepting successful actors as they wished to be seen. In Goffman's account, no person is ever authentic in public behavior toward an audience; authenticity, to the extent it is possible, occurs only in the private sphere. To an audience one shows a persona, rather than revealing one's identity. Goffman (1959, p. 58) draws on Simone de Beauvoir for support: "the least sophisticated of women, once she is 'dressed', does not present *herself* to observation; she is, like . . . the actor on the stage, an agent through whom is suggested someone not there, that is, the character she represents, but is not."

Fashion blogging offers an apotheosis of Goffmann's dramaturgical metaphor. Unlike in face-to-face interactions in everyday life, or conversing with known friends on Facebook, a fashion blogger can display a persona that may be far removed from her real self, a persona she can rehearse and rewrite until she gets it right. Display of this persona seems ill-suited to constructing an authentic self. Therefore, blogging must be an authoritative performance (Arnould and Price 2003). But it is a novel kind, insofar as it is an individually sourced rather than collectively underwritten act, and because it cleaves to fashion rather than tradition. Fashion blogging, interpreted in Goffmanesque terms, expands the category of authoritative performances to include a social actor's successful enactment of style—the authority of her taste.

Fast forward to 2010, and clairvoyance is not needed. As it turned out, fashion bloggers—the successful ones we studied—do not blog to affiliate with a community of like-minded consumers. Bloggers do not exhibit taste preferences to draw boundaries. Rather, per Goffman, bloggers exercise taste in the vertical sense, to draw a mass audience of strangers. Gaining a foothold with such an audience launches a virtuous circle, which cycles between taste displays and cultural capital.

EMPIRICAL EVIDENCE

McQuarrie et al. (2013) describe an empirical study of ten fashion blogs, each of which was launched by an ordinary person, who later gained large numbers of followers. There seemed no point in reproducing here all of the method and results published there. The opportunity, here in this book, lies with introducing ancillary material that didn't make it into the published paper, followed by a brief discussion of key results. The final part of the essay returns to a discussion of the conceptual implications of what we discovered from these fashion blogs.

Method in Consumer Sociology

> I am publicly criticizing my fellows ... Anyone who does this can expect to have their motives questioned. Readers may wonder whether the author is embittered ... perhaps he has been slighted in the past ... [now] gaining his revenge. Or ... deeply flawed as a person, a serial troublemaker ... constantly picking quarrels. (Billig 2013, *Learn to Write Badly*, p. i)

There are few vetted methods in consumer research; too few, to advance consumer sociology. Vetted means approved by journal reviewers; and as I unpack that point, you'll understand why I led off with that Billig quote.

Publish or perish. Everyone knows that phrase, of course, but not everyone knows the corollary, which governs business academia, and consumer research specifically: publish in the inner circle of peer-reviewed journals, the very best ones, or see your academic career go nowhere. For instance, if I were not already retired, and unconcerned with career advancement, I would hesitate to write this book: no matter how successful, it can do little for my narrowly defined academic reputation, my reputation among colleagues who occupy this corner of academia. Books don't count there.

Only journal publications, and only papers in the most highly selective outlets, where 80–90 percent of submissions are rejected during the gauntlet of peer review, can advance a scholarly career in business academia and consumer research. Next, the peers, who review submissions for these journals, are people who have already published there, and perforce, published articles that used some method. Reviewers assume that a submission that uses the same method as they did, is probably sound, so that they can proceed to evaluate quality of execution. But if the method is unfamiliar, then all bets are off. Who knows if the results are any good or not? Who can tell whether the unfamiliar method has even been executed appropriately? The consequence: an enormous inertia in favor of established methods. Peer review, as too few recognize, cannot be receptive to innovative approaches.

Although the journal system is hostile to anything new, the established methods in consumer research struck me as especially unsuited to studying cultural capital among fashion bloggers. There are two vetted methods: the laboratory experiment favored by consumer psychologists, and the in-depth interview favored by ethnographers. A laboratory experiment must force out sociological concepts in favor of psychological ideas: it is a stimulus-and-individual-response paradigm. If you have not been initiated into consumer psychology, you cannot begin to imagine the patriotic fervor with which such experiments are endorsed in business academia. Reviewers schooled within that paradigm cannot envision why any serious scholar would ever do anything other than experiment—the One True Path to Knowledge (see McQuarrie 2004, 2014 for a more sustained skeptical treatment of such laboratory experiments).

More pertinent to sociology is the ethnographic method, especially, in this context, the netnography pioneered by Kozinets (2007, 2009). Before the Web, ethnographers had long engaged in participant observation, living among the natives as it were, and conversing and interacting widely. Alternatively, they interviewed members of a community in depth over time. With netnography, participant observation returned, and researchers began to read blogs and discussion posts, comment back, email questions, and otherwise engage with the online community under study.

By 2010, within the fraction of researchers sympathetic to ethnography, the interview, whether in person or virtual, had acquired the same degree of orthodoxy as the laboratory experiment had got among consumer psychologists. Reviewers could not understand why my co-authors and I did not go out and interview fashion bloggers for this study, or Pinterest users for Essay Three. How can you understand consumers' sense-making, their communally shaped attributions, their psychological processes, their inner life, if you don't interview them? Our retort was: "Who says fashion bloggers are part of a community?" and, "Why do we have to care about their inner life?" To which one reviewer responded, "Community *has* to come into it!" But authors are in no position to retort to reviewers.

Bourdieu was sensitive to the limits and dangers of interviews in a sociological context. Interviews, like all empirical methods, shape what can and cannot be learned. If you conduct an ethnographic interview, you will tend to discover what ethnographers have historically found when using this tool: that is, community. If you interview people using a more diffuse theoretical perspective—interviews are not the exclusive province of ethnographers—then, given the dominance of psychological perspectives today, your questions will gravitate toward motivation, perception, introspection, and sundry other psychological processes. Neither the ethnographic nor the psychological paradigm is conducive to ferreting out what is properly sociological.

Think about it: if interviews were necessary to understand people, history would be impossible—dead people are among the most difficult to interview. If history can yield understanding, then it must be possible for an analyst to immerse himself in written materials, and come away with an understanding that is not private and unverifiable, but public. Our method was historical, even though the bloggers were still alive. The basic procedure was to sample blogs systematically, and then read copious material in blogs, and about them. My co-authors, who handled this portion of the research, immersed themselves in the blogs, sampling posts from beginning, middle, and end, and moving back and forth in time as they read.

A consumer sociology can never emerge from psychological labora-tory experiments. Any sociology that relies on consumer interviews will tend to revert to ethnography or social psychology. If we are to do consumer sociology, we must be set free to examine documents, and to value the historical analysis of all kinds of documents, whether from blogs, online reviews, or pinboards, or from more traditional sources such as advertisements and correspondence. The tyranny of interviews must cease.

Findings: Blogger Trajectory

Initial position
These ten bloggers began as ordinary consumers outside of the fashion system. McCracken (1986) describes the fashion system as composed of the designers and manufacturers of fashion clothing and accessories; the media institutions that promote such clothing in editorials and advertising; and the social elite, especially celebrities, who engage in the vast public relations machine of television and movie roles, special event appearances, and talk-show and gossip magazine placements (compare the gift system defined in Giesler 2006). These are the traditional, professional sources that govern the determination of what is fashionable, also recognized by Bourdieu (Rocamora 2002). None of our bloggers was a fashion insider or professional and no family connections to the fashion system were uncovered. When their blogs launched, these ten individuals were indis-tinguishable from the millions of ordinary consumers who make up the market for fashion clothing. Ordinary, in this usage, does not mean average or typical, nor does it exclude extraordinary skill, as in the taste displays to be discussed. I mean ordinary in Turner's (2010) sense: neither endowed by family connections nor credentialed by professional or institutional position.

These bloggers may never have intended their blog to be only a per-sonal journal online. The blog titles are rhetorically stylized and replete with complex, allusive forms of wordplay: *Fashion Toast, Style Bubble*. Mass advertisers use wordplay to attract consumers by aesthetic appeal (McQuarrie and Mick 1996). These bloggers devised blog titles to accom-plish the same goal. The rhetoricized titles signal to the prospective audi-ence that aesthetic judgments will be offered.

From personal journal to taste display
Early posts sometimes give the impression of a consumer who uses her blog as an online journal for personal disclosure (Chittenden 2010; Hodkinson 2007; Kretz and de Valck 2010; Reed 2009; see also Box 1.1):

> just got home from teddys, decided to not go to the after party, we had a great night as it is. me, z and deb went, paparazzi snapped pictures of us all night long ... they are so clueless ... the gastineau girls were chillin at a table by themselves, still a foreign concept that the mom and daughter party together. random other models and celebs partied really hard ... cant help but love la! time for bed as hollywood continues to party. (*BIA* 03/25/07)

This post, with its casual focus and lack of attention to spelling and punctuation, describing a night on the town, would pass unnoticed on Facebook or any other social media site. Fashion blogging is undermotivated: almost anything that can be posted on a blog could have been posted on a personal page at a social media site. The key difference: with a blog, you can reach an indefinitely large audience of strangers.

Posts to these ten blogs soon cease to resemble private social media, and evolve toward public displays of taste. Here is an example, from later in one of the most popular blogs.

> Found the perfect gray socks while shopping at Uniqlo in Tokyo with my mom/ favorite shopping partner (she's always down to stop randomly to eat and shares my love for finding wearable things in unlikely places). Vaguely sheer and just the right length. This sounds extremely trivial, and sort of is, but I've been looking for something like them forever now. (*FT* 05/12/10)

This post came to be read by more than 30 000 people. It received 174 comments, such as "OMG Rumi, you are my greatest inspiration EVER, you just rock with your amazing outfits and with your breathtaking photos. You are the best style icon EVER." Get past the demotic vernacular, and you see appreciation for the blogger's aesthetic acumen.

Choosing to display gray socks is neither here nor there with respect to taste as distinction-between. These gray socks do not serve as a badge of membership in some group (Berger and Ward 2010). Likewise, the socks are not a signal inviting affiliation with other marginalized youths over against a fictive mainstream (Thornton 1996); the blogger is, after all, shopping with her mom. It is not the display of gray socks per se on a fashion blog, but selection of a particular brand, length, and opacity of gray socks to display—and choosing to pair them with leather shorts— that makes a display of taste leadership. And such displays can be recognized as taste leadership insofar as these attract and hold a large audience (in this case, more than 30 000 people).

Consider next the post reproduced in McQuarrie et al. (2013, Figure 1), from another blog. The picture is captioned: "Everything I'm wearing is Vintage, except the Doc Martens. Those babies are fakes, and now the black plastic is peeling away, which I kind of love." The blogger claims to be tasteful, by making a risky choice. Who knew that peeling plastic fakes could look good, look right—be fashionable?

Further insight: "Vintage" is not a stray capitalization error, but the name of a brand of clothing which, according to the manufacturer's website, "is a premier streetwear brand that was born out of the free thinking and creative spirit of the underground music and art cultures . . . [designed for] lyrical wordsmiths, crate digging-vinyl loving deejays . . . fed up with the mediocre mainstream brands from malls and major department stores." The Vintage clothing brand lays claim to the heritage of the club, hipster, or indie culture studied by Thornton (1996) and Arsel and Thompson (2011), where real Doc Martens shoes are worn. But by wearing peeling plastic fake Doc Martens, this blogger lays claim to a distinctive personal style. She takes a risk, and invites her audience to judge her: "How does this look?" She exercises taste and makes a public display of it.

These posts build a persona, in Goffman's (1959) terms, an elaborate statement of who the blogger proposes to be: "I am a woman of style. I combine the indie brand of Vintage with the punk brand of Doc Martens yet openly acknowledge I wear fake footwear, while on another day I may pair a real fur hat with a Chanel bag. I make my own fashion statements." Rather than affiliating with a community, the blogger declares her taste: "I think this looks good." What will be judged tasteful, in a concrete instance, is not something "that can be learned in school," to use Thornton's (1996, p. 13) formulation. Rather, audience members with a passion for fashion clothing know taste when they see it. Hence, each taste display by the blogger represents a risk. The blog is an ongoing performance that could bomb at any time (Deighton 1992).

It is because the blogger takes risks, and is judged tasteful more often than not, that she may be said to accumulate cultural capital. Taste as judgment power can't be learned in school, but it can be developed through repeated exercise. A blogger accumulates cultural capital insofar as she succeeds again and again in being judged fashionable, and as a result, develops more and more capacity to take fashion risks and succeed. To use the metaphor of Bourdieu and Wacquant (1992), once a poker player has amassed a large pile of chips, she can play differently than one who has got only a small stake.

Cultural capital accumulates by means of iterated displays of taste that are favorably received; displays which draw, hold, and grow an audience. What elevates the successful blogger? She exercises better taste, reflecting her greater degree of judgment power (Gronow 1997). In the realm of clothing, she makes aesthetic judgments that are both good and adventurous. We know she shows good judgment, when a large number of consumers, exposed to that picture of grey socks with leather shorts, viscerally respond, "that is fashionable," or "that is to my taste." With the aid of the Web, a display of taste can win her an audience. In turn, that favorable response increases her capacity to exercise taste, and encourages her to invest in further displays. The blogger acts as a connoisseur with a megaphone.

But the taste display has to be adventurous as well. As Bourdieu (1984, pp. 91–92) recognized, there is an element of bluff in taste leadership—it demands flair. Any catalog picture will show attractive people wearing nice-looking clothes correctly combined. But fashion is not a matter of right or wrong according to an explicit and ascertainable standard; fashion is not a dress code (Bayley 1991; Gronow 1997). Fashion doesn't stand still, so that repeating what has already been done cannot secure attributions of fashionable or stylish. To stay within the confines of established selections and combinations of clothing, wins no accolade. To be received as a taste leader, and accumulate capital, the blogger must take risks, such as wearing a Vintage outfit with fake plastic boots, or pairing a real fur hat with a Chanel bag. In fashion blogging, we found consumers exercising verbal and visual connoisseurship, and riding a trajectory toward an economic and social position they lacked at the outset. Here aesthetically discriminating taste judgments lead to an advantageous social position, rather than a privileged social position producing a favored taste judgment.

From community to audience

These blogs develop over time in a second respect. Just as bloggers begin by sharing moments in their personal life, early in the blog they adopt a community orientation toward others who browse their blog. Initially the blogger is thrilled to receive comments, and answers questions and suggestions with her own comments (Chittenden 2010), or in her next post, as this example illustrates:

> Thank you so much for all the kind words and congratulations! I'm going to answer all the questions in that post today, just want to make sure I address them well. One of you mentioned that headbands/scarves would be fun and it inspired me to dig up one of my favorite vintage silk scarves today. Kind of adds a more boho element to the leather skirt. (*FT* 02/25/08)

Seeming eager to please, bloggers will ask their followers what they would like to see on the blog. Likewise, early in their trajectory, bloggers will provide personal information in response to questions, such as weight, height, and ethnicity, and tell where to find specific fashion items.

The early interaction between blogger and follower is consistent with the treatment of virtual communities in Mathwick et al. (2007), who approach Web-based discussion forums as sites for the accumulation of social capital. They define social capital in Putnam's (1995) terms, as a collective possession, and not in Bourdieu's (1986) terms, as connections an individual can use to gain preferment. Mathwick et al. (2007) show how norms of reciprocity play a key role in producing collective social capital within an online community (see also Giesler 2006).

Fashion bloggers begin in the same vein, acting as if the blog were a collective good from which all can benefit, through sharing ideas about fashion clothing, and where all can participate in shaping the content that appears on the blog, per the account of authoritative performances in Arnould and Price (2003). Initially, the blog proceeds as if a virtual community was going to be built, with the blogger acting as one participant among others. But this complex of behaviors soon disappears, as the blogger begins to build an audience.

As her audience grows larger, the blogger's behavior changes. She stops interacting with her followers. She avoids answering questions, ignores suggestions for posts, and refuses to address issues raised in comments. Interestingly, this doesn't bring the growth in audience numbers to a halt. Follower comments become more uniformly positive, as the blogger ignores her followers more and more. As bloggers gain autonomy from their followers' desires and wishes, they appear to be perceived as more worthy of an audience.

An important contribution of early research on online consumer behavior was to establish the existence and reality of virtual communities (Muniz and O'Guinn 2001; Rheingold 2000). It has even been argued that "community is the true 'killer app' of cyberspace" (Jarrett 2003, p. 339). However, this analysis of fashion blogging suggests that community is not the only thing that consumers seek online. In the end, the bloggers studied didn't affiliate with or construct a community—they built an audience.

To this point, consumer research has not considered the value, to ordinary consumers, of becoming an audience rather than joining a community. One explanation comes from the organization theorist Karl Weick (1995, p. 54), who remarked: "when you are lost, any old map will do." Late Capitalist society can be a confusing place, offering the overwhelming freedom to dress any way you please (Davis 1992). Holt (2002) hypothesized that many consumers would buckle under such freedom, and look to "cultural specialists" for guidance (see also Durrer and Miles 2009 on cultural intermediaries). Consumers may be looking for fashion guidance they can't get from professional and institutional sources, such as brand advertisers and other credentialed members of the fashion system (McCracken 1986). Consumers who wander, somewhat lost, provide a ready audience for a peer consumer who has the taste resources to risk taking a leadership role. Comments from fashion blog followers support the idea that blogs offer aesthetic inspiration and exemplary taste:

> Your dress is amazing, too bad it's vintage, now I can't buy it. But that makes it even more beautiful. With ur chain, clutch, and shoes makes ur outfit perfect! (*SW* 06/26/10)

> I absolutely LOVE your blog. Your outfits are amazing, and it gives me so many more ideas. Thank you! (*SW* 06/26/10)

What bloggers offer their followers is not a supportive community, or a badge of group membership, but an exemplar of taste. Bloggers engage in an enterprise of distinction-over: in their posts, they show combinations of clothing that may never have occurred to the consumer reading the blog, but which nonetheless strike her favorably. Bloggers establish themselves as better at fashion style than others: leaders, not fellow community members. Taste leadership makes a blog valuable to other consumers, and builds an audience for the blogger.

Findings: Blogger Outcomes

These fashion bloggers garnered both economic and social rewards. Economic rewards included gifts of branded fashion clothing and other merchandise, paid ad placements on the fashion blog, and paid sponsorship of their blog contests. Other paid assignments included modeling branded clothing, designing clothes and accessories, and writing for publication. Bloggers' social position improves, as they receive invitations to exclusive parties, runway shows, designer open-houses, charity appearances, and mentions in the media. By the time we studied them, these bloggers had gained a role within the larger fashion system unavailable to an ordinary consumer, no matter how involved she may be with fashion clothing.

Any Bourdieusian capital—a status reserved in this book for cultural capital—can be exchanged for economic capital; and economic capital can be exchanged for almost anything else, here in Late Capitalist times. The fungibility of money helps to explain the unruly proliferation of capitals in Bourdieu's work. Since cultural capital can be converted to money, and money can buy social connections, an elite education, and so on, it becomes all too easy to slip into speaking about social capital, educational capital, capital this, capital that. But this tendency has to be fought. If we take seriously the money metaphor underlying cultural capital, then its convertibility into money is a given, and money by definition is fungible. No need to go slapping the label of capital on everything in sight. The task, rather, is to tease apart the sources of cultural capital, and trace how it may be leveraged.

These bloggers won an audience by making public displays of taste. Positive response, to their initial displays of taste, stimulated bloggers to develop their taste further. They take risks and make taste ventures. These developments iteratively produce a larger audience and a more favorable audience reaction, which charge the cycle once more. Figure 1.2 depicts this process.

As their audience continues to grow, bloggers come to the attention of promoters in the fashion system, who send economic resources their way, in terms of gifts of merchandise, money for ad placements, and so forth. These resources, which fuel further taste ventures, grow the blogger's audience, which keeps resources flowing, and sets up a positive feedback loop. As their audience grows, bloggers also gain social connections to prominent insiders within the fashion system, which lends bloggers more prominence, which enhances the size of their audience of ordinary consumers, while conveying to this audience that the blogger really is a taste leader (Pham 2011 describes this as a "prominence dividend"). Having and growing an audience makes bloggers valuable to marketers and to fashion insiders alike. The interest of both acts to enhance her audience size, and its approbation for her, which recharges the inner two feedback loops in Figure 1.2.

Countless ordinary consumers, highly involved with fashion, dream of such success, but it is unavailable to all but a few. Our successful bloggers accumulated cultural capital from the small seed with which they began: their ability to make aesthetic discriminations judged suitable by, and novel enough to be of interest to, a mass audience of other consumers. Taste as judgment power fueled these bloggers' success.

Findings: Maintaining an Audience

Practices of misrecognition

Once they gain an audience, bloggers appear motivated to hold on to it. Here, these bloggers have an advantage over *Vogue* and other institutionally sanctioned fashion outlets on the Web, which also compete for an audience. Since clothing is an extension of the self (Belk 1988; Entwistle 2000), believable taste in clothing requires that the blog follower, an ordinary consumer, be able to see herself in the taste displays she encounters on the Web. Can this occur, when the clothes are worn by a supermodel, in a setting impossible for that ordinary consumer to attain? By contrast, a blog follower can look at the taste display of an ordinary consumer, such as the bloggers studied, and believe, "I could look good in that."

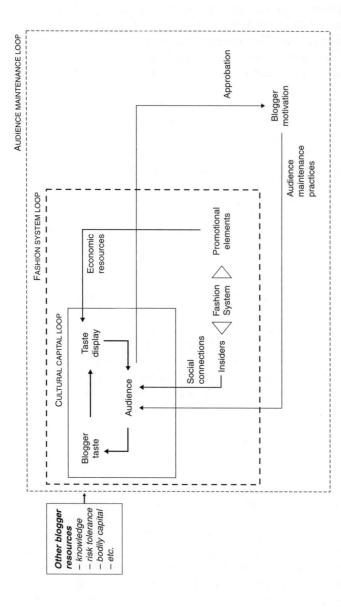

Note: Three feedback loops are shown. In the innermost loop, a blogger's capacity to make taste displays gains her an audience, and this feedback increases her cultural capital, expanding her capacity to exercise taste and make a display of it. In the next feedback loop, once her audience has increased past some threshold, it becomes valuable to the fashion system. Prominent fashion insiders (for example, a magazine editor) now provide social connections to the blogger, which tends to increase her audience further. Likewise, the promotional element also desires audience access, so it sends gifts and payments to the blogger, which further enhance her taste displays, and thus her audience. In the third loop, having a mass audience motivates the blogger to keep it, which leads to misrecognition practices that maintain it. Each of the loops thus charges the others.

Figure 1.2   Feedback loops involving bloggers' cultural capital

However, once a blogger gains a mass audience and enjoys privileged access to the fashion system, she is no longer truly an ordinary consumer. This poses a threat of loss of audience, and hence of her newly gained position. One solution: practices that deny the existence of boundaries that separate them from followers (Schau et al. 2009; Warde 2005). Two discursive practices fit this description: bloggers feign similarity, and self-deprecate.

Bloggers feign similarity with their followers by referring to mundane and ordinary aspects of their lives that downplay the glamour and rarity of being a fashion insider, with its special access and privileges. Here, for example, the blogger complains about her small closet while posting about her attendance at London's Fashion Week and the gifting of clothes to her by designers:

> I leave for Fashion Week on Thursday. I am so excited to be back on The Strand . . . probably stumbling all over the place on the impossibly unpredictable cobblestones of Somerset House. Also looking forward to seeing some of the most inspiring people I know. And best yet, I have some exciting clothes coming my way . . . So I hope to see you there! By the WAY: Have you noticed the size of my wardrobe in these photos?! Have you seen how painfully SMALL it is? About a quarter of my clothes fit in there, the rest are folded in piles that are forever circling my room: from my desk, to the floor . . . and I have even resorted to under my bed. It is a distressing situation! . . . One day I'll have the walk-in wardrobe that I actually have vivid dreams about at night. (*F* 02/14/10)

Note how the blogger says she hopes to see her followers at Fashion Week, even though the event is attended by invitation only. In this way, she maintains similarity with her followers by deliberately misrecognizing their inability to join her at the event.

A related practice, which again serves to make the blogger appear less distant, is to express self-deprecation and self-ridicule, and to downplay accomplishments. For example, in the *Frassy* post (above), the blogger states that she will be stumbling all over the cobblestones, implying that she cannot walk in high heels. In other examples, the blogger insults her own appearance, even as she announces her involvement in premier fashion events (McQuarrie et al. 2013).

In self-deprecating, bloggers may mention physical characteristics, bad habits, or embarrassing moments, but deprecation never ventures into the realm of fashion. Bloggers do not ridicule their own taste in clothing. A blogger might say she has a small closet, but she would never say she doesn't know what to pair together from her closet. A blogger might say she stumbles in high heels, but she would never say she had trouble figuring out which brand and color of heels to buy. Self-deprecation and feigning similarity emerge as strategic practices, which misrecognize the blogger's

actual social position vis-á-vis her followers, consistent with the dramaturgical perspective of Goffman (1959).

Fashion bloggers use strategic practices, of feigned similarity and
self-deprecation, to deny boundaries and misrecognize distinction-over.
This contrasts with past discussions of cultural capital, in which taste is
exercised to exclude others and to enforce distinction-between (e.g., Arsel
and Thompson 2011). By contrast, bloggers amass their cultural capital by
drawing and holding an audience. To continue this success, bloggers must
misrecognize the boundaries that come to separate them from followers.
Fashion blogging shows how cultural capital can operate in unsuspected
ways, to efface rather than enforce boundaries.

Misrecognition of social position is discussed by Bourdieu (1991).
However in his examples, misrecognition takes the form of substitution-up,
as when a student in the Paris of Bourdieu's day, and his examiner, mis-
recognizes his exam performance as due to intellectual merit, rather than
to a mere affinity of shared tastes and social background (see the extensive
analysis of the grading sheets for the essays used to select students for
elite schools in Bourdieu 1996). Fashion bloggers show the reverse form
of misrecognition, a substitution-down, in which they deny their factually
privileged position relative to followers.

Misrecognition and authenticity

Authenticity has been widely studied in cultural sociology as well as consumer research (see Chapter 2 in Johnston and Baumann 2010 for an integrative review). As a rule, people seek authenticity in the uncommon, and
in opposition to the mainstream (Thornton 1996). Thus for Holt (1998),
to seek after authenticity is to avoid market-constructed meanings, and
to resist mass culture or try to mask its influence (Beverland and Farrelly
2009; Campbell 2005; Rose and Wood 2005). Arsel and Thompson (2011)
similarly find that greater amounts of cultural capital help hipster consumers to reject meanings imposed by mainstream culture, and preserve the
authenticity of their taste preferences.

This description of authenticity presents a puzzle. These successful
fashion blogs were replete with commercial endorsements of mainstream goods. Why do consumers not reject and disdain these blogs as
inauthentic, as happened to some of the bloggers studied in Kozinets
et al. (2010)? Each fashion blog contains many commercial messages and
each photo is captioned with a list of all the brands worn, down to the
nail polish. Many brands are endorsed, including retailers and online
shopping sites; most are well-known, mainstream fashion brands, rather
than artisanal or craft brands. Often, the items displayed on the blog
are sponsored or gifted by fashion manufacturers, as freely admitted

by bloggers. Nonetheless, the response of blog followers remained very positive.

Why does the commercialization rampant on these fashion blogs not produce the jarring effect found by Kozinets et al. (2010)? Perhaps authenticity, in Holt's (1998) sense of rejection of marketplace meanings, is only central when a blog presents itself as a personal blog, an online journal where identity work will be performed (Chittenden 2010; Parmentier and Fischer 2011). Marketing efforts, when these intrude upon personal blogs, do transgress. Successful fashion blogs represent something else: a public display of taste. Fashion products and their brands are intrinsic rather than extrinsic to the taste asserted. The appearance of free gifts on the blogs ratifies the blogger's taste leadership, rather than violating trust.

Another explanation stems from the effective misrecognition which bloggers practice. If followers live vicariously, through consecrating the blogger (Bourdieu 1991), then when the blogger receives invitations, gifts, and deals, these perks only reinforce the consecration. That is, unusual privileges and a bounty of gifts confirm the blogger's taste leadership. Consumers accept overt marketing in these blogs without scorning the lack or loss of authenticity.

DISCUSSION OF FINDINGS

Bourdieu on the Web

In the first part of this essay, I pruned and redirected Bourdieu's ideas, to tie cultural capital back to financial capital: a liquid thing, an asset that consumers can invest, risk, and accumulate (Bourdieu and Wacquant 1992). Under this dynamic account, fashion bloggers act as cultural capitalists, amassing capital as they make venturesome displays of taste. Once these taste displays have acquired a large enough audience, bloggers can convert their cultural capital into economic and social resources, as the established fashion system begins to assimilate them. Once they join the system, audience acquisition becomes self-reinforcing, as positive feedback loops leverage institutional elements of the fashion system, a circuit kept open by bloggers' practices of misrecognition.

I've depicted the Web as a causal factor that midwifes new forms of consumer behavior. Past consumer research has tended to treat the things consumers do online as analogues of what they do offline, and to view the Web as only a new location. Thus, researchers have asserted that market-place communities can be established online same as offline (Muniz and O'Guinn 2001), norms of reciprocity govern online communities same as offline (Giesler 2006; Mathwick et al. 2007), and consumers' postings online correspond to word of mouth offline (Kozinets et al. 2010).

By contrast, a focus on consumers' new-found capacity, courtesy of the Web, to acquire a mass audience, suggests that something new and different occurs there. Ordinary consumers could not gain such an audience before the Web. There is no offline equivalent of a verbal–visual blog, a Yelp restaurant review, or user-curated images published on Pinterest. Before the Web, only professionals holding an institutional position could publish their writing or images. Ordinary consumers were confined to their immediate social networks and communities; they could not grab the megaphone and acquire a mass audience of strangers for their acts of consuming. As a consequence, the value some consumers place on acquiring a large audience of strangers, and the value other consumers place on being part of such an audience, had not been glimpsed. The megaphone effect, combined with ideas from Bourdieu and Goffman, makes these new consumer acts visible and comprehensible.

The distinctiveness of the megaphone effect, as manifest in fashion blogging, may emerge more clearly through a contrast with earlier studies of online consumer behavior by Schau and Gilly (2003) and Giesler (2006). In their study of personal websites constructed before blogging had diffused as a widespread practice, Schau and Gilly found consumers who undertook to communicate to an unknown public without institutional support, in rough parallel to what we found in fashion blogging. However, there was a key difference: the websites in their study were ultimately intended to reach individual unknown others, in order to set up a dyadic interaction; as, for instance, with future romantic partners or potential employers. Giesler's (2006) study of peer-to-peer file sharing through Napster defines a gift system, parallel to what we, following McCracken (1986), refer to as the fashion system. For Giesler a gift system is not merely a set of dyadic gift-giving relationships, or a bounded community of reciprocal give and take, but an overarching socio-cultural structure, one that rests on, and provides an opportunity to demonstrate, social distinction (cf. Bourdieu 1980, pp. 98–101). Likewise, we represent the fashion system as a locus where ordinary consumers, by means of the Web, can attain distinction. The key difference: taste leadership played no role in the file-sharing gift system studied by Giesler (2006), whereas here, it is taste that drives bloggers' distinction.

My adaptation of Bourdieu highlights the role of taste in consuming, especially online, even as it shifts the emphasis away from existing theories of how taste operates. In the past, consumer researchers focused on the horizontal operation of taste: the ways in which taste preferences group consumers together and serve to divide an Us from a Them:

distinction-between (Lamont 1992). This study, of how mass audiences are built on the Web, shifts the focus to the vertical operation of taste: the way that judgment power—the capacity to make aesthetic discriminations that can win an audience—enables a select few consumers to distinguish themselves as above the rest. When we apply a sociological lens, and put aside the ethnographic lens, we discover that consumers can place as much value on achieving prominence, as securing an authentic identity (Goffman 1951, 1959).

Ideology of Giftedness

In adopting Gronow's (1997) definition of taste, based on judgment power and aesthetic discrimination, in one respect I deviated from Bourdieu's position. To be more blunt, there is one area where I rejected Bourdieu's view, rather than trying to retrieve or refashion it. This rejection is teased out next.

Throughout his career, Bourdieu was hostile to what he called the ideology of giftedness (Bourdieu 1990, p. 109): the supposition that aesthetic ability or good taste was inborn, a personal gift independent of the social position and historical context of the bearer. Bourdieu also rejected the related assumption, that objects themselves could be beautiful, tasteful, or fashionable, as opposed to being deemed such by culturally and socially situated individuals. In Bourdieu's experience, to assert good taste often meant only to assert the taste of the ruling class, taste judgments legitimated by the social position of the person doing the judging. As Gronow (1997) notes, this position is unsustainable, given the fluidity and mobility of modern consumer society, and is peculiarly unsuited to the sphere of fashion, where mutability is of the essence.

We can nonetheless be sympathetic to Bourdieu's project, and his reasons for inveighing against the ideology of giftedness. As developed earlier in Box 1.6, sociologists are keenly aware of, and vigilant against, the tendency to naturalize, and thus misrecognize, matters that belong to the domain of the culturally local and arbitrary. Most attributions to human nature have to be looked at with suspicion, once this sociological mindset has been grasped. What bothered Bourdieu, I believe, was the attitude of Enlightenment Rationalists (never absent from France) and socially well-off aesthetes—who might be one and the same—in which they knew, really knew, that this one is beautiful and that one is humdrum, this shows taste and that does not, this has aesthetic value and that does not. "Balderdash!"[14] Bourdieu might have spluttered. "What you perceive to be your gift of discernment is nothing but your social position projected onto compatible objects. You elevate supposed art over supposed kitsch to elevate yourself over others." Bourdieu had a fractal model of the social and aesthetic spheres, in which the structure of the one was projected and reprojected onto the other, almost as if two funhouse mirrors were arranged face to face. Certain objects were perceived by certain refined people as more refined than the humdrum objects esteemed by the common sort who lacked refinement. This hermetic circle naturalized taste as a gift, possessed by a special few of the better sort of people.

But in rejecting the idea of a personal gift for aesthetic discrimination, a gift of judgment power, a beautiful baby got thrown out with the dirty gray bathwater. Bourdieu's efforts to expose the misrecognition, of social position as aesthetic judgment, called into question the idea that anyone could have better aesthetic judgment than anyone else. Consistent with the Copernican and Darwinian spirit of modernity, this skepticism leads inevitably to Boaz's ethnographic position: no one can have good taste across groups—no one cultural product can be judged better than some other culture's product—even as everyone has taste within their group of affiliation, can recognize and celebrate objects consecrated in their own group or culture. From the rejection of giftedness it is a short step to the rejection of all taste judgments as culturally arbitrary, on a par, a matter of the group with which you identify; nothing more to be said.

With the post-Kantian demise of the idea that taste hierarchies are universal, the horizontal operation of taste came naturally to the fore, in consumer research as elsewhere. Taste was made relative and particular to communities and subcultures. Nonetheless, selectivity, exclusion, and hierarchy continued to operate in spheres such as clothing. Mainstream mass society endured and flourished, and aesthetic judgments about consumer goods continue to be made and contested there. I've argued that tasteful, in the vertical sense, now consists of intuiting what might be to the taste of a mass audience of involved peers. Taste in fashion can once again be treated as a gift that a select few consumers possess. By means of the Web, these select few can leverage that gift to acquire cultural capital, and convert this capital to social position and economic resources.

What distinguishes the megaphone effect is the absence of institutional mediation. These fashion bloggers acquired their initial audiences on their own. This separates the megaphone effect from reality television on the one hand, and fast fashion on the other (Ferdows et al. 2004; Crane and Bovone 2006). In fast fashion, a clothing manufacturer—an institution—seeks out fashion innovations on the street among the people, and puts these street fashions into production. As with reality television, originally demotic elements get picked up and presented to a mass audience; but in each case media and manufacturing institutions retain control. Fashion blogging, online reviewing, and user-curated images represent something different. Here, institutions are only ancillary, not determinative.

Some consumers have the gift of good taste. That gift explains why some fashion bloggers gain a mass audience. Whether by nature, nurture, or both, some people go beyond involvement with the clothing category to demonstrate good taste—judgment power, aesthetic discrimination. The presence of this gift may bear some relation to family social position; I'd wager that most people who show judgment power for clothing enjoy at least some discretionary income. The argument stands, as long as judgment power does not vary in lockstep with increasingly advantaged social position.

The Web changes things. The gift of taste can now be leveraged outside an immediate circle. The leverage is provided by the megaphone effect: the newly available possibility of reaching a mass audience, without first having to gain a favored institutional position. Before the Web, no ordinary person, acting on their own behalf, had much chance to gain a mass audience. This is new.

LIMITATIONS

A more extensive discussion of limitations appears in McQuarrie et al. (2013). Here I only touch on some limitations of the empirical work reported, to begin the transition to the next essay, which will switch focus, from fashion clothing and blogging, to restaurants, Yelp, and online reviews.

The taste leadership displayed in the fashion blogs we studied, and its role in explaining how they acquired a mass audience, may not generalize to explain the success of other kinds of blogs, such as technology blogs, or even other kinds of fashion blogs, such as those undertaken by men, or originating outside the developed Anglo-Saxon societies where our blogs were situated (Pham 2011). Nor need taste leadership be the only explanation for the success of young female bloggers, some of whom may blog in pursuit of an identity project, or as a means to affiliate with a subculture (Scaraboto and Fischer 2013).

Likewise, we studied blogs at a particular juncture in the diffusion of Web technologies. Whether blogging, on fashion or any other topic, will continue to let ordinary consumers grab hold of the megaphone, is unknown. The megaphone effect seems likely to endure for awhile; but the routes by which consumers get hold of that megaphone may shift or evolve.

Not All Goods Are Taste Goods

The rule laid down in this essay has been: if no exercise of taste, then no accumulation of cultural capital. To back up this rule I had to define taste, in the consumer sphere, narrowly. Taste only pertains where, per Thornton (1996), "things that can't be learned in school" are central. When knowledge that can be learned in school provides expertise, or when professional and institutional experience provides knowledge, taste ceases to be pertinent. I have tried to preserve cultural capital for consumer research by making it specific to taste, and drawing tight limits around the sphere of taste. The heart of the strategy: separate taste from knowledge and skill. The stakes are high. Wherever Becker's (1993) idea of human capital, derived from the exercise of knowledge and the practice of skill, can explain consumer behavior, there is no point in bringing in cultural capital (Ratchford 2001). Beauty dare not tread where Truth makes his bed.

Within this first limit, a second may be glimpsed: not all taste judgments produce cultural capital. Taste is present wherever an aesthetic discrimination can be made; but the exercise of taste can only accumulate cultural capital when preferment is possible. That is, taste leadership, rather than simply taste clustering, must be possible, before cultural capital comes into play. In this study, taste leadership meant acquiring a mass audience; other routes may exist.

A third limit confines the applicability of a dynamic conception of cultural capital. I do not deny the continued pertinence of a static notion of cultural capital, wherein large amounts of it come into your possession as a family endowment, as a result of institutional position, or from education. High levels of taste—taste ratified by large numbers of social peers—can still be produced by birth, or by acquiring a favorable social position. But the reverse sequence, in which the exercise of taste leads to a higher social position, is now possible, courtesy of the Web. Our fashion bloggers, who acquired a mass audience online, supply an anchor case for this trajectory.

Pulling together these threads, a dynamic conception of cultural capital should be fruitful in three broad categories of consumer goods: (1) fashion clothing and accessories; (2) food, including restaurants (Johnston and Baumann 2010); and (3) home décor, including any visible aspect of the abode, whether interior or exterior (Arsel and Bean 2013; Lynes 1980 [1955]). The cultural arbitrary governs these domains (Bourdieu 1984, p. 78). These three categories appear often in post-Bourdieusian scholarship on taste (Bayley 1991; Falk 1994; Gronow 1997; Warde 1997). A question for future research is whether taste operates more widely in consumer behavior, and if so, where. Although food, fashion, and home décor are good places to start, for exploring the role of taste leadership in consuming, there may be yet others.

Consumer Culture, Consumer Sociology

Consumer researchers have learned much about the pursuit of identity (Arnould and Thompson 2005; Parmentier and Fischer 2011), the role of community in supporting identities formed in opposition to the mainstream (Thornton 1996), and how authenticity can be claimed or disputed (Arnould and Price 2003). Less is known how consumers go about improving their social position, or pursue mainstream success, or gain preferment outside of an institutional path. This research suggests that many consumers wish to join audiences, not just participate in communities, that a select few ordinary consumers desire an audience for their consuming, and that both actions flourish online.

Muniz and O'Guinn's (2001) innovative treatment of community among consumers marked a swing of the pendulum in social history. As originally conceived by German sociologists such as Tonnies, the marketplace was portrayed as the antithesis of community, and even, the agent of its destruction. Following Muniz and O'Guinn, researchers have explored how consumers construct marketplace communities, including virtual communities (Mathwick et al. 2007). That work has supplied a corrective to individually centered and purely psychological accounts. But under a sociological lens, consumers do not only affiliate with communities—they also seek positions in society, vis-à-vis a mass of strangers. These positions not only shape, but are shaped by, and even attained by, consuming. Courtesy of the Web, a new kind of social position has emerged: that of the taste leader who takes hold of the megaphone, builds an audience for her consuming, and gains a position she didn't have to start.

But the megaphone effect is not the only new thing on the Web.

NOTES

1. Some sentences in this essay appeared previously in McQuarrie et al. (2013); the duplication is greatest in the "Findings" sections. Before and after, the material has been largely rewritten and greatly expanded.
2. The idea of specifying a baseline period, and locating it then, comes from me, not Turner.
3. Yes, I know that the original phrase was "to the manor born." I want to highlight the pun.
4. Much later, in the epilogue, I'll challenge the supposed distinction between metaphor and theory; but here, I conform to ordinary usage, in which the word metaphor has to be prefaced by a diminutive like mere.

5. Another argument for getting rid of (Bourdieusian) social capital, in the service of pruning and strengthening the important idea of cultural capital: too many other theorists have laid claim to the phrase, and mean something quite different by it than did Bourdieu. In the United States, social capital is most famously associated with Putnam (1995). He is not alone; to learn about other claimants to ownership of the term, see Baron et al. (2000). Bourdieu is unusual in making social capital the possession of an individual; other traditions locate it outside of individuals, in the collectivity. In consumer research, see Mathwick et al. (2007). In sociology, see Erickson (1996) and Lizardo (2006).

6. This diagnosis may be specific to the small corners of academia I have occupied: a business school, and the interdisciplinary association of consumer researchers, most but not all of whom are located in business schools. Whether historians or sociologists encounter this mindset in their departments and associations, I cannot say.

7. To describe, in English, phenomena associated with pretension and status claims, there are an astonishing number of words borrowed from French: parvenu, arriviste, poseur, nouveau riche, jejune, déclassé. I'm not sure why that is.

8. I don't think Goffman intended quite such a restricted meaning for restrictive practice, but I find it convenient to assign him thus, the better to tease out the differences between the intuitive, quite specific application of restrictive practice, and the broader applicability of Lamont's idea of drawing boundaries that include as much as they exclude.

9. This ideology has able exponents, but has never appealed to me. To be frank, as a favorably dated Baby Boomer, born into the middle class, I've lived too well in material terms, while rising too far in what has seemed a very stable academic hierarchy, to be able to believe that things have fallen apart and the center cannot hold. It's perhaps an easier ideology to adopt if you have been a maltreated female professor in the Humanities, perhaps an adjunct paid a pittance, or at least a person of color, rather than, like me, a white male living a life of plenty in the USA.

10. Of course, much brand advertising is directed at climbing this steep hill, and infusing cultural identity into products that carry none (Marchand 1985).

11. Major kitchen appliances are an interesting liminal case, since they are machines but also home décor.

12. A complicating factor: I don't have high levels of taste in any of the domains I will be discussing; surely not clothing, although maybe home décor, since I was designing a house as this was written. But if taste is real, and not a habitus of class or a function of group identification, my lack of it should not produce insuperable problems for this scholarly study of it.

13. This dances around a philosophical elephant in the room, that has caused a ruckus since at least Kant; see Gronow (1997) for an illuminating discussion.

14. Bourdieu would have used some pungent French phrase, of course, but I'm writing for an Anglo-Saxon audience.

Interlude: From cultural capital to social formation

Next I look at online reviews, taking as my exemplar Yelp, now the most successful of the dedicated hosting sites. Yelp also reveals something new, but it is not the same novelty seen in fashion blogs. Yelp brings authorship to the masses. With Yelp, more consumers than ever before can publish. Only a few fashion bloggers attain a mass audience. That made concepts of distinction, and cultural capital to fuel that distinction, apropos in Essay One. But with reviews, millions of people can gain an audience of strangers; too many for the concept of distinction to illuminate.

Accordingly, the conceptual apparatus in Essay Two shifts away from Bourdieusian ideas of capital, toward an older dialogue among sociologists, about the new social formations appearing in the modern world. The term social formation is from Simmel (see Gronow 1997), but the dialogue draws in many of the early sociologists, beginning with Tonnies, and his famous dichotomy between *Gemeinschaft* and *Gesellschaft* (see Nisbet 1966 for an integrative thematic account of how the founding fathers of sociology dealt with these issues). Today, the debate centers on the nature of community in a modern, and now Late Capitalist world. As will become apparent, Yelp is not a community. Yelp creates a new social formation.

Just as fashion blogs provided the occasion to critically examine, and ultimately overhaul Bourdieu's ideas about cultural capital, online reviews provide an entry point for criticizing Tonnies's now ancient and far too simple contrast between *Gemeinschaft* and *Gesellschaft*, intact community versus fractured mass society. Modernity gives rise to many new social forms. Some of these new social forms are best studied by examining consumers—not people, or citizens. Understanding consumer-centric social forms allows consumer sociology to contribute to sociology in general.

Next, if I were to heed Billig (2013), I should always refer to social forms, not the more clunky social formations. But the two extra syllables make a point: these locate social structures in history, as dynamic entities, becoming rather than being. Social form, used throughout, would be too Platonic. Form implies eternal and invariant. But social forms come and go, and I will stick with social formation, the better to emphasize their historical character.

Essay Two proceeds through three phases. First I describe online reviews and mash up economic, psychological, and sociological perspectives, to bring out the unique perspective of sociology. Next, I elaborate the *Gemeinschaft–Gesellschaft* dichotomy into a more comprehensive typology of social forms. Only then can Yelp be located, as a machine for making publics. The final part of the chapter probes more deeply the shortcomings of a strictly economic perspective on reviews. Here I beat up on market explanations, which have become so hegemonic today, and develop the benefits of treating Yelp as a new kind of designed social formation, offering fresh solutions to old problems of trust.

Throughout, online reviews are exemplified by reviews of restaurants—a taste good. Ideas about taste goods link Essay Two back to Essay One, and on to Essay Three.

Essay Two: Yelp and the soapbox imperative

with Shelby H. McIntyre and Ravi Shanmugam

WHY DID REVIEWS EXPLODE?—Experience Goods—Offline versus Online Reviews—Word of Mouse?—What Distinguishes Online Reviews from WOM?—Reviews are not WOM—Potential Psychological Explanations for the Explosion of Reviews—But Wait!—Probing the Economic Explanation—The Social Psychological Alternative—Transition: From Individual Consumer to Social Formation—SOCIAL FORMATIONS—A Simple Polarity of Social Forms—Problems with the *Gemeinschaft–Gesellschaft* Axis—More Elaborate Typologies—Tying up Loose Ends—CULTURAL SOCIAL FORMATIONS—Yelp Gives Ordinary Consumers a Public—The Printing Press and the Web—Benefits and Value of Having a Public—The Megaphone versus the Soapbox—The Meaning of Publics after the Web—YELP AS A SOCIAL FORMATION—Can Writing Reviews Produce a Gain in Status?—How are Web Publics Structured?—Can Sociology be a Science?—MARKETS AND YELP—Yelp as a Competitor in the Hosting Market—Invisible Hand or Visible Social Structure?—Market Competition and the Structure of Privately Controlled Publics—Not a Community—Reviews as Marketplace Exchange? What is Quality Market Information?—TRUST—The Skeptical Sociologist—Feedback to the Rescue—Is the Crowd Wise?—The Problem of Tastes—A Sociological Take on Trust—INSTITUTIONAL LOGIC AT YELP—Logic of Friending—Honor Logic—Summary: Institutional Terrain and Socio-Technical Design—Transition to Data Analysis—DATA—Feedback Studies—Trust Studies—Comparative Study—LIMITATIONS—CONCLUSION

Online reviews are evaluative texts, written by ordinary consumers about goods that can be bought, and aggregated and organized by a Web hosting site. What is new online emerges by contrasting what came before: offline reviews, not written by ordinary people, in print. Book reviews, even dedicated newspaper sections like the *New York Times Book Review*, date back to the 19th century, as do newspaper restaurant reviews. Newspapers had reviewed music, movies, and popular culture for perhaps a century before the Internet. *Consumer Reports* flourished more recently, a creature of Late Capitalist, post-World War II affluence in the USA, but still predates the Internet by decades. In short, reviewing predates the Internet. It's the explosion of amateur reviews, posted to the Web by ordinary consumers, that is new.

WHY DID REVIEWS EXPLODE?

Amazon.com was the first hosting site to gain prominence, allowing ordinary consumers to post reviews of books and music they had bought. Later, sites like epinions.com developed, to host reviews of almost any consumer good, extending far beyond taste goods to the appliances and convenience items that populate *Consumer Reports*. Yelp came later, and not alone, as City Search and Yahoo (Wang 2010), and then Google+, introduced reviews of local businesses. By 2011, Walmart, Best Buy, and many other retailers had copied Amazon, to host consumer reviews of any product within their vast assortments. As of 2015, across all hosting sites, millions of reviews had been posted, by millions of consumers, concerning tens of thousands of products and services. Box 2.1 provides a guide to major online review sites.

In this essay I will focus more narrowly, on restaurants and Yelp. I take taste goods, and reviews of local businesses, to be central. It is the explosion of these reviews that has to be explained. See Box 2.2 for the scope of the empirical data used.

BOX 2.1   GUIDE TO ONLINE REVIEW SITES CIRCA 2014

I had hoped to reproduce screenshots from the websites discussed, especially for the reader who comes upon this book a decade hence. However, their inclusion would have raised difficult questions of copyright law (see Lanham 2006a for a more general discussion of the impediments to adopting new media in scholarly publication). This box provides a substitute.

If you are a contemporary reader, you can use the URL given to go directly to the site, and navigate there to explore the look and feel. If you are reading this book some +years hence, that look and feel will have evolved (assuming the website is still in business, or has not been subsumed under a new corporate name). You might go to archive.org and use their "wayback machine." This non-profit organization takes snapshots of the Web at various intervals, and compiles them by date in a searchable archive. Enter any of the URLs below, and click on the 2014 links that appear. Some links will only show a placeholder page, in cases where the website rejected the attempted snapshot. Others will show what a yelp.com or other website page looked like at that point in time.

Major Review Sites

www.yelp.com
Yelp is the leading hosting site for local businesses, treated in this book as an
    exemplar for review hosting sites in general.

---

www.amazon.com
Amazon may have been the first review hosting site to achieve prominence. Reviews are an adjunct to the main line of business, which is retailing.

www.epinions.com
A dedicated review site, the focus here is durables and other goods, rather than the local businesses reviewed in Yelp, or the cultural products reviewed at Amazon.com

www.tripadvisor.com
Also a dedicated site, TripAdvisor reviews focus on hotels, resorts, cruises, and vacation homes.

Plus.google.com
If you search google.com for a restaurant, the top link may go to Yelp or another review site, or you may see a link to a review at plus.google.com. If you create a google+ account, you can see all the reviews of that restaurant written by google+ members, post a review yourself, or see what other members of your Google circle thought of it.

www.citysearch.com
The CitySearch site predates Yelp (see Wang 2010), but seemed on the way to a moribund state when I started my research. Some reviews here were written by professionals.

Other Review Hosting Sites

By 2014, all major retailers with an online presence (for example, Walmart.com) had imitated Amazon in providing a review capability to support shopping. Searching for goods on the site (for example, "Whirlpool washing machines") brings up a page with tabs containing descriptive information obtained from the manufacturer, and also reviews posted by customers. Also by 2014, the software needed to host and manage reviews had been integrated into commercial packages for managing a website, allowing any online business to add review functionality.

New sites for hosting reviews may yet emerge. The Web is dynamic, and young. Enter a consumer good of interest in a search engine, couple it to the word "review," and you may find niche or emerging hosting sites.

Future Research

When I began this research, there was not much scholarship available on the topic of reviews. I expect that to change. To keep up with new scholarship, I recommend a search strategy on scholar.google.com that uses terms such as "online reviews," "eWOM," or the name of a particular review hosting site ("Yelp"). The search needs to take place on scholar.google.com, or on some other scholarly database; if you use a general search engine, you'll simply be directed to a set of review hosting sites, rather than to scholarship about them.

BOX 2.2   SCOPE OF THE REVIEW DATA

The data underlying this essay are Yelp reviews of restaurants in the San Jose, California area. Yelp got its start in California's Silicon Valley, and its review system had been operating in the San Francisco Bay Area for more than five years when we began collecting data in 2011. Over time, Yelp expanded elsewhere, and continues to grow today, especially overseas. Restaurants were the most common category of Yelp review in 2011. Although my topic is online reviews, not Yelp or restaurants, to keep the narrative concrete, I will say Yelp, and restaurant, to avoid cumbersome locutions like "the online review phenomenon," or "review objects."

By 2011 in San Jose, Yelp had reviews posted for more than 4000 restaurants. Some restaurants had more than 1000 reviews posted, and hundreds of restaurants had garnered more than 100 reviews. In our samples, described in later boxes, the average review was more than 100 words in length, with many in the 500–1000-word category.

Across the sample, comprised of several thousand reviews, we found hundreds of consumers who had written hundreds of reviews, and dozens with more than 1000 reviews to their credit. Some had been writing reviews for years. Other consumers had joined more recently. Regardless of when a consumer joined, different rates could be observed: some people wrote almost every day, while others poked along.

Experience Goods

Although thousands of products and services have been reviewed online, this bald statement misleads: it suggests that reviews are catholic in covering the universe of goods sold in Late Capitalist America. Not true. A small number of product categories account for the majority of reviews posted by ordinary consumers. Experience goods, not search goods, dominate the review space.

Nelson (1970) introduced these labels to call out two different kinds of buyer behavior. With search goods, you can ascertain quality before buying. You can know whether a vacuum cleaner will work, before committing to purchase, because you can search for facts. As a machine, it can be tested in a lab. You can search for its test results, and judge, reliably, whether the vacuum cleaner is good enough for the use you intend. By contrast, restaurants are experience goods, whose quality cannot be determined before purchase. You can never be sure how good that meal will be until you experience it. Many services are experiential goods: restaurants, clubs and bars, hotels and resorts, even home remodeling contractors. Entertainment, including popular books, music and movies, also fits here.

All the high-volume review sites focus on experiential goods: Yelp, TripAdvisor, Angie's List, Amazon, and Imdb. Conversely, for search goods there is epinions.com, which is far smaller than Yelp and its ilk, and the captive review sites of Walmart, Best Buy, Home Depot and the like, where the review count for any of the myriad models sold will often be low or zero. The population of online reviews is concentrated and biased, within the larger universe of goods for sale. Experience goods draw reviews by the hundreds and thousands; not vacuum cleaners, or stereo speakers, or furniture. The explosion is a shaped charge, going off in one direction.

In Essay One, vacuum cleaners and similar mechanical appliances figured in a different contrast, with what I called taste goods. Taste goods share properties with an early extension of Nelson's framework, termed credence goods by Darby and Karni (1973). In credence categories, quality may be difficult to ascertain even after purchase. Medical services provide the classic example. How can you tell if that colonoscopy was of low, medium, or high quality? You're not a doctor. It can't be described as an experiential good; you were unconscious during it. A consumer cannot know the quality of a medical or other specialized service, even after purchase; he can only believe, rather than know. A liberal arts education provides another exemplar of a credence good (the juxtaposition with colonoscopy is accidental). Ask any professor, around the time course evaluations are distributed, whether students are able to judge the quality of the education they received . . .

Credence goods show that quality may be difficult or impossible to discover, whether before or after purchase. Taste goods are analogous. Their defining feature: quality, as typically applied in the evaluation of search goods, sinks into irrelevance, playing a *de minimus* role in choice. Quality remains a floor; few want to dine at a cockroach-infested dive that failed its Health Department inspection. But "dine only at restaurants with a clean bill of health" won't narrow your restaurant choices by much.

Rather than quality, in taste good categories consumers focus on suitability, what might be described as quality-for (me) rather than quality-of (good for sale). Tastes vary. The steakhouse that I find comforting, familiar, and safe, you may consider to be a fossil, patronized mostly by doddering geezers courting a heart attack. And pleasure in dining can be very idiosyncratic. I am fond of sushi, especially the mouth feel, but of course, the idea of eating raw fish continues to give many Americans a shudder. I can sympathize: once, when I dined at a not very Americanized Japanese restaurant in the Bay Area, most of the menu items there made *me* shudder.

I still enjoy sushi, even after learning that what I call sushi, in California, is to native Japanese cuisine what chop suey is to Mandarin cuisine. Curiously, I continue to enjoy the taste of a hamachi nigiri with the right amount of high-sodium soy sauce and fake wasabi. Yes, I was disconcerted to learn, that what is served in California as wasabi relates to the Japanese original as Tang relates to fresh squeezed orange juice. Even so, I continue to prefer sushi with the green paste. It tastes better to me that way. *De gustibus non est disputandam.*

Nelson's distinction between types of goods, and its expansion to taste goods, draws a line in the sand. Quality, understood as a continuum between good and bad, is fundamental to classical economic explanations of what consumers do. Quality is what consumers trade off against price. But for restaurants and other taste goods, quality, in the straightforward sense of good or bad, need not drive choice. The consumer uncertainty is whether I will experience this restaurant as good, whether it will be to my taste. The information gap, which causes consumers to seek out reviews, is ignorance about this restaurant's suitability, its quality-for-me.

The remainder of this essay presents a sustained assault on economic and market explanations for online reviews. Ideas about experience and taste goods are the wedge to pry you loose from the idea that reviews are written to help buyers decide what to buy (Simonson and Rosen 2014). Isn't that what reviews are all about: information, for buyers? No. I hope this preface jostles your certainty about why reviews exploded.

Offline Versus Online Reviews

Before the Web, offline reviews were written by professionals and published in conventional mass media, such as newspapers and magazines. The professional might be named, and write dozens or hundreds of reviews per year, as in the case of a food critic for the *New York Times*, or a movie reviewer for the *New Yorker*. In time, and if the publication was prestigious enough, a critic might gain the status of public intellectual, widely known, esteemed (or maybe feared), and either way, an influential figure in cultural life, and a member of the local or even national elite. Or, as in the case of *Consumer Reports*, the professional might be an anonymous inspector in a white lab coat, with the review written by a staff writer, who might or might not get a byline. At the other extreme, public intellectuals and prominent people, whose reputations had already been established in other contexts, might be invited to write a review, lending their prestige to bolster the authority of the hosting publication. For example, the *New York Times* might invite Henry Kissinger to review a new biography of Metternich.

In the offline case, only people holding an institutional position, or those credentialed in another context, could get hold of the megaphone, and publish their reviews, their taste, to a mass audience. Reviews had the authority of their source, that of the author or the hosting publication, and were credible to just that degree. At a well-regarded publication, readers could reasonably expect that each reviewer had been vetted to have expertise, and that the content of the reviews appearing in the paper had been vetted, in the same way as field reports concerning news of the day. In short, offline professional reviews could be expected to be true and credible, and reviewers could be expected to be experienced, judicious, and expert.[1]

Two points emerge from this initial contrast between offline and online. First, online reviews represent a demotic turn, same as blogging (Turner 2010). With online reviews the mass media, now in the form of websites, open up to ordinary consumers. Second, online reviews, even more so than fashion blogging, are unnecessary; an undermotivated event requiring explanation. Most of the time, except for the newest or most obscure restaurant, a professional, expert restaurant review would already be available from a newspaper archive. Except for the minor and obscure, the same would hold true for books, music, or movies. Hence, the Internet could have developed along a path in which newspaper archives were quickly digitized and made widely available, so that there was neither occasion nor need for ordinary consumers ever to write a restaurant review.

Even under this scenario, one exception might have attracted consumer reviews: niche cultural products, the Long Tail as it is sometimes called (Anderson 2006). Here the ethnographic perspective discussed in Essay One might have applied, as vegans found one another via the Web, and swapped notes on restaurants too obscure to earn a professional review from a mainstream newspaper. Small clusters of neo-punk reggae fusion music lovers might have used the resources of the Web to find one another and congregate on a small site, where they could construct a virtual community based on shared tastes. But that is not what happened. Instead, amateur reviews of mainstream products exploded, dwarfing in number all those contributed to any niche community.

Another development that could have occurred, but did not: online reviews might have ended up a minor affair, with the staying power of Pets. com. Consider restaurants: the initial enthusiasm for all things Web—if you weren't around during the dot.com boom of the late 1990s, that enthusiasm may be hard to grasp—might have led people to experiment with posting local restaurant reviews, among the profusion of other attempts to exploit the possibilities of the Web. A blogger might have started to post reviews of where he dined, and got some readership, whereupon other bloggers in other cities might have attempted the same. Someone else might have put up a national directory to such blogs. Or, enthusiastic or upset diners might have found a way to post comments on a local discussion board about some heavenly or hellish restaurant experience. And then, after a year or two, the whole thing might have run out of gas, and gone the way of MySpace. Who wants to read an anonymous rant about a restaurant across town that you never intended to visit anyway? What vegetarian cares to read a steakhouse review? What good is a directory that doesn't offer a review of that one restaurant you were considering for tomorrow night's dinner? For that matter, who cares what random strangers think about a restaurant, when you could equally well ping your friends on Facebook with a query about where to dine?

But instead of petering out, the number of consumer reviews of experience goods exploded, pouring out in a seemingly inexhaustible flood. One year in the 1990s there was a trickle of reviews concerning a few books on Amazon, focused as much on whether the book had shipped on time and in good condition, as to whether it was a good read; and then a decade later, there were millions and millions of reviews online, for thousands of experiential goods, often hundreds of words in length. It is important to recognize, and contemplate, the sheer magnitude of what occurred, even within the narrow domain of restaurant reviews, on Yelp, in one state, for one city (Box 2.2).

This is new. Never before had there been mass publishing, a mass of willing and successful authors. The explosion of reviews written by ordinary consumers is the central fact to explain: why so much writing, so often, by so many?

This unnecessary explosion of reviews lets me pitch a sociological account against explanations from psychology and economics. Consumer researchers today are to psychology and economics as fish to water. This essay is critical in aim, as I set up putative psychological and economic explanations for the explosion of online reviews, and then knock them down. Sociology made nemesis. The danger that I deal only in straw men will be acute. The goal is to show that neither psychology nor economics has a good explanation for why online reviews exploded, or why the explosion occurred in one sector, for experiential and taste goods, and not for all goods. Only then can a sociological explanation proceed.

Word of Mouse?

To further appreciate the novelty of online reviews, it helps to compare these to a second foil. During the period before the Web when reviews were written exclusively by professionals, ordinary consumers were not silent about which restaurants they liked or didn't. Dining picks and pans have been shared among ordinary people since the beginnings of modern consumer society. By Late Capitalist times this was labeled word of mouth, or WOM (Arndt 1967; Dichter 1966; Katz 1957). While professionals controlled access to the mass media in terms of providing neutral judgments of products and services, and marketers controlled access to those mass media for advocacy appeals via advertising, this professionally sourced verbiage, although it monopolized the mass media, did not exhaust speech about products. Consumers spoke among themselves.

In this essay I treat WOM, and the substantial academic literature that has accumulated around this concept (Berger 2012), as merely a foil. I confess that journal reviewers would have none of it. My reluctance to treat online reviews as a subspecies of WOM was automatically a cause for manuscript rejection, time after time.[2] In journal world, online reviews had to be old, had to be a subspecies of WOM; could not be a new thing requiring new theory.[3] This painful experience taught me much about the inherent conservatism of journal reviewing, and led me to publish these thoughts in a book. Journal reviewers, it appeared, could not bear the thought that all that theorizing, accumulated to explain consumers talking out loud to one another, back in the 1959–1995 baseline period, might have to be bracketed. Online reviews could not be new. No, no, no! WOM! WOM! WOM!

I got mad, and wrote the next section to lay out, in painstaking detail, the gulf that separates the new online review from the old activity—which has by no means disappeared—of word of mouth communication. Consumers still talk to one another about goods for sale; it makes little difference if they now talk by trading Facebook posts, rather than leaning over the back fence, or hanging around the water cooler. Consumers continue to converse about products within their circle of friends and acquaintances, on and off the Web; nothing new there. Online reviews are something else.

What Distinguishes Online Reviews from WOM?

The key difference: online reviews are produced, stored, and found on websites dedicated to this purpose, and these review sites provide an institutional infrastructure that is absent in the case of WOM (Scaraboto and Fischer 2013; Nicosia and Mayer 1976). What separates online reviews from WOM is not the content of what is said, but the novel context within which consumers confer, and the effects of this context. Although WOM tends to be oral, and eWOM written, as in a Facebook, blog, or Twitter post, both are embedded in a context that is not primarily about market information. Ordinary WOM occurs as a side-effect of consumers going about their everyday life. By contrast, online reviews have to be deliberately produced, and are written and read only when a consumer steps out of her everyday life and goes to an institutional setting dedicated to reviews. Online reviews are opt-in.

In the default state no review is produced. A special effort is required for an online review to be written, or read, and this remains true no matter how many reviews have been written or read in the past. By contrast, ordinary WOM is almost unavoidable, occurring spontaneously every day. Even if you are disinclined to talk about stuff to buy, others around you may broach the topic. Conversation, in a consumer society, necessarily includes talk of goods for sale, causing WOM to occur ("I found a great sushi place"). No special effort is required; on the contrary, consider the lengths you would have to go to, to avoid hearing any WOM for an entire week.

Here are five more points of difference.

Social ties

WOM occurs within an ongoing social relationship (termed the organic inter-consumer model by Kozinets et al. 2010; see their Figure 1A). The consumer who offers WOM and the consumer(s) who receive it are linked by personal, familial, or community relations. These social ties may be distinguished as strong or weak (Granovetter 1973), but there will be a tie of some kind—WOM occurs between consumers who know one another, have a history together, and can look forward to future encounters.

In contrast, reviews are written and read by strangers who are anonymous. A social relationship need not predate the review, no relationship is needed for reviews to be sent out or received, and only rarely will an interpersonal relationship result. The review writer and reader enter into some type of relationship, and the aggregate of reviewers and readers constitute some kind of collectivity; but these have not yet been analyzed.

Situated dialogue versus repeated emission

WOM (and eWOM) take place in conversation: a dialogue that occupies a brief, bounded interval. A recommendation or evaluation may be unsolicited, or a response to a request, and may be queried, or otherwise engaged, over multiple conversational rounds. WOM occurs as a conversational turn (Sacks 1998).

Reviews are collated and not part of a dialogue. Reviews are not requested, and in most cases, do not trigger a text in response (Box 2.3 compares blogs, discussion forums, and social media, where, unlike reviews, posts may lead to comments or other responses). Reviews may be rated by readers, as part of the infrastructure created by online review sites, but this rating is not a conversational turn. Likewise, reviews may be read years after they were generated, reviews whose date of production is separated by years may be read in juxtaposition, and dozens of reviews may be read one after the other. A review is not a conversational turn. It is a document stored with thousands of other documents in an archive.

Occasional and evanescent versus accumulated and archived

Next, most WOM occurs as a one-off. A consumer may have multiple WOM encounters during some period, but each is specific to its occasion,

---

BOX 2.3 TYPES OF ONLINE COMMUNICATION

Online reviews are one type of consumer-to-consumer communication and influence, or CCCI. At the top level, we can distinguish in-person from computer-mediated CCCI. Next, computer-mediated CCCI can be either one-to-one, or one-to-many. One consumer, texting another one about consuming, using a smartphone, is no different from that same consumer, leaning over his backyard fence to speak to a neighbor. To post a photo to your Facebook page, showing a new hat, is not so different from showing off that hat at lunch. But to publish a blog, which can be viewed by tens of thousands of other consumers, has few parallels in offline consumption.

Blogs are not the only example of newly emerged, one-to-many CCCI. Since the personal computer era began in the late 1970s, bulletin boards and discussion forums have flourished. When a forum focuses on consumption, it becomes a computer-mediated marketplace community, as argued by Muniz and O'Guinn (2001). Discussion boards and forums allow for threaded, dialogic communication; that is, peer-to-peer conversations (Mathwick et al. 2007).

Online consumer reviews represent a third instance of computer-mediated CCCI. As with discussion forums, which can be stand-alone entities or adjuncts to some other enterprise, online reviews may appear on a site dedicated to hosting reviews, such as Yelp.com, or reviews may be added to a site focused elsewhere (for example, Amazon.com). Online review sites differ from both blogs and discussion forums. A blog is one consumer engaging in one-to-many communication: a series of utterances from a single source. A discussion forum is dialogic and threaded: a set of conversations, few to few, occurring many times. By contrast, an online review site hosts many consumers, who engage in multiple one-to-many publishing acts, and who may participate on both the sending and receiving end. Reviews are neither dialogic nor threaded, and are not utterances from a single person going out to many.

Reviews are different from blogs and forums. Reviews can't be grasped using ideas that apply to traditional oral WOM, Facebook posts, blogs, or discussion boards. Reviews are new.

---

and these occasions are not institutionally embedded. The roles of WOM sender and receiver, opinion leader and follower, are informal and tacit. Sender and receiver roles may be swapped on another occasion, or in the case of some other product. Opinion leadership may or may not be widely recognized within the speaker's social circle, but will not be documented. Recipients of WOM may not be aware of how many others have received that piece of advice, or of how much or little WOM is produced by that source.

By contrast, on a review hosting site every reviewer has a dossier.[4] Depending on the website design, you can browse his or her complete set of reviews, which may accumulate into the hundreds, and see the reactions of others to these reviews, in the form of feedback. At more specialized sites, such as Yelp, a lot of information may be provided (Box 2.1). Unlike conversations, online reviews leave an archival trace. Reviews are supported by an institutional infrastructure; WOM is not.

En masse[5]

A fifth point of distinction is the mass audience provided by an online review site. Traditional WOM is dyadic speech between sender and receiver. eWOM adds a narrowcasting component, as when a Facebook post is seen by dozens of friends, or a personal blog post is read by hundreds of followers. Group conversations are also possible in WOM and eWOM, as in online discussion forums, but participation is limited to group and community members. By contrast, an online review may be read by thousands of strangers. A consumer is likely to receive WOM from more than one friend or acquaintance. But at an online review site, you can read hundreds of reviews for a restaurant, and do the same for dozens more places to dine. You have access to reviews written by millions of people. Online reviews are mass communication in which both writers and readers engage with a large population of strangers.

Publication versus conversation

Writing an online review is a public act: a publication of one's views and tastes. The ordinary consumer becomes a writer who publishes. As always in publishing, a review goes out to an unnumbered audience of strangers. It may never be read by anyone, or it may be read by thousands, and you cannot know, while writing, how big an audience you will get. By contrast, WOM is always a speech act: it is conversation with known others, within your social circle or community. To describe online reviews as publishing draws together, under a single heading, engagement with strangers, mass audience, broadcasting, collation, and the bridging of time and space.

Reviews Are Not WOM

Here are three questions posed by the novel features that distinguish online reviews from WOM. The first two questions will not be explored until later in the essay, but are included here to give a sense of where it is headed:

1. What kind of collectivity is Yelp?
    a. Deciding that Yelp is not a community doesn't tell us much, except that it reinforces the insight that community ought not to be an all-purpose term, applied to any social formation whatsoever.
    b. Here is a trick question: how many types of collectivity are there in Late Capitalist times? What are their names?

    c.   At present this would be a hard question for most scholars in consumer research to answer. That difficulty animated the quest for the typology laid out later. If community cannot serve as a catch-all term for all supra-individual groupings, where are the dividing lines, that separate community from other kinds of social formations? Where does Yelp fall on that map?

2.   How does a collectivity like Yelp function? What are its central structures, and how do these structures support those functions?[6]

    a.   These questions are necessarily vague here at the outset. But a social formation is more than a name. Social formations are not just categories in a classification scheme. Each has properties that shape what members do.

    b.   Collectivities are sites where human action occurs. Not every social formation need have a function; perhaps a family can just be. But, as pointed out above, online reviews are unnecessary. If review collectivities were to fulfill some function for participants, either uniquely or in a superior way, this could explain why Yelp and the rest emerged and flourished.

    c.   Different functions presuppose different supporting structures. Sometimes structures are more visible than function. To study structure provides one route to discovering function. The two are best investigated together, as mutually illuminating standpoints, the better to understand, in sociological terms, what happens.

This next question will occupy the remainder of the opening section of Essay Two, and provide a bridge to the following sections where the first two questions will be pursued. It will soon emerge that this question can't be answered without taking up the first two:

3.   Why did online reviews explode, rather than wither away? What sustains participation in a social formation such as Yelp?

    a.   Note the absurdity of this question if translated into a traditional WOM context. It makes no sense to ask, "What keeps consumers talking about goods for sale?" Duh—it is not possible, in a consumer society, not to talk about things you can buy.

    b.   The answer to the second part of the question could be relatively sociological in emphasis, or more psychological. If sustained is translated into motivated, a psychological perspective is imposed; if translated into supported, a more sociological stance is allowed.

Good consumer sociologists know where their turf peters out in favor of psychological explanations. Consumer sociologists do not wish to be

imperialistic. Economists and psychologists, however, do tend to be imperialistic, with claims to offer a complete explanation of human action.
Therefore, marking out any turf for sociology requires drawing a line
that psychology and economics aren't able to get across; to show where
economic and psychological explanations fall short. And I link psychology and economics, because they both focus on individual actors to the
exclusion of collectivity.

Potential Psychological Explanations for the Explosion of Reviews

A psychologist looking at this explosion, and respecting the factors that
distinguish reviews from WOM, might speculate that an unsuspectedly
large number of ordinary people have a need to be read: a drive to write for
and be read by strangers, of the sort familiar from the study of novelists,
journalists, and others who pursue professional careers in writing.

Alas, this psychological explanation is circular. Moliere satirized this
circular style of explanation, using the example of a dormitive principle, as
in the question, "Why does opium make people sleepy?" Answer: "Opium
has within it a dormitive principle [that causes them to sleep]." The dormitive style offers a name, not an explanation. The failure to explain is most
obvious when the supposed explanatory factor—need for readership—is
newly minted upon observing a new behavior. Why do ordinary people
write online reviews? Because they have a need (to have their writing read).

In response to this flawed opening move by the psychologist, a feeble
attempt at sociology might counter that sustained production of reviews,
or more exactly, differences in the level of review production, stem from
social capital (see Essay One). Reviewers who have lots of friends on
Yelp—who have amassed social connections there—will continue to write
reviews in quantity, while those who lack social capital will tail off and
stop.

I call it a feeble attempt at sociology, because it is so vulnerable to
redescription by the social psychologist, who states: "What you call social
capital I call social facilitation: an external context that shapes behavior."
You see other people posting reviews. Then you post one yourself, after
you had that awful meal at Chez Tout. That was easy enough, so you start
posting more reviews, because, well, because other people are doing it too.

This social psychological gambit has to be faced. Under it, there is
no need to discuss collectivities. No need to delve into their structure
and function. Social facilitation is one of many external forces acting on
individuals, and social psychology has successfully explained many other
behaviors using the same model:

Situational Factors → Behavior. No sociology needed.

But Wait!

By this point at least a few of you may have slammed the book down (hopefully not thrown it across the room), wanting to scream, "*It's obvious! Don't you get it?*" Online reviews help consumers choose with more confidence what to buy (Simonson and Rosen 2014). Online reviews are market information (Stiglitz 2002). Consumers want to know whether a restaurant is any good, and, whether it is good for their purpose (for example, anniversary dinner), and, if it will suit their taste (match the utility function characteristic of their segment, an economist might say).

Markets work better when more information circulates more widely. For the economist, that's why WOM exists in the first place, and that's why online reviews came into being and soon exploded. Yes, some information on restaurant quality was available before the Internet, in the form of professional reviews or Michelin guides, but when it comes to market facts, more is better.[7] Online reviews flourish because they increase the overall welfare of consumers. Folding his arms, the economist reminds us that Adam Smith → free markets → greatest means of wealth creation ever seen → no need to complicate matters with this sociology stuff.

Although laid out tongue in cheek, there are far more sanguine proponents of this economic explanation. As a social scientist located in a business school at the turn of the millennium, I've had ample exposure to economics, to habits of economic explanation, and above all, to the serene confidence of economists to know the answer, the entire answer, with respect to anything whatsoever having to do with consumers. As a discipline, economics (of the Anglo-Saxon sort) is as much the rival of sociology as psychology (Reckwitz 2002). Both economics and psychology are totalizing disciplines, predisposed to the belief that no other behavioral or social science is necessary to explain what people, especially consumers, do. Economics and psychology have their differences, concerning the role of rationality in consumer choice, but they are united in their indifference to, and distance from, properly sociological explanation.

All the theoretical questions laid out earlier are pointless, if a perfectly good economic explanation for online reviews is already in hand. There's no need to ponder what sort of collectivity Yelp might be, if Yelp only assists the exchange of market information. And there is no need to ask what sustains the production of reviews if online reviews = WOM = exchange of information = the usual and customary behavior of market participants. Note also that if the economic explanation is correct, the thesis of the book fails: there is nothing new about the exchange of market facts, so that no new theory is needed, certainly not sociological theory. Move along folks, nothing to see here.

Under a market information account, the differences between traditional oral WOM and the new online review are irrelevant. Yes, the details of information exchange differ, but in both cases, facts are exchanged using whatever capabilities are at hand. Market information has got to flow; there's money in it. Like water under gravity, it flows through any available channel. Online reviews exploded? Yes, and water runs out a dam when the sluice opens. Not new.

Probing the Economic Explanation

If you are sympathetic to sociology, I hope you see the need to recognize, and confront directly, the alternative explanation for online reviews offered by economic theory. (I'll turn to face the psychological challenger later.) Time to lay out the economic account in a systematic way, and probe it for shortfalls: predictions made and not confirmed by Yelp data, or pertinent Yelp facts not predicted and hence not explained.

But perhaps I only set up and knock down a straw man. Here is a scrupulous attempt to give the economic explanation a fair shake. In outline:

1. When it comes to markets, the more information, the better.
    a. This is a theoretical postulate not open to questioning by non-economists.
2. Because market information is so valuable to participants, it circulates by all available means.
    a. Therefore, when a new channel opens up, it will always and soon be exploited to circulate market facts. That's why newspapers, soon after their appearance, began to run ads, as did magazines, and then radio, and then television. That's also why the Web began to carry banner ads almost from the beginning. Market information has got to flow.

These first three steps in the argument explain both the existence of online reviews and their rapid explosion and subsequent flourishing. The opportunity for consumers to post and consult reviews was a new channel for the exchange of facts, which was perforce rapidly exploited. Yes, professional reviews were already available, and yes, a rich exchange of traditional WOM continued. But because more information is better, the explosion of online reviews had to occur. It is no longer undermotivated:

1. What needs to be exchanged is information about the quality and suitability of goods.

a. Sellers must inform buyers of the existence and availability of the good, and provide some means for the buyer to determine its quality and whether it is suitable to his purpose. You can't sell to buyers who can't find you or don't know what you have.

b. Buyers rationally fear that the fewer facts they have, the greater the risk of error. Error means waste; waste means loss; and the buyer seeks to be better off, not worse, by exchanging money for goods. Buyers are utility-maximizers. Therefore, buyers have as much incentive to seek out market information as sellers have to offer it.

2. However, seller-provided information is inherently problematic. Sellers are like the rhetoricians who so concerned Plato (Bender and Wellbery 1990): more motivated to say what works than to tell the truth. Sellers hope the buyer will conclude that the good on offer is high quality and perfectly suitable, even if it is not. Sellers seek to maximize their own utility, not the buyer's.

3. Buyers know this, expect it, and seek out information from non-sellers, hoping for a more neutral and objective perspective; for better information. Therefore, buyers are highly motivated to consult anyone but the seller, and acquire whatever facts these other market players know.

4. It's not just about objectivity: peer-provided information helps you learn about suitability. While a newspaper review of the restaurant, if available, might tell you about quality, a newspaper reviewer is unlikely to have exactly the same tastes as you.

5. Therefore, buyers will be interested both in reading peer-written reviews, and in reading many of these, as they search for a peer with compatible tastes, to judge whether the restaurant is both good and suitable.

A complete explanation for the explosion of online reviews comes into view, couched in strictly economic terms. It starts with the imperative need for facts. There must be an explosion of online reviews, once this channel becomes available. There must be an avid readership, among consumers, for reviews written by peers, because the suitability of a restaurant is as important as its quality. Because tastes are diverse, information is greatest if many consumers write reviews of each restaurant; exactly as we observe in the Yelp data. Because there is a guaranteed and avid readership for consumer-written reviews, businesses like Yelp have an incentive to provide an infrastructure to support the writing and reading of reviews. Yelp can sell advertising against its eager, devoted—each time I dine out I must choose where to dine—and potentially very large readership. Yelp can make money.

Although seemingly airtight—if I have done my job and been scrupulous about putting the best foot forward for the economic perspective—there remains one loose thread. Before I begin to pull on it, ask yourself: what aspect of online reviews has not been explained?

Unexplained: why ordinary consumers bother to write reviews of restaurants, or more exactly, why millions of people choose to write, and write, and keep on writing reviews. Under a market information account, sellers have an incentive to provide information, and buyers have an incentive to read reviews; but there is no economic incentive to be a reviewer. Yelp imposes no penalty for freeloading. Consumers get to read Yelp's reviews by browsing to the site: no membership is required, and there is no quid pro quo, in which you must contribute a review before you can read the reviews of others. Yelp has an incentive to motivate reviewers, to attract readers and sell advertising to monetize that readership. But Yelp does not recruit or pay reviewers, and it violates the terms of service for a member to generate a review for compensation (it is necessary to sign up as a member of Yelp to post a review). Yet, restaurant reviews on Yelp are written in huge numbers, on an ongoing basis.

There is one possible economic explanation. It definitely is a straw man that I don't believe anyone takes seriously, but it has to be mentioned, for completeness: that some consumers write many reviews because they get utility from writing reviews. This veers toward a dormitive principle explanation: (1) consumers always act to maximize utility; (2) there are many kinds of utility, to encompass the diversity of tastes; (3) if some consumers write reviews, it is because they derive utility from writing reviews. The explanation in terms of market information does not require that all consumers, or even many consumers, have to write reviews. With at least 1 million adults in the San Jose area, and about 4000 restaurants, if 1 percent of adults have this peculiar utility function, and write about one review per month over a period of two years, then every restaurant will average in excess of 50 reviews, perhaps enough to capture the diversity in local taste regimes.[8]

The utility function explanation is most risible at the level of "some people derive utility from writing reviews of Vietnamese noodle shops, on the possibility that these might be read by some other people they've never met." It is more plausible at the abstract level of "some people gain utility from writing." It is easy to accept this more encompassing statement. I love to write, but to the best of my knowledge, none of my neighbors do, nor do many colleagues at the university, who get more utility from teaching.

Here the economic explanation, based on diverse utility functions, merges with the psychological explanation, which attributes a need for readership. Two differences are worth noting. In economic theory, utility is a point concept. It means one thing, the only thing that explains behavior.

Utility is always the same single thing, but people derive it from different sources, that is, from engaging in various behaviors. In psychology, needs are diverse within limits: numbered, and nameable, and not equivalent. Needs or motives are also structured. Needs may be located in hierarchies, as in Maslow, or organized into sets, as in self-determination theory, which separates out what used to be called intrinsic versus extrinsic motivation (Deci and Ryan 2002).

Second, a psychologist speaks of need for readership, not need for writing. This puts the act of writing into a larger context, and invokes a relationship between writer and reader, and perhaps even a theory of mind, since if you want to be read, you must make assumptions about what the reader wants to read. In short, and to no surprise, psychology offers more tools for dissecting the anatomy of individual behavior than economics. Economists are after different game, where it is mathematically useful to posit that buyers maximize utility, in constructing a much larger system of equations, designed to predict events in markets, more than to diagnose the behavior of individuals.

Unfortunately, even the strong-form psychological explanation, much less the weaker explanation in terms of utility functions, runs into problems explaining why people write online reviews. For instance: if I have a need for my writing to be read, why not write an email to my mother, who will read it? Or post to my Facebook account, about the restaurant where I dined last night, and how much I liked it.[9] This Facebook post may be read by dozens of people, and might even strengthen my relationship with them, as they comment back about a dinner they enjoyed there, or tell me about another restaurant I might like. This sounds more satisfying than writing for potentially unresponsive strangers.

"No, no, no," say the psychologist and economist. In speaking of utility from, or a need for, writing or readership, we meant writing to an audience of complete strangers, not your mother or your friends. The behavior that satisfies the need or provides utility is to publish one's writing, not send a private email. That's where this particular need or utility is focused: on writing for people you do not know, who do not know you, whom you have not met and are unlikely to meet, and who may never read what you wrote.

Although this riposte descends toward a dormitive principle explanation, I have a better rebuttal: if that is the specific need, why not post to your blog, rather than post on Yelp's site? It's just as easy; you have far more control over formatting, style, context, and content—you can blog about anything—and blogging would appear to satisfy the urge to write for strangers to the same degree as posting a review on Yelp.

If the next rejoinder is any form of, "No, people get a specific utility from writing reviews that they can't get from writing exactly the same words on their blog," then we are smack back to the dormitive principle style of explanation. Second, and reverting to the psychologist's language, this need to write, for strangers, who may not read what you wrote, is a strange sort of need. We are a long way from need for food, or need for shelter, or even the need to belong or to enjoy autonomy. Of course we could tie review writing back to Maslow's need for self-actualization, but what does that mean? And again, why satisfy that need this way, by producing restaurant reviews, rather than by the countless other ways it can be satisfied, and was satisfied, before online reviews became possible?

Here the sociologist might tentatively raise his hand. No social formation of any kind has played a role in these psychological or economic explanations. Everything has been explained in terms of individual consumers and their needs or utility functions. So try something different: let readership, or having an audience—a public—be a social formation. Now situate this social formation historically, and examine its structure as compared to other, more familiar groups such as a village community. Explore whether to gain a public, an audience for one's views and tastes, might fulfill some need less denatured, than maybe to be read by strangers. And then ask, is there something about online reviews that makes them well suited to obtaining that outcome?

"Not so fast," interjects the social psychologist. The economist was perhaps too easy a target for you. Dismissing the utility function explanation doesn't begin to address the much more subtle account a psychologist can provide of the needs and motivations that characterize a social being. You were too hasty in dismissing attempts to explain review writing by enduring psychological needs.

The Social Psychological Alternative

Let's set the economic explanation aside, and consider a more heavyweight challenge to a sociological take on reviewing. Once the unexplained element has been fingered, as the voluntary, unpaid behavior of some people, and once their actions have been exposed, as not rational by the standard of utility maximization, psychological explanations properly come to the fore. Hardly any consumer psychologist believes that an economic explanation, based on maximizing utility, provides a complete account of consumer behavior; the field was born out of that discontent toward the end of the 1960s (Kassarjian and Goodstein 2010). The parent discipline of social psychology is replete with examples of how ordinary people rely on heuristics, faulty calculation, and irrational decision-making (Kahneman 2011). Social psychologists have no problem with people doing things for free, or that are not in their self-interest. Foolishness is rife, self-deception the norm, and most of us, if not easily duped, are all too readily distracted. Some of us are materialistic, others more free-spirited. Any number of motives might underlie review writing.

Two specific motives that a psychologist might connect to review writing are the need to belong, and the drive to gain status (Deci and Ryan 2002; Lampel and Bhalla 2007). Both make tacit assumptions worth holding up to a sociological lens.

The desire to belong is deep-seated, and is sometimes twinned with a desire for autonomy as two fundamental pillars of human motivation (Deci and Ryan 2002). Humans—or more properly, the Late Capitalist, young, middle-class persons who provide the bulk of social psychological data—want to be free, and don't want to feel alone. Angyal (1973) saw human motivation as oscillating between the poles of homonomy (togetherness) and autonomy. In a post-Maslow world, these can be depicted as root desires that play out in many contexts. Yelp's promotional pitch to new members presumes the potency and relevance of the need to belong, inviting you to "join the community." And the more community-like is Yelp's membership, the stronger the argument that review writing comes from a desire to belong. Conversely, if Yelp proves to be a looser and less intimate social formation—like being a member of some airline's loyalty program—then it becomes less likely that people write reviews to secure a sense of belonging. Consumers join frequent-flyer programs to get free flights, not to feel a sense of belonging.

If Yelp was structured as a community, unpaid review writing would be easy to explain. Either pure altruism or voluntary reciprocity might be the cause (Andreoni 2007; Bergstrom et al. 1986; Bolton and Ockenfels 2000). Emotional bonds forge community. Reviews might then be donated, for the collective well-being of the whole, out of some combination of *agape* and *caritas*. Alternatively, if we take ongoing interaction as the defining feature of community, review writing might be an instance of voluntary reciprocity, in which consumers who have benefitted from reading reviews "give something back" to the community, by writing a review in the hope that other consumers will benefit. Reading reviews, and donating reviews, enter into a virtuous circle, of getting and giving.

Unfortunately, there's a problem with explaining Yelp in terms of community. We deal here with mundane goods and mainstream, conventional services: restaurants, bars, beauty salons, dry cleaners, and the like. At the extreme, we have expensive indulgences by an affluent clientele: a swell who might drop $300 to dine at an expensive French restaurant, and who wants to know whether the pâté made from the liver of tortured geese will suit his taste. With children starving in Africa, this is where ordinary people direct their *agape* and *caritas*? Oh come on!

Marketplace communities, as introduced by Muniz and O'Guinn (2001), do exist, and can exert emotional force. But the conditions for marketplace communities are more likely to be met in the case of niche products, or marginalized tastes, or oppositional subcultures (Thornton 1996). Writing Yelp reviews of mainstream restaurants—steakhouses and barbecue joints—does not fit the bill.

But we cannot judge the fitness of this first social psychological explanation, until we analyze Yelp as a social formation. Even if we concluded that Yelp was sufficiently community-like to offer a sense of belonging, we would still have to connect this motive to review writing. You can join Yelp as a member without having to write a review, and need not ever write a review to sustain membership. As a member, you can befriend others, give feedback and send compliments, and participate in Yelp's discussion forums. Yelp will also send emails announcing events where you can meet other members. True, you cannot receive feedback unless you write a review, and you may not receive friend requests if you never write one; but much of the belonging you can obtain from Yelp is gained by joining as a member and spending time on the site. You need not write a single review, much less hundreds. As a motive, the need to belong fails to explain sustained review writing, and woefully fails to explain copious review writing.

By contrast, the status motive does explain why some people write hundreds of reviews for Yelp. Once a dossier exists, review authors can be distinguished by their review count. To see how this distinction arises, imagine that you are a utility-maximizing buyer, browsing a set of restaurant reviews. These reviews do not speak with one voice, and you struggle to decide whether the restaurant is suitable, and of sufficient quality. The Yelp display indicates that Tom has written 12 reviews, Dick has written 16 reviews, and Harry has written 216 reviews. If everything else is equal, to whose review would you give the highest weight? How might readers—and there may be hundreds or thousands of readers, for a popular restaurant in a large urban area—regard Harry, relative to Tom and Dick? Presumably, in a favorable way, parallel to how an academic would regard another with a long string of publications,[10] or a sports fan would regard a pitcher with more strikeouts, or a movie buff an actress with more film credits. Review count provides a simple index of more. Harry is more than Tom and Dick because he has done more.

Perhaps you can even manufacture distinction, elevate yourself by the bootstraps, by authoring reviews on Yelp. Unlike a blogger, who cannot compel followers, no matter how many blog posts are made, and who may not even be found, among the millions of other bloggers, all a Yelp reviewer has to do, to be distinguished by a high review count, is to invest time in writing, while avoiding the Yelp filter. Avoiding the filter becomes easier after accumulating a dozen or two reviews, as the filter is harshest on new reviewers with no track record. (I'll have more to say about the filter later.) Depending on your energy, reviews can be quickly accumulated. You don't have to pay for 100 restaurant meals to write 100 reviews and be so distinguished in the Yelp display; any local business can be reviewed. Nor need the reviews be very long, making it possible to write several per day if motivated.

Nowhere else in contemporary society can an ordinary person build a favorable reputation simply by producing. This is especially true in the knowledge and taste spheres. You can get into *Guinness World Records* for many a stunt, but it is otherwise difficult to distinguish yourself by effort alone, at will.

To approach review writing as status-seeking has several merits. Egotism makes it attractive to be the reviewer who wrote hundreds of reviews, compared to others who have mustered barely a dozen. Egotism drives you to write hundreds rather than a handful of reviews. Status-seeking accounts for an aspect of Yelp that few other explanations can: why so many Yelp members contribute not one review, or ten reviews, but hundreds. To gain the esteem of others is often thought to be a fundamental human motivation. What easier way to attain distinction, than to seed 100 reviews in the hothouse of Yelp?

Most importantly, the status account explains why it is online reviews that are produced by ordinary people, and not blog posts or discussion boards or Facebook posts or email, or any of the other new opportunities for writing. Only on review hosting sites, and especially sites like Yelp, that supply a rich dossier, can you compel distinction by dint of effort. And, to stand the economic explanation on its head, it is only because of the hunger for market facts that it is commercially viable to host a review site. And to turn things inside out, it is only because of the enduring need for the esteem of your peers that reviews are written, in quantity, to satisfy that need, at a price the hosting site can afford, which is to say, for no money payment at all.

Nonetheless, a social psychological explanation based on status-seeking does have two vulnerabilities. The first problem: it may be more folk theory than psychological science. To assert a fundamental human desire for status enhancement turns out to be no more scientific than cynical throwaways of the form, "it's the money, honey."[11] The term "status" does not appear in the index to Deci and Ryan's *Handbook of Self-Determination Research*, nor does "prestige" or "distinction." (Self-determination theory is the current name for a research stream that began by exploring the difference between intrinsic and extrinsic motivation.) The related concepts that Deci and Ryan (2002, pp. 24–25) do consider appear in this context:

extrinsic aspirations (at least within American culture) are wealth, fame, and image . . . Whereas people might feel happy about attaining their extrinsic aspirations . . . pursuit and attainment of extrinsic aspirations will not contribute to . . . well-being. . . . In fact, the pursuit and attainment of extrinsic aspirations may actually detract from need satisfaction by keeping people focused on goals that are not directly need-related.

The authors cite research to show that extrinsic aspirations, such as fame or image (the words they use in place of status), arise where real needs have been frustrated, so that even attaining these external goals leads to poor health, depression and other forms of ill-being. Turns out that seeking status—social materialism—is not a fundamental human need. Naming it so only reflects folk theory, the fashionable cynicism of "everything comes down to money."[12]

Real fundamental needs are: (1) belonging, per the first social psychological explanation; (2) autonomy; and (3) competence (Deci and Ryan 2002). Only when these real needs have been frustrated do derivative motives like gaining status emerge. That is the position of self-determination theorists, who do have standing as scientific psychologists. It does not follow that the status-seeking explanation fails; there are lots of frustrated and dissatisfied people here in Late Capitalist America, more than enough to contribute 1 or 2 million reviews, and fuel at least the initial success of online review sites. But the status-seeking explanation, now bereft of support from psychological science, becomes more suspect, as an explanation for how and why review writing can sustain itself over the long term, as appears to occur at Yelp.

The second vulnerability stems from how the goal is defined. What, exactly, is this status, or image utility, as the economists call it (Kossmeier et al. 2009)? It's not like being blond, which I can acquire from a bottle, or like money, which I can hold in my hand and exchange for almost anything else of value, or like ocean-view property, which I can enjoy every day, while being envied by others. Status is not a personal characteristic or a possession. It is manifest as a particular sort of regard by others. I don't have status unless other people see me that way. This is the pretext for countless romantic comedies, where status is of no avail when it goes unrecognized. Status as image utility is an attribution made by others, and I won't feel I have such a status, unless I can believe that others regard me that way. Status is an attribution to me, relative to others within some social formation, made by fellow members. Status locates me on a vertical axis specific to a social formation.

As with sense of belonging, the social psychological explanation of reviews, in terms of status-seeking, can't be evaluated without examining the tacit sociological assertions that undergird it. The status gained from having written hundreds of reviews on Yelp isn't like the status gained from having noble birth, or a recognized family name, or movie star celebrity, or wealth, or fame. Is status even an apt term for what results, when you write hundreds of reviews, in a social formation where most people write only a few? And even if status is an apt term, for some part of what you gain from writing 100 reviews, was that your goal in writing? Once again, we cannot proceed, until we identify the social form that is Yelp.

Transition: From Individual Consumer to Social Formation

The next section lays out a typology of social formations, and locates Yelp as an instance of a special type: a public. Once that material is in hand, I return to contesting rival explanations, from economics and psychology, for what happens on Yelp. The status-seeking explanation has been bloodied, but not defeated; at least, not as much as the idea that a profit-seeking corporation, hosting millions of members, can act as a community that provides a sense of belonging. And although the economic explanation trips on the problem of reviewer motivation, that is not its only shortfall. But neither of these contests can be pursued until we get clear on the structure of social formations. What underlying principles organize the space of social possibility?

SOCIAL FORMATIONS

Consumer research has not developed a vocabulary for social formations. The origins of consumer research were primarily psychological rather than sociological (Nicosia and Mayer 1976). For decades, work focused on person–object relations (for example, brand attitude), not multi-person relations. Regarding collectivity, only three terms have gained any currency. There is a literature on subcultures (Arnould and Thompson 2005; Schouten and McAlexander 1995); a newer literature on institutions that draws on theories about organizations in the management literature (Scaraboto and Fischer 2013); and by far the most common, a flourishing discussion of marketplace community (Muniz and O'Guinn 2001; Schau et al. 2009). As suggested earlier, a reflexive response among consumer researchers would be to describe Yelp as a community, and Yelp describes itself that way, in its pitch to prospective members.

Online reviews force a rethinking of where communities fit in the larger domain of social formations, and invite us to explore collectives that are not communities. Nothing is known today about how terms like community, subculture, and institution could be integrated, nor how these three concepts might be differentiated from crowd (Surowiecki 2004), tribe (Cova and Cova 2002), organization (Weick 1995), audience (Goffman 1959), public (Arvidsson 2013; Warner 2002), social field (Bourdieu 1984), or discursive regime (Arsel and Bean 2013), to name but a few. In the absence of a theoretical vocabulary, salient and familiar terms, such as community, get pressed into service as all-purpose descriptors for any supra-individual thing.

Consumer researchers need a framework that locates online review sites as one type of social formation. However, we can't just port an existing sociological framework. Sociologists have been thinking about sociability for two centuries (Nisbet 1966). A welter of contending perspectives exists, many of which are only distantly related to consumers. There's no shortage of frameworks for arranging social formations; the difficulty lies in their profusion. What's needed is a sociologically informed but customized framework, one adapted to things consumers do, such as writing and reading reviews. To devise such a framework is the task of this section.

A Simple Polarity of Social Forms

One of the oldest attempts to divvy up social formations is Tonnies's contrast between *Gemeinschaft* and *Gesellschaft*, adapted for consumer research by Muniz and O'Guinn (2001). In plain speech, this is the difference between the sociability seen in a small pre-modern village, versus that found in a large urban society after the Industrial / Scientific / Technological / Capitalist (I/S/T/C) Revolutions. It's too bad this contrast comes down to us as polysyllabic German, guaranteed to derail a dinner conversation. But intellectual history is not ours to choose, and although we need not linger long, *Gemeinschaft* and *Gesellschaft* are where a consumer sociology must start.[13]

The intellectual heritage behind these terms yields insight. They were conceived as an opposition: *Gesellschaft* is other to *Gemeinschaft*; a society has a different structure and hosts functions not seen in a community. The two terms are typically placed in a historical relationship: *Gemeinschaft*, in Tonnies's view, was disappearing, with the tight bonds of an intact community beginning to dissolve, and give way to the more distant and rationalized relations seen in a mass society structured by market relations, as summed up in Weber's views on disenchantment. As a consequence *Gemeinschaft* carries connotations of nostalgia, and gets lauded. *Gemeinschaft* is the utopian ideal of how humans should live together; *Gesellschaft* is the dull reality of modern life in a mass society, from which the traditions and loyalties that anchored meaning in a *Gemeinschaft* world have been purged (Lampel and Bhalla 2007).

The *Gemeinschaft-Gesellschaft* contrast lends itself to polemical usage: *Gemeinschaft* groups get celebrated, while *Gesellschaft* arrangements get disparaged. At the extreme, *Gesellschaft* ceases to refer to a true collectivity, and describes instead a social nadir, a mere aggregate of individuals, a Hobbesian crowd of all separated from all. *Gesellschaft* gets emptied out to mean only market society, social existence as nothing but a market composed of atomized self-interested individuals, rationalizing action in all spheres, everywhere disenchanted, under a market rule of marginal utility. An achievement of Muniz and O'Guinn (2001), in establishing the existence of brand communities, was to show that *Gemeinschaft* elements have continued to exist, develop, and thrive even in the heart of the marketplace. Community has by no means vanished from what is polemically characterized as our rationalized, disenchanted, atomized market society.[14]

This history of polemical usage has an unfortunate consequence: community comes to be opposed to the individual, setting up a second, shadow polarity. What could have been a fruitful continuum, joining two polar types of social reality, gets reduced to an antinomy: there are atomized individuals or *Gemeinschaft* communities, nothing else. In this truncation *Gemeinschaft* absorbs every form of collectivity; what isn't a community can only be a mass of atoms. Community becomes the vehicle for whatever is not a property of individuals; community arrogates to itself everything social. The insight which gets lost: there are at least two kinds of social relations among consumers, more than one alternative to depicting consumers as isolated, atomized, asocial buyers. That insight slips out of more pejorative and ideological accounts, where *Gesellschaft* comes to mean the anti-social.

Understood positively, the idea of *Gesellschaft* sociability carves out a space, for social phenomena that have nothing to do with community. Theories to explain *Gesellschaft* phenomena aren't going to be the same as those that explain intact *Gemeinschaft* groups. Sociology does not draw upon the same body of theory as ethnography. The idea of an *ethnos*, a people, is shot through with *Gemeinschaft* elements, conveying the sweet scent of emotional bonds, the delights of reciprocity, the comfort of shared custom, and the juice of voluntary, wholehearted commitment. A sociological perspective on the social, aimed at collectivities toward the *Gesellschaft* pole, will focus on relations among strangers: people who may not have any emotional bonds or shared traditions. However grim that sounds, a focus on how strangers relate to one another allows us to consider social position, not just community bonds; rank, as well as reciprocity; distinction, apart from identity; and interested rather than altruistic behaviors. Consumers need not be portrayed as atomized individuals, but they don't only participate in communities.

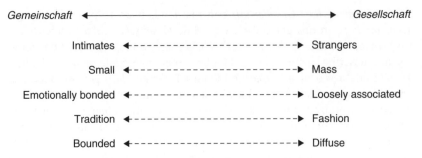

Figure 2.1   Simple polarity model of social formations

Gemeinschaft collectives differ from *Gesellschaft* collectives as the conceptual frame of ethnography differs from that of sociology. For both disciplines, much of what a consumer does is assumed to be socially and culturally constructed, rather than autochthonous. But the two disciplines conceive the source and manner of that construction differently. Recall that an ethnographic perspective emphasizes the horizontal operation of taste, its use to bond and bound groups. Perspectives that emphasize the value of community, or the emotional and personal elements in social relations, or the attractions of belonging, of having an ethnos, can likewise be characterized as ethnographic. Sociology is cold where ethnography is hot. Sociology comes into its own when we focus on the looser forms of association that occur near the *Gesellschaft* pole. Sociology lets us approach Yelp as something new, as a social form that offers something other than the hot, personal, intense bonds of community.[15]

The simple polarity uniting *Gemeinschaft* and *Gesellschaft* is graphically represented in Figure 2.1. Several polarities bundle together to mark out the *Gemeinschaft* or community pole. These include strong versus weak social ties, intimates versus strangers, ongoing interaction versus one-off contacts, and small and tightly bounded groups versus larger and more loosely bounded aggregates. The *Gemeinschaft* pole captures intimate relationships among known others with whom you have enduring bonds and ongoing interactions that are in turn shaped by shared traditions and values (Nisbet 1966).

In a *Gemeinschaft* collective, emotional bonds link members of the community. At the extreme, members of a *Gemeinschaft* share a history of interaction, are well known to one another, and are bonded to one another: the welfare of the community has standing, apart from, and even on the same level as, a person's own welfare. Shared traditions, intimate knowledge, and emotional commitments create trust. Accordingly, altruism is expected, and can flourish, in *Gemeinschaft* collectives. Coming back to online reviews, in a communitarian and ethnographic frame, the motive for contributing online reviews might be reciprocity, to strengthen bonds; or even altruism, to reflect the power of existing bonds, and renew commitment.

We must apply a different conceptual frame to study *Gesellschaft* collectives. Here the prototype is relations among strangers: people who lack a history together, who may be unknown to one another, and lack any acquaintances in common; people to whom no duty of care is owed. Trust is not automatic, and disinterested altruistic behavior is less likely because it is not clear that any two strangers, engaged in a transaction, share membership in . . . anything. The anonymity of a city differs starkly from life in a village. *Gesellschaft* collectives will often be large; the word mass may apply.

The benefit of describing social reality in terms of the *Gemeinschaft–Gesellschaft* axis: we learn to question whether there can ever be an asocial, purely individual consumer; the autochthonous buyer studied in economics and psychology. Sociology is not ethnography, but neither is sociology economics. On a sociological perspective, the autochthonous buyer, whose choices are self-subsisting, based only on rationally derived utility, comprehensible without reference to social considerations, is a fiction specific to our historical era (Bourdieu 1990). At the *Gesellschaft* pole, the rationalizing influence of markets, and the attendant atomization, may produce the appearance of asocial individuals. But this isolation is incomplete, leaving consumer experience no less socially constructed, albeit according to different principles than in a *Gemeinschaft* context.

Problems with the *Gemeinschaft–Gesellschaft* Axis

Recall that the *Gesellschaft* pole was initially conceived in pejorative and ideological terms, as the loss of community, a fall away from real, intimate relationships based on shared values, into urban anomie and alienation, in which strangers interact at arm's length and in superficial ways. This is why the *Gesellschaft* pole was readily assimilated to market relations, and to critiques of the market as a defective or hollowed-out social formation (Muniz and O'Guinn 2001). In ideological usage, *Gesellschaft* sociability was a remainder, all that was left after the I/S/T/C Revolutions had destroyed intact *Gemeinschaft* relations.

The first problem with the polarity graphed in Figure 2.1: it asserts that every type of collectivity can be ordered in terms of a single bundle of properties (for example, intimacy + ongoing interaction). Such one-dimensional models cannot take us very far. A more subtle problem: Figure 2.1 does not show a bipolar axis, but rather, depicts community versus its absence. A collectivity either has one of the properties that define community—for example, strong bonds—or it lacks this property, to a greater or less degree. Tonnies-style descriptions fail to construct a typology of collectivities, inasmuch as the *Gesellschaft* pole, defined as a negation, becomes an empty vessel. The axis only generates predictions about community, with predictions about the *Gesellschaft* pole limited to negating these assertions. *Gesellschaft* is left with no substantive meaning. It's defined as the absence of something else.

A simple axis, with tightly bonded communities at one end, and . . . not much at the other, fails us. It does no good to force all social formations onto the Procrustean bed of community or not. Consumer researchers need a more complex typology.

More Elaborate Typologies

In the business disciplines, we improve on simple polarities by introducing a second contrast at right angles to the first, to produce what's known as a 2 x 2, or quadrant, or Harvard model. To find the second axis, we look again to the sociological literature. A good candidate, almost as well established as the *Gemeinschaft–Gesellschaft* axis, is to distinguish between social structure and individual agency, as alternative causes of events and outcomes. To grasp the distinction, consider the difference between a corporation with 1000 employees and a crowd of the same size. The corporation is differentiated with respect to job roles; these roles are ranked hierarchically; and policies and directives shape the activities of the agents who occupy these roles. A crowd has none of these, so that agency is relatively unconstrained—anyone can throw the first rock—but also unsupported, so that individual agency may amount to little, unless agencies happen to align, and the crowd surges in one direction, or begins pelting the police with rocks, bottles, and pieces of street. The crowd can't stop throwing things, or even concentrate its fire, because it has no structure, no internal organization.

For a more positive example of agency predominating over structure, consider an Adam Smith-style free market: a rug *souk* in Istanbul, say. Market structure is limited to supply and demand, equilibrated by the pricing mechanism, and to the role division between seller and buyer. Else, individual agency is the rule, as sellers choose what merchandise to offer and set an asking price, even as buyers choose whether to buy, and which rug to buy, and what price they are willing to pay. Such a market, while it represents some kind of social formation, is not a community; but a market is not the same kind of non-community as a corporation or crowd.

Figure 2.2 provides a suggestive ordering of non-community collectives

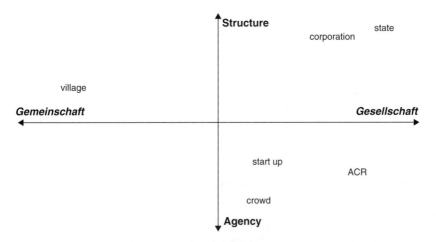

Note: ACR = Association for Consumer Research.

Figure 2.2 Quadrant model of social formations

using a quadrant model. It reveals a new problem: most of the differentiation offered by structure versus agency occurs on the *Gesellschaft* side. It is large collectivities that vary in amount of structure; communities don't vary in this way. Alas, this calls into question the depiction of the typology as two crossed axes. A good old 2 x 2 will not do.

The two-dimensional picture in Figure 2.2 suffers from another problem. Culturally based collectivities are missing; thus, state is shown, but not Church; corporations are placed, but not subcultures. It appears that two dimensions may not be enough to account for the diverse collectivities that consumers inhabit. Quadrant models, because they consist of only two dimensions, fall short for the same reason as one-dimensional continua: not enough differentiation. Lop-sided quadrant models call the whole game of crossed axes into question.

Figure 2.3 is a first attempt to go beyond the limits of a 2 x 2. It represents the space of collectivities as a three-dimensional conic projection. A cone has interesting properties: it allows for no differentiation at one extreme, as it narrows to a point, and two axes of differentiation at the other, where it widens out. In this model, community is not differentiated but treated as one undifferentiated thing; in evolutionary terms, community is the *Homo sapiens* baseline: 50 000 years ago, the only form of human collectivity was the small tribal band. All other kinds of social formation evolved later, after populations expanded, first with the Agricultural Revolution, later with the I/S/T/C Revolutions. The conic

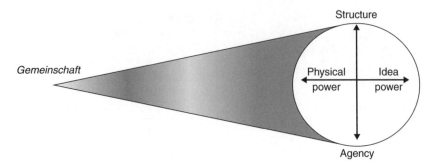

Figure 2.3   Cone projection model of social formations

projection captures this evolutionary ordering. In conceptual terms, community is one thing: a small, bonded, bounded group of people interacting together on an ongoing basis, with intact traditions. The intensity of community bonds varies, the robustness of tradition may vary, and longevity may also vary. But community is a unitary type of social formation. It does not need to be further differentiated.

By contrast, *Gesellschaft* collectivities can be differentiated along at least two dimensions: structure versus agency, and physical versus ideational authority. The latter is approximately the difference between state and Church, between the power to kill and to provision, versus the power to make sacred and to damn. Put another way, it is the difference between social structure, which controls how bodies interact, and cultural structure, which controls how ideas and values get selected and arranged: what makes sense. With this third dimension, it becomes possible to locate entities such as subcultures and taste regimes within the typology. Likewise, we can distinguish relatively loosely bonded associations, such as the Association for Consumer Research, which exert only ideational control, from the more tightly bound corporation, which exerts physical control, through the coercive power to hire and fire, promote or demote.

Although more promising than one-dimensional axes, or 2 x 2 quadrant models, the conic projection in Figure 2.3 still presents difficulties. Most notably, at the broad *Gesellschaft* projection, we are again stuck using only two dimensions to structure the enormous variety of modern, extracommunitarian social arrangements. At the wide end of the cone, it's back to the 2 x 2.

Better: a spherical projection in *n*-dimensional space, as shown in Figure 2.4, provides an even more flexible model. It places community at the center of the sphere, to acknowledge the evolutionary truth that in the beginning, there was only one kind of human sociability: a small, bonded,

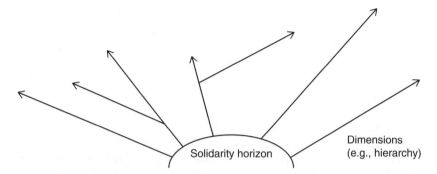

Figure 2.4 N-*dimensional model of social formations*

tightly bounded group of individuals who interacted in an ongoing and traditional way. Placing small intact communities at the center of an *n*-dimensional space, rather than at the tip of a cone, allows for a much wider spectrum of emergent outcomes, as first the Agricultural Revolution, and then the development of cities, and then the I/S/T/C Revolutions, and now the Web, introduced many new possibilities. This center–periphery model captures the insight that community is one thing, while *Gesellschaft* collectivities take many forms. But it improves on the conic projection in Figure 2.3, because it allows for as many dimensions—as many different types of social formation—as the facts require, while still placing these within a conceptual frame. These dimensions, and the properties these reflect, become central to comparing and explaining social forms.

To represent social space as *n*-dimensions radiating out from a center, rather than as a few regions, as in the simple quadrant model, is powerful. Here's why: we can visualize each dimension as a ray, and view each ray as a theoretical property that distinguishes social formations. Social formations can be compared by plotting their relative locations on the relevant dimensions in social space. Less relevant properties can be placed on the other side of the sphere.

As an example, consider the difference between a corporation and a combat unit, each of which falls relatively high on the structure dimension. Each will also be located high on a second dimension, which might be termed hierarchy; but the combat unit will be located low on a third dimension, call it role differences, while the corporation will be located higher up. Every soldier has essentially the same task of overcoming the enemy, while corporate employees pursue distinct tasks, organized into roles such as sales, accounting, and manufacturing. Some soldiers wield rifles, and other handle mortars or bazookas; but this difference is smaller than the difference between a salesperson and a bookkeeper.

Now think of a dimension that might be relevant to some other social forms, but which scarcely applies to large bureaucracies or army groups: fluidity. Neither corporations nor armies are usefully differentiated by varying degrees of fluidity; this dimension, this ray, points away from both. Fluidity would be more important in the study of voluntary associations, or the social scene down at the club. That's the power of locating social forms in an *n*-dimensional space with a center: we can differentiate as much as we please, while still linking everything together.

As this example suggests, we do substantive theoretical work on social formations when we identify the dimensions that apply to a social form, and generate predictions, based on whether that social form is located high or low on each relevant dimension. The predictions get grounded in the dimensions: the effects of more hierarchy, or less role differentiation. The dimensions are made central. Social theory develops by identifying dimensions, each of which plays a causal role in determining how social forms shape the actions of participants, and what outcomes will follow from an event, or from an act performed at that *n*-dimensional locus.

Had the model elaborated in Figure 2.4 already existed, I could have moved directly to examine relevant dimensions of online review sites. I could not take that step without laying out this model, because in its absence, the dimensions developed to describe online review sites, and bring out their character, would float in a theoretical vacuum.

An important feature of the model is the solidarity horizon. There aren't many traditional *Gemeinschaft* groupings left in the developed world: it is rare to find small, physically co-located groups, bound from birth by an enduring bond, and interacting on an intensive and exclusive basis with one another, as was true for millennia in the peasant village or tribal band. And yet, many sociologists believe that community is something that almost everyone seeks and something that can potentially be recaptured, even in the modern or post-modern world (Nisbet 1966). The term solidarity marks out social formations that resemble traditional *Gemeinschaft* arrangements. Solidarity allows community-like to be applied to social formations that in physical terms look nothing like traditional *Gemeinschaft* groupings. Degree of solidarity might distinguish employees of a start-up from those of a Fortune 500 corporation, while members of a special operations combat unit might have more solidarity with one another than any soldier feels toward the Army. To speak of solidarity converts community from a particular social formation, to a property that can be present to a greater or lesser degree, across social formations. This again was Muniz and O'Guinn's (2001) achievement: to show that consumers, traditionally thought of as anomic market participants located far out on the *Gesellschaft* pole, could nonetheless experience a meaningful degree of

solidarity with one another, within smaller and more intimate social formations organized around a brand or product category.

Latent in the model is the thesis, per Angyal (1973) and Nisbet (1966),
that to lack solidarity is painful. It hurts, not to experience solidarity with
some group; to have no one, be part of nothing larger. More subtly, everyone in a *Gesellschaft* world feels that hurt, that damage, that emptiness, to
some degree some of the time. Therefore, the attempt to recapture solidarity drives participation in many *Gesellschaft* social arrangements. Alone in
a crowd, we look for solidarity wherever we can find it. This thesis will help
me explain why the ersatz form of sociability offered by a Yelp nonetheless
sustains actions such as writing reviews, giving feedback, and spending
time on the Yelp site. Solidarity drains out of the disenchanted *Gesellschaft*
world, even as we try to cup it in our hands, to slake our thirst.

Tying Up Loose Ends

Institution does not appear anywhere in Figures 2.1 through 2.4. There is
no institution (noun, singular) that is not also an organization, whether
corporate, governmental, or otherwise (despite the academic shorthand
in which scholars point to their university by saying "at my institution").
What do exist are institutional logics; in other words, structure. Each
Gesellschaft social formation has structure, and diverse social formations
are linked together by kinds of structures. This is what Scaraboto and
Fischer (2013) studied: the institutions of modern mass marketing as they
apply to fashion clothing; that is, the institutional logics that determine
whether a consumer group can obtain desired outcomes and by what
avenue.

Structure is a wonderfully neutral-sounding word, and institutional
logic has a clean, Apollonian sound to it. Nothing could be further from
the truth. Social structure is like the Borg: it is drilled into our brains, and
violates our individuality. *Gesellschaft* persons are no more free than the
Borged units stomping around the *Starship Enterprise*. Foucault's great
contribution in *The Order of Things* was to convey how the coils of social
structure wrap around and penetrate our heads. I'll return to this theme in
the Epilogue.

Now we can locate the meaning of Bourdieu's social field: it refers to
any space in which multiple social formations interact; or more exactly, in
which people who are members of different social formations, sometimes
simultaneously, interact with one another. It is not itself a social formation
but a space which contains social formations. In turn, the Anglo-Saxon
terminology of institutional logics maps onto what Bourdieu described as
force fields, or rules of the game.

Finally, an attractive feature, possessed by any center–periphery model laid out in n-dimensional space, is that dimensions may cluster, and also diverge. Role difference and hierarchy go together. They are not the same property, but they co-vary. Conversely, structure and agency are orthogonal. Dimensions that cluster with one another, and diverge from other clusters, mark out regions in social space. For example, physical coercion, and the different means of coercing individuals, might demarcate one region; ideational authority, and its different bases, including religion and nationalism, would cluster in a different region.

CULTURAL SOCIAL FORMATIONS

From here on out, I have to set aside the general model displayed in Figure 2.4, and begin the return to Yelp, to examine its properties as a social form. The context has been set. Time to drill down. I locate Yelp in the cultural region of social space. Let's see what that means.

The ideational power that infuses cultural social formations (hereafter, cultural formations) can shape consumer behavior no less than the physical power exerted by governmental social formations. And cultural formations may fall within the solidarity horizon or not, same as social formations. A cultural formation need not be a community, or very community-like, to exert a potent influence on consumers. Within contemporary society, diverse types of cultural formations flourish. These cultural formations are distributed along multiple dimensions in n-dimensional social space. Therefore, the term subculture, as it has been applied within consumer research (Schouten and McAlexander 1995), does not encompass all cultural formations, but represents only one type.

The cultural formations consumers inhabit have been neglected most of all. The omni-application of community and subculture, to all social formations whatsoever, blinds us. To divine the nature of online reviews, we must unpack the region of cultural formations, and put aside subculture: Yelp is something else.

The term subculture, insofar as it describes consumers, should be reserved for cultural formations that oppose some mainstream (Thornton 1996). Take it as short for subaltern culture: a subjugated alternative. As oppositional groupings, subcultures attract members who, sometimes by choice and sometimes because of identifying stigmata, are marginalized relative to mainstream groupings. Youths, clubbers, motorcycle riders, immigrants, minorities, and gays, for example, may develop a subculture. When people within an oppositional subculture begin to socialize exclusively with fellows, forging a high degree of solidarity, we might even speak, metaphorically, of a tribe (Cova and Cova 2002).

Yelp cannot be a subculture under this definition, nor can any review hosting site. It has too many members, these members are too diverse, and the restaurants reviewed on Yelp are too mainstream. To talk of steakhouse subculture, or French restaurant subculture, or the barbecue (BBQ) tribe, is a category error. It is not the nature of online behavior that drives this error: the Web could have spawned subcultures around reviewing. Rather, Yelp and its ilk are not subcultures, due to the mainstream character of what is reviewed, and because the people who write reviews are not marginal. I can imagine vegans, in some small Midwestern meatpacking city, launching a website such as VeganReviews.com, devoted exclusively to reviews of local vegetarian restaurants and evaluations of the purity and caliber of the vegan options on offer. Vegans might be sufficiently marginalized, oppositional, and small in number to constitute a subculture, and a review site patronized by vegans could be a site for enacting a subculture. But Yelp, Amazon, Google+, epinions.com are too big, and the content is too mainstream.

Yelp Gives Ordinary Consumers a Public

To capture what Yelp is, we need the idea of a public, defined as a potential audience for cultural products, especially written work, whose members are not physically co-located and only loosely bounded in number, and who will typically be unknown to one another and to the author. A public is a cultural formation, high on the fluidity dimension. It is an extra-community relation, among strangers. A public comes into existence whenever a piece of writing is published. Publics are work-centered cultural formations; there are at least as many publics as there are cultural productions. Unlike religions and many other cultural formations, publics have no existence apart from works; publics need not endure, as traditions must. Unlike the values, icons, symbols, scriptures, or practices which provide the base for some cultural formations, publics are many rather than few, because publics come and go, as works are published or disappear.

A public is a distinctly *Gesellschaft* form of sociability; there can be no public in a world of tribal bands or village communities. A public only becomes possible, could only come into existence, after the invention of the printing press: the first instance of mass media. To have a public is an opportunity restricted to moderns. Publics are new, relative to urban settlement and *Gesellschaft* formations, which are thousands of years old.

Writing is far older than the printing press, of course. That is why it does no good to treat online reviews as providing utility from writing. An email to Mom is written, but it is not addressed to a public in the way that online reviews are. And *pace* Billig (2013), best not to refer to public writing; better to stick to the noun, since there can be publics for non-written cultural productions as well.[16] And I say writing for the same reason I say restaurant, not review object; and refer to Yelp, not to the online review phenomenon. Terse, concrete—better.

The idea of a public remains slippery. To get a firm grip, it helps to distinguish several analytic levels (Warner 2002). At the base level lies the possibility of a public, any public—the sheer potential for this historically recent human experience to occur. At this first level, public means the opposite of private: a diary is private, as is my email to my mom, and any missive that does not go beyond my circle of intimates. What is public is other to what is private. Second, at a more granular level, are the many publics that come into being as cultural works are produced; each cultural work brings about a public. Third, at a macro level, we have "the" public, all of us within a nation or other political unit. This level—The People— has been the focus of political science and philosophy. Many scholars who discuss the public do so from the standpoint of political discourse. Approached slightly differently, as every person located in some media market, this macro level identifies the public in public opinion, in public- ity, and in public relations. In a media-soaked and -marinated society like Late Capitalist America,[17] the public, in a national media context, merges with the public that concerns political science. Much scholarship in jour- nalism and media studies focuses on this public (see the literature cited in Warner 2002). In both cases, "the" public means all of us in reach of some media vehicle. Only the first two levels are germane to this account of online reviews; but because public, like taste, is a contested concept, claimed across multiple disciplines, it seemed best to lay out the whole picture first.

The possibility of there being publics, any public, is historically situated, a development brought into being by a major technological innovation, one often located at the root of modernity: the printing press. Warner (2002), as a literary theorist, is perhaps too fond of the paradoxical and self-reflexive character of the publics created by each act of discourse. The possibility of there being any such public contains no paradox, but follows directly from technological innovation, and the larger historical move- ment, away from a world of *Gemeinschaft* sociability toward the modern *Gesellschaft* age, of distant relations among strangers. A brief historical tour will secure the point: a public is a social form made possible by and founded on technology.

The Printing Press and the Web

Before modern times, outside of a *Gesellschaft* context—the two phrases verge on redundant—writing was not writing to a public. In the first instance it was epistolary writing, speech at a distance to a fellow community member. Pronouncements by a government, as when the King sent out written copies of a new law to be read in each town, are similarly speech at a distance. In the third instance it was writing designed to capture oral traditions, as in the case of much religious and literary writing (the Bible, Homer), and also scholarly writing, which captured oral teaching and colloquia (Plato and Socrates). Most other writing prior to print was to establish a permanent record, as in bookkeeping by Sumerian scribes, temple inscriptions, memorial stele, and the like. The writing done by ordinary citizens was not public, and the writing by holders of an institutional office, that was addressed to all, was incidental to carrying out the duties of that office. These people acted as officials, not authors. No ordinary person had or could have a public in the modern sense. The secular and sacred ruler each had a public, or better, there was a public sphere around any ruler; but no person, other than a ruler, had or could have a public for texts that they wrote.[18]

What became briefly possible, following the printing press, was the opportunity to write to unknown others, not already part of one's social circle, outside of any institutional role. Kings and other authorities could always address strangers, but their writing was limited to amplifying speech, initially made in the court or church, about decisions and actions undertaken in their institutional role. With print, for the first time, a layperson could write to multiple other laypeople not physically present and not known individually, and this writing could be about . . . anything. The work-centered public became possible. Habermas (1991) writes eloquently about the development of what he terms the public sphere, a new space opened up in the body politic during the early centuries of modernity, presenting new possibilities for governance. But as commentary by Warner (2002) makes clear, the Habermasian public sphere is a concept in political science and philosophy, and not the same thing as the sheer possibility of a public, available to anyone who wants to be an author.

First pamphlets and then newspapers began to take advantage of the development of a literate public, as people became accustomed to receiving writing broadcast by strangers not holding any office. Reading what peers had written, on some topic of mutual interest, gradually became a regular and ultimately daily practice among the literate, whose ranks expanded throughout this period, in part because of the printing press and the greater availability of written material. Coffeehouse culture came into being in London and other urban centers in Europe (Warner 2002), where members of a public could come together, to discuss the written work which had brought them into being as a public for that writing. Of course, in this era only a narrow sliver of the populace was engaged as a public for one another, a group tightly circumscribed by gender and economic and social position. But the gentlemen, merchants, and professionals who thronged London coffeehouses, and argued about what they had read in the *Spectator*, a piece which may have been written by one of them, were ordinary people, who did not hold any institutional office, but who were able, courtesy of the printing press, and the affluence of early mercantile capitalism, to gain a public, and to be a public, for any one of their company.

In this early period when the public sphere was born and then flourished—perhaps the 17th through mid-18th centuries—most of the material written and shared could not be described as marketing. That absence is important. One of the attractive features of the economic explanation was that it explained why online reviews exploded: because more market information is better, each new media channel must get rapidly colonized, the better to exchange facts among buyers and sellers. Yet the early development of publics-for-anyone, while not an explosion, did come to engage large numbers of people, not limited to specialists such as journalists and scholars, as came to be the case in Late Capitalist times. And this first expansion of publics had little to do with market information. To have a public must be valuable, independent of whether it is market facts that are published. People wanted to have a public, and to be a member of publics, once this became possible.

As consumer society developed and flourished in the 19th and 20th centuries, under the warm sun of the I/S/T/C Revolutions, fluid, open, and democratic access to the mass media gradually dried up. By Tarde's time in the late 19th century, the contemporary, Late Capitalist structure of the mass media was freezing into place. Access to a public was once again limited to holders of institutional office, even as the nature of these offices changed relative to the medieval period. Professional journalists, members of the commercial elite, government officials, and credentialed cultural producers could reach a mass audience; but everyone else was restricted to the role of reader or audience member, and could no longer gain a public for their views and tastes. Ordinary people could be a public, but could not have a public. As always, people conversed, and their talk may have been about what they read, but they could not publish, only converse and write epistles, as had long been the case, in the millennia after writing diffused, and before the printing press cranked into gear.

The Web broke up these old structures (Turner 2010). The demotic turn made it possible once again for ordinary people to have a public. Some few were able to grab the megaphone, as in the case of select fashion bloggers, and gain a truly mass audience. But a much larger number of people got the opportunity, through online reviews, to step up on a soapbox, and gain a public for their written work.

Benefits and Value of Having a Public

What do I get if I gain a public? I get more than the chance to reach out to strangers. That's the visible behavior, and some stranger reading what I wrote is the obvious outcome. But another, less obvious outcome is captured by the word published. A published work exists independent of its author, in a way conversation never can and an epistle rarely does. Once I am published, I become more than I was before; I gain entry into a new field, as Bourdieu might have said. I come to exist on a second plane apart from the earthly plane on which my body dwells. I become immortal; my publications can continue to touch people long after my body returns to dust. To enter the public sphere is a pale imitation of going to the Christian heaven: it brings everlasting life, a continued incorporeal presence, available to anyone everywhere, like an angel.

That sounds a lot less abstruse than writing to be read by strangers! The potential for everlasting life, continued existence beyond the grave, moves this outcome, of gaining a public, closer to widespread and deeply felt yearnings.[19] To have a public is to be a cultural producer, a culture maker, no longer just that guy over there. I am larger than before, and I escape the limits of the humdrum. What I think and feel is ennobled by publishing it. If substantial numbers of strangers, people with whom I have no concrete social tie and who owe me nothing, are willing to read me, then I must be somebody. I can act at a distance, even as I sleep. I exist beyond my immediate location, active everywhere at once, a demiurge.

This status has been enjoyed, by a few, from the onset of mass media. Novelists, public intellectuals, artists, and their ilk have had the possibility of a public for several centuries, as have holders of an institutional office, which could be as simple as employment as a journalist, or a tenure-track position in academia. But, absent an institutional role or credential, access to publics was scarce. Take the case of a would-be novelist, whether in 1850 or 1950. First, you had to pass the gatekeeper at some publisher (countless *New Yorker* cartoons come to mind here, along with jokes about manuscripts that come in over the transom, unsolicited). It costs money to print up a book, and many would-be novelists must be denied, as poor commercial risks. Second, to have a public of any size, enough to get a second book published, and thereby gain a more secure and ongoing access, could occur for only a select few aspirants. Selection was fitfully a matter of talent, editorial taste, or the author's social connections, but however executed, the winnowing was severe. There could be no mass access to a public, for those lacking institutional office, except as they passed through the eye of the publisher's needle, however intense and widespread the desire for such a public might have been.

Outside an institutional role, fame or celebrity also conferred the ability to reach a public. But here again, access was limited to the lucky or the freakishly talented, and to gain a public was to get hold of the megaphone; one had a mass public, or none at all. To have a public was an elite status, rare and controlled. There was no demotic participation, except as passive audience, or as conversation partner to other audience members, discussing what the celebrated had done or said.

For millennia nobody had a public; this social formation did not and could not exist until *Gesellschaft* conditions took over. After the printing press was introduced, publics became possible, and for a period, there was widespread access to publics, within a narrow privileged circle. As the I/S/T/C Revolutions rolled along and population expanded in the 19th century, a mass society came into being, with mass media to match. Open access to these mass media was lost, and only those holding institutional roles, or who had run the gauntlet to fame and celebrity, could have a public. Then, the Internet came along, and the possibility of having a public once again opened up to anyone, restricted only by a basic requirement of literacy, and enough distance from necessity to have something to say to a public.

With this history, I've converted the pallid and arid exercise, of writing for strangers, into something more momentous, something nearer to deep yearnings and abiding desire. With this insight, the sociologist can give an alternative account of why online reviews exploded, and what sustains the writing of reviews. The price was to invoke a hoary parallel between printing press and Internet, and commit to a fraught theory that technological innovation drives social change. But, having maybe lived too long in Silicon Valley, I do find the analogy sound. The Internet today, in making it possible for ordinary consumers to gain a public for their views and tastes, works exactly as the printing press had, for a select population of gentlemen centuries before. This raises the darker prospect that just as the opening of the public to the public, occasioned by the printing press, lasted for only a brief epoch, so also this new opening, occasioned by the Internet, may likewise slip away. But no one knows the future.

The Megaphone Versus the Soapbox

Fashion blogging was explained in terms of a megaphone effect, using concepts of cultural capital and audience. For online reviews, the key concept is a public, and cultural capital is no longer central. Online reviews differ from blogging. The soapbox imperative is not the megaphone effect.

The tie between public and soapbox dates to the 19th century. Even after the mass media had frozen out the ordinary person, for a brief interval crowded cities still offered a public space. Enough people thronged the squares and boulevards that an ordinary person could get a public, albeit a fragile and temporary one, by dint of standing on a soapbox and beginning to speak in a loud voice. The people who did were mostly cranks, zealots, and malcontents, but still, these were ordinary people, not holding institutional position: anyone could get up on a soapbox. And people did. You have probably never seen a physical soapbox, much less tested its ability to hold your weight; but you know the cliché. The survival of the cliché, long after its physical anchor disappeared, testifies to the enduring appeal of having a soapbox, the appeal of gaining a public, a potential audience for one's views and tastes.

Before the development of electronic amplification, standing on a soapbox in a public place provided enough prominence to be able to address and gather to oneself an audience. The soapbox supplied just enough elevation to distinguish one from many. From the standpoint of distinction—the perspective of Essay One—the salient element in the soapbox metaphor is the fact of elevation: to stand on a soapbox is to elevate oneself above many. Here in Essay Two, the salient element is the opportunity to speak to a public, to express your private thoughts, to reach strangers outside your circle. The key metric is the fact of an audience, a realized public, and not its size. There can be no expression without a public external to one's private self.[20] But it only takes a handful of strangers to realize a public.

To probe further the difference between soapbox and megaphone, let's compare audience and public. Public is the broader term. An audience is a concrete instance of the potential for a public, a realized public. The audience some fashion bloggers achieve exploits one possibility, from among the many publics newly available in an Internet age. Audiences can be counted. That was important in exploring cultural capital, which invokes a money metaphor, with money anchoring the idea of a countable social good. Because audience can be counted, it can be converted into other countable things, like money. Because an audience is a realized public, it can accept concrete descriptors like large or mass. Hence, the megaphone effect describes one of the new phenomena made possible by the availability of a public for any member of the public. Fashion blogging supplied one instance of how the Web broke the monopoly over the mass media held by institutional players.

Essay One described the newfound possibility of gaining a mass audience. Essay Two examines a different new thing: mass access to a public of indeterminate size. Recall that only a few fashion bloggers obtained a mass audience. The title of Lovink (2008) speaks the gloomy truth about the vast majority of blogs: *Zero Comments*. Millions of blogs attained no audience, beyond members of the blogger's social circle; and one's circle is not a public. What separates reviewing from blogging? Simple: an online review is guaranteed an audience. A blog is not guaranteed an audience, hence may fail to realize the possibility of a public. Or, in a few cases, a blog may gain a mass audience, and this will be an audience for the blogger, herself, with all the distinction that may result.

A writer of online reviews is unlikely to gain the mass audience achieved by some fashion bloggers. It is Yelp the corporation that has a mass audience, and it is Yelp whose capital increases with audience count. But, by the same reasoning, an online review on Yelp, of a restaurant in an urban location, will never have an audience of zero. It will be read, by dozens, maybe hundreds of peer consumers. And if you write more than one review, especially if you sustain the practice of reviewing over months and years, you may gain an audience of thousands. You have a public for your writing, of an elastic size, that may grow quite large.

Recall that the economic explanation, which rests on the imperative to exchange market information, explains why there are millions and millions of people interested in reading restaurant reviews. Market facts are always in demand. An unsatisfactory dining experience may be very unpleasant, and a successful one, highly rewarding. Overall consumer welfare increases, the more we can avoid the former and secure the latter (Mayzlin et al. 2012). But the economic account failed to explain why millions of people were willing to write reviews for no compensation. In economics, nothing is ever given away for free. There must be compensation—utility—of some type.[21] Otherwise, the whole framework, where utility must be maximized, collapses.

Knowing what a public is, and appreciating the intensity of the desire to have one, and how widespread is that desire, we can turn the economic explanation inside out. Online reviews exploded because, given the value of market information, a public is guaranteed for your written texts: every one you write. Review hosting sites provide what blogs cannot: the certainty that if I go to the trouble to write a review of something consumed, then other consumers of it, strangers to me, will read it, and I will gain a public. It won't necessarily be thousands, or even very many hundreds, but it will include many people who are strangers to me now. I will be published. My review will endure, and may be consulted months or years from now. It doesn't matter who I am. I don't have to be famous, I don't need any credentials, I don't need a college degree, I don't need any education. I need only navigate Yelp's quite straightforward user interface, make enough sense that nobody complains, and not run afoul of Yelp's filter.

I can't get a public by posting to Facebook, which is only an electronically mediated conversation within my social circle. I can't be sure of gaining a public by writing a blog or sending out tweets. And I still cannot appear in the pre-Web mass media, because I lack institutional position and I'm not credentialed as an artist or a celebrity. But, because of the value of market facts, I can be confident of gaining a public if I write a restaurant review for a website that has a mass audience. And once such a website became technologically feasible, all it needed, to draw a mass audience, was a critical mass of reviews, enough good enough market information. Therefore, Yelp.

Cultural capital need play no role in explaining reviewing; it is unnecessary here. What sets apart online reviews is the mass participation of consumer authors, rather than the elevation of a few. On Yelp, many get something, rather than a few getting a lot, and what they get is valuable: a chance to publish.

As with any other trait, the desire to publish will be distributed across the 300 million-some American consumers. That desire will be stronger for some people, weaker for others. Therefore, although there will be mass authorship at Yelp (it's not rare to desire a public), some reviewers will participate more heavily than others, because their desire for a public is stronger. But having 1000 reviews to one's credit won't produce the same result as having thousands of followers did for a few fashion bloggers. The soapbox is not the megaphone.

The Meaning of Publics after the Web

Returning to Warner (2002), from a literary standpoint the creation of publics, plural, is rather mysterious. In his self-reflexive account, he asks rhetorically, "Where is the public for this book before it was published? How does a discourse create a public for itself? [my phrasing]." Plodding forward as a dull social scientist, rather than a brilliant literary theorist, to resolve this conundrum I proposed separate levels of analysis.[22] These levels distinguished the possibility of there being publics, from any given public. I rooted the possibility of anyone having a public in technological change. Once publics became possible via the printing press, uncounted publics coalesce into being around specific cultural products, especially written texts sent out beyond one's social circle. Only in this sense does a discourse create its public; and a better formula might be that discourses are coeval with their publics, within a system of possibility created by the advent of the mass media, first the printing press and now the Web.

To use a metaphor, the printing press spread tinder about, each publication strikes a flint, and audiences are the flames. Pushing the metaphor, a blog post that no one reads is like a spark that fell some distance from any tinder, while a fashion blog that gathers 10000 followers is a bonfire. Pushing the metaphor further, as the mass media of the 19th and 20th century took control, it was as if they sucked up the oxygen: sparks struck by people lacking an institutional position could no longer ignite the tinder lying around. Only sparks struck under the media's oxygen tent could ignite into audiences.

The Web shredded those media tents, spilling out oxygen all around. Tinder continued to be spread about, albeit in clumps, so sparks could again ignite a flame, converting the possibility of a public into a realized audience—if the spark fell near tinder. The taste of some fashion bloggers acts as a sixth sense for locating tinder piles. To complete the metaphor, Yelp comes along as a lumberman with a rake, gathering diffuse bits of tinder into a vast plain of neat piles, so that almost any spark struck on that vast plain will fall near tinder, and make a flame. But it is only here on the market information plane that tinder is piled, and close together; elsewhere, as on the blogging plane, tinder may be scarce on the ground, and scattered not piled, so that most sparks fizzle.

YELP AS A SOCIAL FORMATION

With a typology of social formations in hand, and the idea of a public called out, we can return to the contest between economic and psychological versus sociological explanations for online reviews. Earlier, I argued:

1. Economic theory explains why there should be an explosion of review readers, in light of the value of market information, but does not explain why the number of review writers expanded to match.
2. Psychological theories, of what motivates review writers, are conditioned on the social formation in which review reading and writing occurs, and gain traction only where theory matches formation.
   a. The motive to belong presumes community, a social formation within the solidarity horizon. A profit-seeking entrepreneurial venture, with millions of participants, cannot provide that solidarity.

b. The motive to gain status was more difficult to dismiss. It presumes a *Gesellschaft* arrangement, which Yelp is, and large numbers of participants, as in Yelp. It also explains why there are ordinary consumers who write hundreds of reviews: piling up your review count is how you gain status.

I concluded that the status explanation was bloodied but unbowed, and could not be dispatched until we pinned down the nature of the social form taken by Yelp. We now have an alternative explanation, in which Yelp is a device for providing a public to any consumer who wishes, with the desire for such a public widespread. But devising an alternative motivational explanation is not the same as a rebuttal. Let's resume probing the status account for weakness.

Can Writing Reviews Produce a Gain in Status?

To be a reviewer with hundreds of reviews, on a site where most have written less than a dozen, and many have written none, is to be elevated. Simply to have a public, a realized audience, is likewise to be elevated somewhat. Bourdieu's term distinction might be applied: copious review production creates distinction. This reviewer is distinguished by having done more, which ties back to capital, or money, the simplest social index that divides more from less. But is this elevation, achieved by productive reviewers, properly described as status?

Following Lampel and Bhalla (2007), who draw on established socio-logical accounts, status is defined as "that which, upon recognition, pro-duces deference in response [my phrasing]." Deference means that you give priority to that other person and their needs and desires. This definition is advantageous because it separates the sources of status from the thing itself. In Late Capitalist America, and the modern, Western societies from which it developed, there are a handful of traditional sources of status. Those who hold office in the state—that social formation which has a monopoly on the legitimate use of force—gain status. Most Americans would feel deferential, if ushered into the office of the President, as would the subjects of kings and princes ushered into court. Noble birth produces a deference response, even in Americans (if you doubt this, read any of the breathless genealogical web posts where—OMG—an ancestor is discov-ered to be of noble birth). Wealth, and historic family name, great profes-sional success, or even being a physician can produce deference.

So defined, it is hard to see how status can have anything to do with Yelp. Deference is not the response to noting that this reviewer has 329 reviews and this other one, only 14. Credibility, maybe, and credit, probably, in terms of the weight placed on each review in the event they conflict. There may also be more engagement, a greater likelihood that judgments by the author of 329 reviews are pondered, reread, even contested, in silent study or by writing a new review. Because Yelp is an ersatz social form, a virtual organization rather than a real social group, there is no social position or state power to draw on. Reviewers can gain distinction, yes; enjoy credibility, yes; build a reputation and earn favorable regard, yes; but deference is not on offer, and hence, reviewers cannot have or gain status in the conventional sense.

Pace Billig (2013), an ordinary word like status offers a dusty mirror, grimed by too much loose usage. Status is not the motivator behind the writing of reviews. Status is not on offer on Yelp. Reviewers can distinguish themselves by dint of production, the more so by prodigious production. And the distinction of having authored a large number of reviews becomes a social fact, with implications for how members of the review-reading public will respond. But it is the desire for a public that drives the behavior of writing reviews, a desire which is stronger in some people than others. Inside or outside of Yelp, no one defers to you because you've written 300 reviews. You wrote those reviews for the intrinsic pleasure of gaining and enjoying a public (see Boxes 2.8 and 2.9, toward the end of this essay, for more on intrinsic motivation).

How Are Web Publics Structured?

I have not yet said anything about the structure of the consumer publics hosted by a Yelp, Amazon, Trip Advisor, or Google +. Whatever structures may be in place, one function is clear: to provide the possibility of a public, for any consumer who can muster the effort to write, and make that missive meet the genre expectations for a review: an evaluation of something consumed. But the hosting arrangement that supports that function must have structure. Or, there could be several possible structures, no one way to do it. In turn, different structures will shape the functions supported. That vague verb, to shape, conveys that a public structured one way may provide a pleasing experience for an author, while another structure may be more efficient for casual buyers, even as a third is more effective for engaged readers. Providing a public is a new thing. No one knows how functions may vary, nor whether that variability lies in the experience offered to authors or to readers, or whether what varies across sites is pleasure, efficiency, or something else. But we can know that Yelp's structure shapes the functions Yelp performs.

And, as sociologists, we can make these other assertions: (1) there is more than one way to structure a Web public, and these structures will make a difference, be consequential, for what functions get performed; (2) there need not be only one structure, narrowly tailored to executing a single function; (3) there could instead be multiple structures, providing a web of support for one or several functions; and, most important, (4) there will be social structure. There must be social structure if Web publics are to be explained sociologically. And this last point, in a little while, will return us to the contest against economic and psychological explanations, which unite in dispensing with social structure.

But first, let's step back and assess the language here, this talk of structure and function. It is pleasingly abstract, in a rigorous seeming way, don't you think? It sounds scientific, covering noun and verb, property and action. It is free of literary flourishes, and promises to go beyond mere naming of social forms. But is it scientific? Is social structure real? Does it have causal power? These questions about structure are surface ripples. A much larger beast moves beneath.

Can Sociology Be a Science?

This deep uncertainty is worth calling out. It has implications for doing sociology, and more especially consumer sociology, here in the 21st century, in Late Capitalist times. Although every social science must (or should) struggle with this issue, the sociology of social formations, especially new formations, must wrestle this question while high up on a ledge.

Yelp is not a natural thing, but a designed entity. Design compounds the uncertainty about whether science can be done here. And yet, the explosion of online reviews, and the proliferation of hosting sites, is as natural as any human social form, insofar as any historical event can be said to occur naturally. A scientific account of online reviews, a sociology, must grapple with this paradoxical element.

Yelp, as a website, is software code, written to a design that originated in the creative efforts of one or more people, who designed that code to do something that hadn't been done in software before. Even so, it was only at this juncture in human history, and not before, that teams of human coders decided it would be worth their while to write code to do the things that Yelp does. As a simultaneous and multiply sourced effort, controlled and coordinated by no one, the explosion of online reviews can rightly be called a phenomenon, a historical development, even as these terms grate when applied to the Yelp corporation.

Those coders were employees, working for founders and venture capitalists in a start-up, which is a corporate form that predates online reviews by decades, even as each start-up nonetheless represents a new design launched by named individuals on some one day. And start-ups are only one type of privately owned corporation, one type of joint stock company, organizational forms which are but centuries old, making the joint stock corporation itself an historically situated phenomenon. Best to say that the private corporation, implemented as a joint stock company, emerged in history. It seems a category error to say that John Smith and his legislative staff personally created the joint stock corporation, made it happen, in some Act of Parliament passed in the early 1800s; even as enabling legislation was nonetheless crucial to the emergence of the joint stock company, in America and Britain.

So can Yelp and its structure be explained scientifically, or not? Well let me ask you a question: can history be a science? Can there be a science of organizations, corporate and otherwise? (There is a journal called *Organization Science*, if that matters to your answer.) Even so, can a science of designed social forms, which emerge in history, proceed in the same way as the sciences of kinetics and chemistry and genes?

These questions, among scholars in the social sciences outside the History Department, are like batty old Uncle Alfred, whose arrest nobody will ever talk about. It would be bad form in the faculty club to say that the tenured members of such and such a department, all of whom present themselves as social scientists, are not doing science. Although, in my personal experience, many social scientists in business schools do not hesitate to knock the intellectual credentials of scholars over in the Humanities departments. This doesn't count, since Humanities scholars seldom claim to be doing science, and also don't feel the lack of anything so jejune as a scientific understanding of Shakespeare, so these two sides can regard each other with amused indifference, and murmur about C.P. Snow with a diffident grimace. The struggle for scientific respectability is specific to the social sciences. Physicists don't have economics envy, and Humanities scholars do not envy social scientists; but "physics envy" is a well-established term in economics and other social science disciplines: Google it.

In day-to-day university life, concern over the scientific status of the social sciences has been repressed, like Uncle Alfred's arrest. As with anything repressed, it bubbles to the surface here and there, in the fetish for mathematics, and what Billig (2013) decries as the rampant thing-ification of human beings. And the recent crisis, swirling around fabricated data in social psychology (McQuarrie 2014), has increased the muttering among physical scientists, about whether psychology and the rest really are sciences. But no practicing social scientist, nor any journal where these social scientists aspire to publish, pauses to question the scientific status of sociology, economics, psychology, marketing, or any of the rest. Humanities scholars may sniff, and physicists may sneer, but within social science, we only acknowledge that there may be some problems with execution, or some dry rot that has to be knocked out, but we are scientists, yes, yes, really, we truly are. Such is the prestige of science in the modern West.

With advancing age, I've moved toward an agnostic view. I don't know if sociology can be or is a science. To continue the analogy, although it's been decades since I attended a religious service outside a wedding or funeral, I cannot style myself an atheist (too close an encounter with Pascal). The views of a Richard Dawkins seem as over the top as the hidebound religious dogmatism against which he delights to rail. Likewise, the irrationalists pilloried in Stove (2001) are not persuasive. I don't know that a scientific sociology, science as judged by the standards of physics, is not possible. But I'm not certain it is possible, either. If it were possible to have scientific knowledge of sociological matters, that would be an attractive prospect, mayhap. But if it were not possible to have scientific knowledge in the physics sense, here in sociology, it would be a great shame to have spent one's career barking up that wrong tree.

To be a consumer sociologist requires you to be tough-minded, to hold in mind two opposed notions, without succumbing to either: that if you could do science here, you should; but if you can't do science here, you ought not to fool yourself on that score.[23] Whatever the outcome of this internal tussle, you remain a scholar, committed to wresting knowledge from facts.

To thread this needle, we need only accept that there can be knowledge that is not scientific knowledge (whereas, if you press a Dawkins or the typical physical scientist, they will deny that there can be true knowledge that is not also scientific). If there can be knowledge of Shakespeare, there can be knowledge of Yelp, and of organizations, and of social change in history. If there can only be opinions about Shakespeare's plays, and no knowledge, no possibility of truth, then the bind tightens for sociology. I say we can have sociological knowledge, and that this knowledge, even if not scientific, has value. Time will tell.

It will be difficult for most of you to maintain this agnostic view of sociological science, and the more youthful, the more difficult; but I do not think it wise to build consumer sociology on an insecure foundation, and sociology's claim to scientific status, like that of sister social sciences, is not firm. It will do no good to deny the uncertainty; and here I pitch to the younger scholar, whose ideas are not frozen in place.

It may not be possible to have scientific knowledge of a new social form that was designed by its owners, rather than occurring naturally. But we can attempt to learn about it, and know it for what it is and is not.

MARKETS AND YELP

Returning to the nature of Yelp, and whether it is an economic thing or a sociological thing, from this point, the argument grows more complicated. Everything comes back to the fitness, or folly, of attempting a market explanation for online reviews. But more than one market explanation is on offer, addressing more than one aspect of online reviews, and the judgment is not always going to be negative. For instance, Yelp the corporation is a market participant. I am sure of it: Yelp competes against other hosting sites, like Google+, to make money off of hosting. But the Yelp website is not a marketplace in which reviews are exchanged, in the manner of goods being exchanged for money; the Yelp site is a machine for manufacturing publics. As a machine, it has a design. As a machine for manufacturing a social good, this design is manifest as a social structure. The details of this structure determine how well Yelp fulfills its function to manufacture publics, and also its other functions, which include supplying information to consumers, who are buyers in the restaurant market, even if they do not always act strictly as market participants, when they write or browse reviews of restaurants. An economic account of online reviews is not so much wrong, as partial.

We have a lot of markets to keep straight here. Sociologists do not wish to be imperialists. We accept that economics has a sphere of its own, in which its ideas hold true: that there are such things as markets, and markets have the structures imputed to them by economists, and operate in the ways that economic theory describes. But not every human sphere is a market. Sociology has its sphere too, which is the sphere of social being, social action, and social structure.

Yelp as a Competitor in the Hosting Market

Earlier, I made fun of the idea that ordinary consumers post reviews on Yelp as a charitable gesture, pro bono. Yelp is an entrepreneurial firm founded by veterans of Silicon Valley, and funded by venture capitalists. Yelp made its founders and funders rich by its initial public offering (IPO) in 2012, and by the quadrupling of its stock that followed. Yelp is no less a profit-seeking commercial entity than ExxonMobil the oil company, Smith & Wesson the pistol maker, or Monsanto the genetically modified organism (GMO) seed company. It strains credulity to think that millions of ordinary consumers willingly spend their time, writing reviews for free, so that a small group of Yelp owners and executives can make enormous sums of money.[24]

Yelp has a *Gesellschaft* structure. The consumer publics hosted on

Yelp, from which Yelp profits, have a structure which reflects Yelp's goal, as a corporation, to make a profit off them. It cannot be, that having a private party host the possibility of publics, has no impact on the structure of these publics. Privately owned publics are new. Centuries ago in the halcyon age of coffeehouse democracy, the public hosted itself. The newspapers of those days were not the closed mass media of centuries hence. Almost any gentleman with the will could start one, or get a missive into one, and if one coffeehouse closed there were always others down the street. The possibility of a public simply existed, as an overlay on everyday sociability that would have occurred anyway. This free-floating possibility of a public went away, as the mass media developed into its contemporary corporate form, closed to outsiders. This freedom was restored, after the Web, but only in the blogosphere, with the attendant high risk that no audience will be realized: publication without issue. Yelp is neither a restoration of the newspaper–coffeehouse system of the late 18th century, nor the pale shadow of it seen in the blogosphere. Yelp is something new: a privately hosted and controlled site that allows for publics to be reliably realized.

Consumer publics are new. Neither consuming, nor the effort to buy and sell, gave a focus to the first publics, spawned during the era of coffeehouse–newspaper culture. But today the ordinary person, who wishes reliably to gain a public, has to write a review of something consumed: has to act as a consumer to get a public. There is no other choice. A 21st-century person can write about anything he or she pleases in a blog, but can't then be guaranteed a realized audience. And the ordinary person still has no access to the conventional mass media. Online reviews exploded because consumer publics are the only public-with-certainty, publics you can tap for yourself, by authoring a piece of discourse that conforms to genre rules, the rules that make a piece of text into a review.

A consumer public, which is a guaranteed public, is a valuable good. As a publisher, Yelp provides a valuable service. And that suggests, as is the case, that Yelp can't be the only hosting site in operation. In Late Capitalist times, most bona fide business opportunities attract competition. Given more than one review hosting site, these sites, as profit-seeking firms, must compete for both review readers and review writers. Market rules apply to corporate competitors.

Economists have theories about how competition works, whether in the review hosting market or any market.[25] First, each competitor will seek advantage (Hunt and Morgan 1996). In Late Capitalist times, most firms don't want to offer a commodity, but something unique, that has no substitute. If it is the right something, if it matches consumer demand, an advantage will be gained. But not every competitor will get it right. Some review hosting websites will be less successful, and fall by the wayside, even as others thrive. For the scholar trying to understand online reviews—in contrast to the marketer seeking an edge—observing what succeeds, versus what fails, may then yield knowledge, and reveal how different structures support, or undermine, desired functions. Outcomes will vary, and structure may both explain this variation, and be revealed by it.[26]

How does a Yelp compete with a Google+ or a City Search? Consider the business models at work in the hosting market. A business model describes how we get paid; exactly where we make money. In Yelp's business model, millions of buyer readers come to Yelp to get market facts. Yelp is free to them, because, as with any mass audience, Yelp can monetize this readership by selling ad space to businesses: restaurants that wish to improve their traffic. Review readers don't pay Yelp. Business advertisers do. So on first take, a Yelp competes with a Google+ to attract review readers, who become the product, which is sold to advertisers, who pay Yelp. In the vernacular, Yelp sells eyeballs.

Review readers are primarily attracted by the quantity and quality of market information available—or so the economist tells us. The role of quantity is easily grasped: I'm less likely to return to a site if a restaurant of interest had no reviews or not many reviews; and if my search for information comes up empty more than once, I may not ever come back. Hence, on second take, the ability to supply reviews, which means to attract review writers in quantity, determines success in the competitive business of hosting reviews.

Quality is more subtle: facts may be easy or hard to find, as a consequence of website software design. But market information, provided in the form of written texts, can also be more or less useful, and offer more or less value, depending on the nature of the texts contributed by reviewers. A review may be written well or poorly, and be easy or hard to read; likewise, a reviewer may be more or less knowledgeable about restaurants, or perceptive about the pleasures to be got from dining out. But reviews can also be legitimate or fake. Shills are always a possibility, as when a groundless and unduly positive review is written in return for a free meal, or for other compensation. Character assassination and vendetta are also possible, as when a restaurateur, using a fake name, writes a scathingly negative review of a competitor. Fake reviews—false facts—make a hosting site less valuable than otherwise. Lies lower the quality of the information supplied. Bad reviewers, or reviewers behaving badly, produce poor-quality market information, and make a hosting site less competitive, against other sites more successful in attracting quality reviews.

So again, on second take, Yelp and Google+ compete in terms of the quantity and quality of the reviewers they can attract and hold; or more subtly, in terms of the reviewer behaviors they are able to encourage, and also the behaviors they discourage. It's a 21st-century business competition: people who aren't employees, whom you do not control, and can't manage in any conventional sense, are responsible for producing the raw material, the feedstock which you transform into your finished product, which is a mass audience for sale. In Harvard case world, we call this a media business model: the millions who read reviews on Yelp are not Yelp's customers, because they don't pay Yelp. Rather, these readers are Yelp's product, the item Yelp sells to its paying customers, who are businesses, who wish to sell their products to Yelp's own product, its audience for sale.

In short, review sites compete for readers by competing to attract review writers. To succeed in this competition, a site must draw more, better reviewers. Review quality, or reviewer quality—these are two faces of one thing—consists of two elements: how informative the review or knowledgeable the reviewer, but also, how honest and trustworthy the review and reviewer. Competitive success, for a Yelp, means attracting quality reviewers, in quantity, without being able to offer any tangible compensation. It means encouraging their better angels, and discouraging their darker impulses, without having any of the controls or incentives a manager would have, if these reviewers were compensated employees. How can this be accomplished?

Invisible Hand or Visible Social Structure?

Economists have a theory for how one review hosting site, competing against others within a market, will, over time, succeed in providing quality market information in quantity. Simply posit a market, and more particularly a free market, as described in Box 2.4. A defining element of any market account is automaticity, the operation of an invisible hand, in Adam Smith's memorable phrase. Invisible hand means no social structure required. Or, from Billig's (2013) perspective, no human acts. Supply and demand, inhuman forces, equilibrate themselves, through the price mechanism, under conditions of pure competition and perfect knowledge. Left alone, markets balance supply and demand more efficiently than any alternative. Translating back to online reviews: market information, good enough, and enough of it to meet consumers' demand, will emerge automatically, if Yelp and its ilk are allowed to compete freely, without the heavy hand of government, understood in Weber's terms as the exercise of police power: that is, without any coercion, applied by anyone, to reviewers. Put large numbers of buyer readers in touch with enough reviewer writers, in the most efficient and effective way, the one that emerges from a competitive struggle; that's all. The market will provide.

BOX 2.4   HOW A MARKET WORKS

A market consists of untrammeled competition, goods that are substitutes, and perfect information. Given these conditions, when sellers and buyers come together in a marketplace, sellers will seek to maximize profit, buyers will seek to maximize utility, and so long as information circulates freely, the pricing mechanism will equilibrate supply and demand. No social structure is required: a market that satisfies the named conditions works perfectly well without any structure, any institutions.

It is important to appreciate how powerful and successful the idea of a market is within its proper sphere. The economist doesn't need any conception of utility other than "that which consumers always seek to maximize." Neither does he need any social structure to generate, from free market conditions, powerful sets of predictive equations concerning price behavior, and changes in supply and demand. The trouble starts when the economist attempts to treat non-market formations as if they were markets. But if everything has been commoditized, commercialized, and marketized here in Late Capitalist times, might not all human behavior be market behavior? Some economists are willing to go there. Sociology offers a corrective. What other social formations are there, besides markets? Sociologists have to ask, Might the widespread appellation of market be metaphor run amok?

However, returning to Weber, the sociologist can't see how quality reviews are going to be produced in quantity, without social control based on some type of social structure. That's the difference between sociological and economic explanations of the new consumer behaviors seen online: classically, economists expect competition, without an overlay of institutional structure, to automatically and necessarily produce a supply of reviews that exactly meets the demand for quantity and quality of market information, at the price consumers are willing to pay. Sociologists, who've read enough psychology to glimpse the dark side, find this dubious: what about cheaters, slackers, the greedy and the vindictive? Economists remain serene: the shoddy and duplicitous will be weeded out by the invisible hand of market forces. Websites offering poor-quality reviews will fail; sites that survive will offer reviews neither more nor less shoddy than the market, composed of buyer readers, demands.

Sociologists think this a fairy tale. Without social control, a review hosting site will soon be thronged with fake reviews. Positive and negative shilling are backed by immediate financial incentives that dwarf the more diffuse benefits, of gleaning market facts or gaining a public. As with Gresham's Law and counterfeit currency, it does not take too many fake reviews to begin a downward spiral for a website. If humans have a dark side, maintaining review quality will require social control, which will be visible as social structure.

This debate between economists and sociologists takes place in a larger context. In the American newspapers of my day,[27] a great debate rages over the proper role of market versus state. In Late Capitalist times, the market waxes ever larger in heft, and the State—gummint, in the vernacular—is under an ideological assault no less vigorous for being sometimes incoherent, as in "keep gummint hands off my Medicare." That is why it is important to counterpose invisible hand explanations, for how online review sites operate, against explanations in terms of social structure, as I attempt here. Further, online reviewing was created in Silicon Valley, so that it carries the sign, TechnologyInnovationUnboundedFutureGlory, which makes opposing market mechanisms to social structure even more apt. The Valley is full of entrepreneurial visionaries, legends in their own mind, lottery winners who believe with zeal, or find it convenient to believe, that the market, unchained, can produce miracles of productivity and well-being, leaving the tired institutions of the past to eat dust. Faced with such hubris, nemesis proceeds.

Market Competition and the Structure of Privately Controlled Publics

The market for review hosting sites is old enough to examine successes and failures; results of the invisible hand. Two early competitors to Yelp, Citysearch.com, and Yahoo Local, soon stagnated and were no longer competitive when this work began (Wang 2010). Google +, introduced later, in the 2011–2012 timeframe, continues to compete, but despite Google's enormous resources and commanding hold over other aspects of Web search, Google has not as yet overcome Yelp's dominance over local reviews.

Yelp has become the most successful of the dedicated review sites, and has succeeded in absolute terms. Yelp must have cracked the puzzle of how to provide quality reviews in quantity. Adopting market logic, Yelp's success can provide clues about what works in review site hosting. Any practices seen on Yelp which differ from the common run of practice across review sites, would be the place to look for insight into Yelp's success. If these practices are consistent with an invisible hand—if Yelp succeeded, because it set up the most frictionless marketplace for exchanging reviews—that will favor market explanations; if instead Yelp practices represent interventions, the visible hand of social structure, such as the exercise of police power, that will favor more sociological perspectives.

Consulting the review hosting sites described in Box 2.1, we can pull together a description of the generic structure for a website that hosts reviews. Generic means widely shared across hosting sites. Then we can pick out design departures specific to Yelp.

Generic discourse structure in review hosting

All major review sites as of 2012 contained these elements:

1. One or more numerical ratings of the review object.
2. Some text: the review proper. Pictures are sometimes present but optional, whereas there must be text to call it a review, rather than a rating.
3. Some information on the reviewer, even if only a nom de plume.
4. A second-order review, which evaluates the focal review; for example, at Amazon, ratings of how helpful or unhelpful the review had been to other readers. This second-order review will be labeled feedback in most of what follows, except when I want to remind you that reviews spawn their own reviews. On those occasions I'll insert the lumbering phrase, second order.

As presented, these four are elements of discourse structure, not social structure, and pertinent to a rhetoric or poetics of website design, which I have not the space to pursue. Their social uses will soon emerge.

At first glance, elements 3 and 4 seem to be unnecessary: without them, online reviews would continue to exist, and a website with unnamed reviewers and no feedback could still fulfill its basic functions, of supplying facts to reader buyers, and offering a public to reviewer authors. Also element 1, the summary number, although universal across sites, is not necessary, as long as element 2 is present. To speak of reviews requires only text linked to goods for sale, that is, evaluative text that appears when searching for goods, such as restaurant, sushi restaurant, or Sengyo. That elements 3 and 4 are so widespread, even though unnecessary, may provide insight.[28]

Hosting sites treat these four elements differently, and/or add other elements. The differences may be small, such as changes in the number of scale points used in the numerical rating (five is the most common, but not universal) or the label used in the second-order review (useful versus helpful). Or the differences may be substantial, such as providing more data on the reviewer, or adding entirely new elements, such as friend count.

Next are notable elements of Yelp's structure, couched in terms of the generic design, along with departures, in the form of new elements introduced by Yelp.

Yelp's take on the generic website design

1. Three facts about the reviewer are displayed next to each review (Box 2.1). Other sites only give the reviewer's nom de plume, often but not always with a link back to a dossier, or profile, as most sites call it.

2. Reviewers have a more extensive dossier at Yelp than most other sites. The dossier may offer descriptive or lifestyle information, entered optionally by the Yelp member when joining; this may be as simple as gender. Other elements in the profile are tallies of activity, automatically updated by the Yelp database software, beginning with count of reviews written, count of friends, count of compliments received, and including a sortable cache of all reviews, and more (browse yelp.com and click on a reviewer to see an example of a profile page).
3. Yelp contains a more elaborate second-order layer than most, with three types of feedback—useful, funny, or cool—and tabulates this feedback for each review and as lifetime totals for each reviewer.

Yelp's unique or less common elements

1. Yelp provides multiple opportunities for a reader to interact with a reviewer, going beyond feedback on the review to friending, adding specific compliments to a reviewer's dossier, and more.
2. Yelp allows for friending, and friending is integrated into many aspects of website operation. For instance, Yelp foregrounds any reviews written by friends when a restaurant's page comes up.
3. Yelp nominates some members as Elite. The nomination is controlled by Yelp, and has to be renewed annually, but is displayed with each review. Typically, Elite members have high review counts and continue to write reviews at a high rate. Elite members, like Gold or Platinum members of an airline's frequent flyer club, get invitations to special Yelp events and receive messages directed only to the Elite.
4. Yelp has a filter. An algorithm examines reviews after posting, and if flagged, the review goes into a kind of jail. Filtered reviews do not show up on a restaurant's main page; a special link at the bottom of the page gives access (one can visit these segregated reviews, hence my term jail). In the case of another set of reviews, the text is cast out entirely by the filter, and cannot be obtained. These reviews, rather than being suspect, as in the case of jailed reviews, are judged to be violations of Yelp's terms of service, and deleted from public view.

Implications of Yelp's website design and structure
These pallid descriptions of Yelp can be enlivened. I'll list them them as conclusions about the natural experiment under way in the review hosting market, using the stentorian preface: "The *most successful* online review sites . . ."

1. . . . enable ordinary consumers to be public figures, with their accomplishments and personal biographies displayed and connected to their published writing.
2. . . . devise structures that allow for friending and honoring, to burnish the site as a destination for both reviewers and review readers.
    a. For prospective reviewers, these social structures provide the opportunity for a more intimate connection to their public, and for honor.
    b. For buyer readers, these structures help vet the trustworthiness of market facts, and increase the value of Yelp, by foregrounding information likely to be more relevant.
3. . . . provide intrinsically rewarding opportunities for social interaction and personal creativity that engage both reviewers and readers.
4. . . . take on some of the powers of the state, such as police power, the capacity to place some reviews in jail or eliminate them. Yelp, as Weber might say, has a monopoly over the legitimate use of jailing and execution on its website. It is a power that no entity now exercises, over the World Wide Web as a whole.

Not a Community

With the elements of Yelp's social structure in view, let's look once more at the question: is Yelp a community? Neither a free market nor a community has any need for the social structures described above. Both invoke the invisible hand.

In a community—any social formation that falls within the solidarity horizon—members experience bonding, fellow feeling for others. The well-being of people with whom you feel solidarity has the same priority as your own well-being. The type case for solidarity is the loving family, in which parents may make sacrifices to help young children, or adult children may make sacrifices to care for aging parents.

Within the solidarity horizon, it is easy to explain how reviews get produced in quantity and how quality is maintained. These actions promote a feeling of solidarity among and with other community members. Reviews are donated for collective well-being, feedback is offered "for the good of the order," and all are better off through this complex web of altruism and reciprocity. In a community, the sympathies of the heart, and not social structure, act as an invisible hand to produce enough good enough reviews.

This makes sense in a community context, where a small group of people, bound by tradition, enjoys intimate bonds founded on an ongoing history of interaction. It makes no sense in the context of a corporate website visited by millions of people who are strangers to one another.

Community requires a degree of solidarity that is not available in mass *Gesellschaft* formations.

As a privately hosted and controlled *Gesellschaft* formation, Yelp is ersatz, and may be criticized as a cheap knock-off of real sociability. This also means that authenticity, in the modern and postmodern senses of that word, can never be central to Yelp. It's imperative that reviews be real, and come from real people; but real isn't really what authentic means. Authenticity comes from The People, in their resistance to OppressiveCheapenedCommercialNonCulture. This is the authenticity satirized in Lander's (2008) *Stuff White People Like*, and in television shows such as *Portlandia*. Yelp can never offer that kind of authenticity. It is not clear that any mass of strangers, any *Gesellschaft* formation, ever can.

Conversely, it is the death of community, and the scarcity of solidarity in Late Capitalist times, that makes the prospect of gaining a public motivating, and its achievement rewarding. If we were still ensconced in real intimate communities, bound together by tradition, few might bother to write for strangers. But then again, we wouldn't be dining out, but dining in, eating authentic home-cooked gruel, squatting on the dirt floor of our peasant hovel. It's a trade-off: the market giveth, and the market taketh away.

Reviews as Marketplace Exchange?

With community explanations set aside, let's examine how review sites could act as marketplaces for the exchange of information—once more to give the economist his due. Here the buyers would be review readers, the sellers review writers. Buyers obtain utility from the market facts found in reviews, and sellers obtain utility from writing reviews (for the market explanation, it does not matter what this utility is: image utility, utility from writing, whatever). The price that clears the market occurs when the facts found in reviews match, in value, the time required to find and read the review, and meet the reader's need for information. Hard-to-read or fake reviews will be like overpriced goods, which do not sell; that is, do not get read in volume. Reviewers want to be read, buyers want good information, and the invisible hand disciplines reviewers into writing about what buyers want to know.

Economists, especially the enthusiast strand sometimes seen in Silicon Valley (Tapscott and Williams 2008), have a rejoinder to the criticism that such a marketplace would soon be destroyed by a plethora of shoddy and fake reviews. The rejoinder is on point because it explains why feedback— second-order market information—appears to be universal among review hosting sites. This rejoinder also explains why review sites provide a dossier on reviewers.

The rejoinder is: feedback and the dossier provide market information about market information. When positive, feedback provides facts for reviewers, explicitly instructing them, rather than leaving them to infer, which of their review texts have proved most successful in the eyes of buyers. Information on reputation, that identifies reviews and reviewers with high counts of positive feedback, helps buyers to find better facts on the site. In short, if hosting sites are formulated as offering a two-level marketplace, this might explain how the quality of information on the site could be held at a high level, despite the sociologist's skepticism toward invisible hand explanations.

Alas, here a new obstacle presents itself, an echo of an old difficulty: how to explain why buyer-readers bother to give feedback. Second-order market information is not required or compensated, on Yelp or any other site. Not to worry: from the economist's corner, the response is the same as when we looked at reviewer motivation. Giving feedback—producing second-order market information—happens a lot, and the specifics of the motivation can safely be left to the psychologist (reciprocity, a desire to connect to other Yelp members socially, whatever). Under a market explanation, there's no need for any of the social structure laid on by Yelp. A two-level marketplace, with information on information, should be enough to maintain the supply of valuable facts, which draw buyer-readers to the Yelp site, which enables monetization, which keeps Yelp a going concern.

You can't imagine the appeal of this rescue maneuver, among the entrepreneurial elite in Silicon Valley! A month before I wrote, Uber added an overlay of feedback, with drivers rating passengers, and passengers rating drivers. Everybody rates everybody. Everybody keeps everybody honest. The invisible hand slaps and beckons, as needed.

Can second-order market information, in the form of feedback, lend muscle to the invisible hand? First we need to take a slight detour, and examine more closely the nature of first-order market information, which I have been treating as a simple thing: what buyers need to know about quality and suitability, so that they can get more value from their choice of where to dine. But things get complicated fast, once we look more closely at market information on taste goods, restaurants in this case.

What is Quality Market Information?

Review quality, for taste goods, has two aspects: a minimum, which requires that the review be real and not fake, and a second aspect, ideally maximized, that concerns how informative the review is to-me, about the suitability of this restaurant for-me. Now restate this twofold formula in relative terms: any review, relative to others for the same restaurant, can be judged as more or less likely to be genuine, and as more or less useful in helping me decide if the restaurant will be suitable. This relative restatement becomes important when reviews offer conflicting appraisals. Because taste goods are like experiential and credence goods, such conflict is likely to occur; and the greater the number of reviews collected for a restaurant, the greater the odds of conflict, and the more likely there will be multilevel, multifaceted conflict among them. You will never read 100 reviews that speak with one voice. Unless . . . many are fake.

The problem to highlight: economists, if not confronted, may conjure a fantasy review, a paragon. Like this one: "Get their seafood platter appetizer. It includes their best preparations, offers just as much food as any of their entrées, and is priced $3.00 lower."

This review supplies a valuable market fact, in the most concrete sense: how to optimize the price–quantity trade-off. Unfortunately, this paragon is more the exception than the rule, if only because restaurant owners, as rational market actors reading such a review, would be wont to raise the price on the appetizer by $2.50 or so, and include a little less quantity going forward. Markets are, after all, more or less efficient: perhaps the reviewer dined on the first day of work for a new cook, whose generosity was soon corrected by the restaurant manager as training continued. Markets can self-correct; after which, this review text will not be fake, or weakly informative, but mistaken, and no longer trustworthy.

Economists, and their Silicon Valley epigones, are prone to a second fantasy: that reviews will mostly align, making the choice between restaurants easy as pie, once you have this great new technology of Web 2.0. You bring up Yelp on your smartphone, as you stroll downtown, and find that Chez Dolce is rated 4.5, while Chez Barfe is rated 2.5, with verbiage to match. Eat at Chez Dolce. Problem solved.

Ever browsed Yelp? It's never *that* clear. You'll stroll through Japantown in San Jose, and see 12 sushi restaurants from the corner where you stand. They are all rated 3.5, 4.0 or 4.5 (like hundreds of other restaurants on Yelp). The ones rated 4.5 don't have many reviews, which also don't seem perceptive, while the ones rated 3.5 have more and more thoughtful reviews, not a few of which give ratings of 5, mixed in with a few obvious slams. Where you gonna eat?

Here is another paragon review: "The sushi here at Sengyo is as fresh as you can get. Other sushi bars don't do enough volume. At a smaller place, if you order anything but tuna, you are probably eating yesterday's fish, or older, because they couldn't sell it all in a day."

At first read, this sounds like valuable insider information, from someone more knowledgeable about restaurant operations than you. But, is it true? Or do staff and family eat any leftover fish each night, so that small restaurant or large, the sushi always represents today's catch? There's no way to pass off days-old fish—you can smell it. Point: how can you evaluate the knowledge of someone who presents as more knowledgeable than you? Elsewhere we use credentials to assure ourselves; I know I got a good colonoscopy, because I see my physician's Doctor of Medicine (MD) diploma, and another framed document stating he is board licensed. But online reviewers have no credentials.

Alas, review texts are seldom as straightforward as "get their seafood platter because . . ." or "I've got inside knowledge." Most restaurants that stay in business will earn ratings of 3.5 or better; Chez Barfe would have closed long ago if it had earned its 2.5. Markets are efficient, remember? And because restaurants are taste goods, whose suitability varies, most restaurants with 100 reviews will be a mixed bag, with numerical ratings that converge between 3.5 and 4.0 (Box 2.5). Evaluating a review, and weighing conflicting judgments across reviews, is necessarily fraught, when undertaken under real-world conditions, with reviews found on Yelp, as opposed to the paragons that swim through the fantasies of free market zealots.

TRUST

Trust is a big problem when it comes to online reviews. There are no easy solutions to deciding whom to believe. Reviews are not like readouts from instruments in a physics experiment. Conflicting judgments are not like Gaussian errors of measurement, minor perturbations that smooth out in large numbers. Reviewers contradict one another. The same restaurant— the same hamachi nigiri, on the same day—gets a 2 from one reviewer and a 5 from another. Who do you believe?[29]

The problem of trust, which is also the problem of credibility, has two dimensions, corresponding to the two aspects of review quality: (1) Is this review genuine? (2) How much weight should I place on it? Consider the following review texts:

1. "Good food, speedy service."
2. "Just an amazing atmosphere, my waitress was so friendly and welcoming."

Do you get any sense, of whether these restaurants would be suitable, as a place to meet a date after work on Friday? Not so much. Confident these reviews are genuine? Maybe not. Each text is generic, little more than a

BOX 2.5   THE SILLINESS OF RATINGS

Some initial work focused on numerical ratings, not review text. As numbers, ratings hold great attraction for the academic social scientist, given how refractory natural language remains. Most empirical work in social psychology aims to produce numbers from subjects. A cottage industry is devoted to devising "reliable and valid measures," in which college students check a box on a seven-point scale with labeled end points, after which, mathematical prestidigitation produces truth. Thus the attraction of studying ratings at sites like Yelp: here in the field, all the work of generating numbers has already been done; the subjects did it unprompted. You can get right on the statistics.

Within an individualistic psychology—which includes the microeconomics of decision-making—it is easy to assume that the numerical rating at the top of the review supplies the key piece of information. Everything gets focused down to a point value: this restaurant is a 4.5, and this other one, only a 3. Best to eat at the 4.5: you might get sick at the other!

In any laboratory experiment, treatments must be separated; if possible, polarized. It's a hallmark of good experimental design: small samples of human responses are noisy, and to have any hope of getting a reportable effect—a publishable finding—you need to administer starkly different treatments. A good experimenter wouldn't use 4.5 versus 3; she'd compare restaurants rated 1 and 5, and then generalize the findings like this: "more positively rated restaurants were significantly more likely to be patronized by [type of consumer] than . . . ." And to keep the design clean, she'd administer at most two review texts per rating condition.

Suppose we checked that rush to the laboratory. What do we see, in the field, at Yelp? First off, Yelp rounds and truncates: there are no restaurants given ratings of 3.6783 or 3.7512 overall. In these two examples, Yelp would show the one restaurant as a 3.5, and the other as a 4.0. Second, although rounding to the half point gives us a nine-point scale—nine levels of restaurant quality—the extremes are per se unlikely to occur, when we average over hundreds of ratings. Day to day, the Yelp user will see restaurants graded into at most seven levels of quality, 1.5 through 4.5.

But even that reduction belies the level of discrimination afforded a day-to-day user of Yelp. You don't see very many restaurants rated 2.5 or below; you also won't see that many restaurants rated 3.0 or 4.5. The majority of restaurants you have to choose among will be rated 3.5 or 4.0; and I suspect that the typical Yelp user is vaguely aware that at bottom, that means a choice, on the numbers, between a restaurant rated 3.6783 and another rated at 3.7512.

A skilled decision-maker, seeking to maximize his utility, would want to see the dispersion as well as the average of ratings. Yelp has the technology to display dispersion: it does so for individual reviewers, on their profile page. But Yelp does not display dispersion for restaurants; just the truncated, rounded mean. The upshot: the numerical ratings are almost useless for selecting the one right restaurant for you, tonight. Most of the restaurants you examine will be pretty good, in summary, and a mixed bag, in detail.

I conclude that Yelp doesn't think numerical ratings are very important. When will laboratory psychologists take notice? When will the topic of study be redefined, as how real people make decisions under conditions of information overload, where numbers don't help? Based on past research, the best answer may be "never" (McQuarrie 2004, 2014). One might as well ask scholastic philosophers, trained in Aristotelian disputation, to set up a chemistry lab.

numerical rating stated in words. You learn nothing about suitability. If only such weak forms of market information were found on Yelp, or if such weak forms predominated, then online reviews would never have exploded. These sample texts don't supply market information, which is the engine that drives review readership, which motivates reviewers, who attract readers, who attract advertisers, forming the virtuous circle which makes a hosting site successful.

The first two examples yield little information because the text is scanty, and vague. Here are two more examples that are neither scanty nor vague, but still problematic for a reader who must decide where to dine:

1. "This place mocks what a French restaurant could be. It ticks every box: the snobbish, preening waiters who sneer at questions, the tired limp menu of has-been standards, the sauce out of a can presented as fresh, a vast wine menu where none of the under $100 bottles is actually available. Our tablecloth had gravy spots, the soup came cold, they tried to sneak an extra $30 bucks onto the tab, and then they took forever to correct the mistake. Awful place, don't ever go there."
2. "Everything was perfect. We were greeted warmly at the door and ushered to a table right by the window. Our drinks came in a jiffy while we looked over the menu. The waitress was very sweet, so helpful, and answered our every question. Our steaks arrived hot and sizzling, the rolls were freshly baked, and the desserts were scrumptious. When they found out it was Joe's birthday, they brought a little cupcake with a candle and didn't even charge us for it. Best place in town to take a steak-loving hubby out for a celebration."

The first is sometimes referred to as a rant and the second, a rave. Each is problematic. First, would you trust either one? Was the first written by a jealous competitor rather than an aggrieved diner? Was the second written in return for a coupon toward their next dinner, or for other compensation? Second, how much do you learn about suitability? In sum, these reviews offer market facts, but a hosting site with large numbers of reviews like these four would attract few repeat visits, and would not explode in popularity. Reviews such as these don't say much, and what they do say is difficult to trust. The shortfall is greatest for suitability: would this be a good restaurant for-me?

Under a market explanation, websites like Yelp must compete to attract enough good enough reviews. Under a free market explanation, as websites compete for review readers, the invisible hand will make certain that enough good enough reviews are supplied. Buyer-readers will cease to visit websites that offer market information as weak as in the four examples, and

---

BOX 2.6   DIMENSIONS OF TRUST

A basic distinction cleaves the large cross-disciplinary literature on trust. Sometimes trust refers to an internal psychological state, while in other contexts, the focus is whether an external source is trustworthy (Moorman et al. 1993; Rousseau et al. 1998; Wilson and Darke 2012).

When deciding whether to trust a source—a Yelp reviewer, for instance—another separation applies. Rousseau et al. (1998, p. 399) refer to sources who have good intentions and are competent, while Herbst et al. (2012, p. 910) speak of whether the source is dependable and competent. Dependable, well-intentioned sources are honest, truthful, and genuine. Competent sources are informative, accurate and correct. The two senses of trustworthy converge on this question: Can I rely on this source? You can't rely on fake reviews but neither can you rely on incompetent reviews (Giffin 1967).

Given this two-factor definition, trustworthy and credible can be used inter-changeably, as do Hovland and Weiss (1951, p. 636). If credibility gets defined as trustworthiness plus expertise (e.g., Erdem and Swait 2004; Hovland et al. 1953), the sense of trustworthy is narrowed to honest or genuine, and expertise replaces competence; but the underlying division into two factors, and their nature, remains the same (Ohanian 1990). Consumer feedback that can be trusted—credible feedback—is genuine and displays enough expertise to be judged competent.

Consumers confronted by proliferated feedback, from strangers, face a dual imperative. Under conditions of uncertainty and risk, an information source has got to be both honest and competent. In the absence of either, you can't trust that source; which in the context of a review, means you can't believe it. In plain English, faced with large amounts of feedback, from stranger peers, consumers must vet and weigh before they can choose what to do.

This dilemma does not arise when reviewers are professionals and hold insti-tutional credentials. There, reviewer competence is guaranteed by the institution: *The New York Times* wouldn't hire an idiot to be its food critic. His restaurant review is as trustworthy as the *Times*.

But you have no such guarantee, when reading reviews written by ordinary con-sumers. That's why trust is a big problem. Worse: what you must trust, or disdain, is a taste judgment. What does competence even mean, in the sphere of taste?

---

go elsewhere. In turn, reviewers will gravitate toward sites that offer better odds of gaining a public. The self-correcting aspect of free markets works to minimize weak and fake reviews, and to equilibrate the quality of reviews supplied with the quality of reviews demanded. There's never a problem.

I linger on the radical free market explanation, not because I think any academic economist holds this view,[30] but because it runs like a golden thread through the hype and promotion seen in Silicon Valley, where evangelists call out the great new world made possible by technology. The technorati mind has a libertarian cast. So many people here got so rich, apparently by dint of their own entrepreneurial efforts, as to fuel a fervor for markets. If government would only get out of the way . . . free markets, juiced by new technology, will fabulously improve our lives, forever and ever, amen.

The Skeptical Sociologist

The sociologist, in his role as nemesis, denies the adequacy of market mechanisms, for keeping trust, and for ensuring that enough good enough reviews get written.[31] The sociologist can't see how to maintain review quality, absent the exercise of police power, a very visible hand that corrals fakes and weeds out the weak. The sociologist expects to see carrot and stick. What honey must we offer reviewers, so that they write dolce reviews, and lots of these, to attract swarms of readers, so Yelp can make money? The sociologist expects the visible hand of social structure to explain why some sites host a higher caliber of review, that attracts more buyer-readers, so that the site makes more money, and thrives, even as other sites, dependent on free market mechanisms, struggle to survive.

To proceed with the assault on free market explanations, consider this question: why do we have, here in the developed West, health department inspections of restaurants? That seems to show a lack of faith in markets. If a restaurant were dirty, and its food made people sick, would not buyers soon discover this, and avoid it in droves, causing that restaurant to go out of business, and correcting the problem, without any regulatory intervention?

You can probably spot the flaw in that reasoning, but to amplify it, here is a thought experiment: suppose you lived tens of thousands of years ago, in a forest where leopards were a constant threat. Your tribal band has a choice: set rules for children about where they may go, to keep them safe; or, let children learn, by trial and error, the best way to avoid predators. The trial and error approach should have the self-correcting feature characteristic of free markets: the children who don't figure it out will soon get eaten; over time, the survivors will learn from the mistakes of the fallen, until gradually, only the children who figure it out will be left alive, and they won't need external social controls, to help them avoid predators.[32]

The health department and the leopard capture the shortcoming of invisible hand explanations: during the interval where self-correction proceeds, the free market, or trial and error learning, may be hard on the unfortunate buyers or leopard avoiders who came early. And enough innocent diners have to get sick, and enough children have to die, for self-correction to become effective. And these delays in time will be substantial whenever it is difficult to connect cause and effect. How easy is it to trace today's unfortunate stomach upset, to one of the meals you had yesterday?

How can you be sure it was that $^#@! dive of a diner where your friend took you for lunch? Won't you need multiple trials—going back to that restaurant again and again—to reliably make the causal connection? And did your poor cousin go to the wrong watering hole, the one every adult knows to avoid, or was he just unlucky, that day he got eaten by the big leopard?

The same difficulty applies to judging whether a review is fake: how could you discover that, without first relying on it, and bearing the consequences? Dinner and wine for two at a good steakhouse or French restaurant in San Jose might cost several hundred dollars; and this is money down the drain if that great place to take hubby proves to be an old grease pit. That's not in the same league as losing a child to a leopard, but still . . .

The sociologist feels he has grounds to reject the sufficiency of market mechanisms for assuring review quality; their self-correction is too fitful and slow. However, one more counter-argument, one more sally from the economic redoubt, must be turned back, before we can explore more deeply the social structure put into place on Yelp. This last rejoinder reasserts the power of second-order market information: feedback on reviews, posted by readers.

Feedback to the Rescue

To lay down a marker: Yelp can easily maintain a higher quality of review by exercising police power. Yelp can do this in software, by constructing a filter that jails suspect or offending reviews.[33] Writing filter software is like staffing a city health department, but focusing on reviews, not eateries. That makes any software filter tantamount to the heavy jackboot of government regulation, and anathema to free market advocates. Fortunately, a free market alternative is to hand: the opportunity for buyer-readers to give feedback on reviews. Might a site design, that makes feedback available, avert the need to use police power?

Within the hard core libertarian precincts of the market model, not scarce in Silicon Valley, if we institute a feedback mechanism—votes that a review was helpful or not—we correct for any risk of market failure. No reader of the hundreds of reviews for a restaurant can be confident of correctly sorting and grading each review as to trustworthiness. But if many other consumers also read these reviews, and endorse a select few as helpful, then later readers can escape the burden of vetting each review, and accept those with the most positive feedback as trustworthy.

This defense rests on the wisdom-of-crowds thesis (Surowiecki 2004), which has been a staple of scholarship studying online reviews (e.g., Anderson and Magruder 2012; Luca and Zervas 2013). A negative report from the Health Department marks out a restaurant as a poor risk.

Likewise, the presence of negative feedback, or even just the absence of positive feedback, marks out a review as of poor quality, and not to be trusted. Here reputation provides an alternative to social structure for achieving social control (Dellarocas 2011). Reputation supplies market information about market information. Advocates for free markets hope that if second-order facts circulate freely, first-order facts can be kept trustworthy without government intervention, that is, the exercise of police power by the website, to jail or delete reviews.

One count in favor of this rescue attempt: it explains why second-order market information—reviews of reviews, or feedback—is nearly universal. Feedback is made necessary rather than superfluous. Feedback becomes central to preserving review quality. Waxing a little more enthusiastic, proponents extol feedback as multiply effective. Not only does it help buyer-readers to vet and weight reviews, thus improving the information offered by the hosting site; it also informs author-reviewers about how their public responds. Feedback should help reviewers write better reviews to more deeply satisfy their intended public. The prospect of piling up positive feedback, and the dread of seeing negative votes pile up, should discipline reviewers to write better reviews. Typically, people who care about writing for a public also care about how that public regards them; the ego of writers is notorious. The fruits of this discipline attract more buyer-readers, and turn the virtuous circle once more. What's not to like?

Is the Crowd Wise?

High hopes are placed on second-order feedback. It will rescue market mechanisms from themselves, and obviate the need for social controls on the review marketplace. But can feedback, and the reputation mechanism that it underwrites, deliver on this promise? The sociologist thinks not.

First, if the crowd is wise, why not resolve conflicts in favor of the majority judgment among the reviews, in the form of the average rating? The hundreds of numerical ratings that accompany reviews of a popular restaurant already represent the judgments of a crowd; why should the second crowd—the source of the second-order feedback—be any wiser than this first crowd?

To compound the problem, examining sites such as TripAdvisor and Yelp shows that while large numbers of hotels and restaurants have hundreds of reviews recorded, few of these reviews acquire even a dozen instances of feedback.[34] Where then is the second-order *crowd*?

All forms of Web-based, stranger-sourced feedback are subject to an infinite regress: if first-order market information can't be trusted, neither can second-order information in the form of feedback; alternatively, if first-order facts can be trusted, then feedback is not needed. Likewise, if first-order information can be gamed, as when a business owner hires a shill to write favorable reviews (Gonchar 2013), then second-order feedback can also be gamed (Kornish 2009). Feedback comes from strangers whose true motives cannot be known. Worse, feedback takes the form of a bare tally, while first-order information may be a lengthy written text that offers additional signals for judging trust. Worse yet, on many review sites first-order feedback comes from a named reviewer, and that name is connected to more facts: at the least, how many reviews have been written under that name, and their text. Feedback has no attribution: it is present only as a numerical total. In short, second-order feedback can't be more trustworthy than first-order reviews, and will typically be less trustworthy, because it lacks context and carries less information. How can such a weak reed guarantee trustworthy reviews?

The Problem of Tastes

The wisdom-of-crowds thesis has a second problem. Each review text is more or less idiosyncratic in its judgments. None of these idiosyncratic judgments is likely to have a crowd behind it. For instance, a review of a BBQ restaurant focuses on the sauce, and the reviewer's love of BBQ sauce. It received two "useful" votes. The review just below it describes and evaluates several entrées, without mentioning sauce. It got no votes of "useful." The two reviews give the same rating for the restaurant overall. Any signal sent by feedback concerns these idiosyncratic remarks. Unfortunately, these remarks aren't comparable. We don't have to decide which one to trust.

Judgments of restaurants are, literally and figuratively, matters of taste; and there is no disputing matters of taste (see Gronow 1997 for a more detailed parsing of *de gustibus non est disputandam*). With no attribution for the two votes accorded the first review, the reader has no way to judge whether those votes come from people who share his tastes, making them pertinent, or who have different tastes, making them irrelevant. If the reader cares most about sauce when choosing a barbecue restaurant, he could have extracted this data from the review; feedback adds no value. In taste goods the problem of idiosyncratic preferences is acute. Worse, the review text, as a complex, stylized document, is also subject to taste judgments, so that feedback may be awarded for style points rather than facts. How useful a market signal is that?

Second-order market information has all the problems of first-order information, while creating new problems besides. Again, why should buyer-readers bother to generate feedback? There's no penalty for free-loading. Review authoring can be motivated by the prospect of gaining a public presence. But feedback, which is anonymous, does not convey that benefit, except that on Yelp, the reviewer (but not the public) receives a private notice that so-and-so voted a review as useful or cool or funny.

To explain why feedback occurs, we are driven back to motives of altruism or reciprocity, community traits that do not apply to a mass *Gesellschaft* formation like Yelp. It is absurd to suppose that market mechanisms, supposed to maintain the quality of market facts, require non-market concepts, such as altruism, to be effective.

It is easy to offer social explanations for feedback and its ubiquity. But these social explanations, to the extent that they are valid, make feedback even less able to serve economic goals. For instance, Yelp lets members friend one another, and the site is designed so that reviews by friends, if any, appear at the top of the reviews displayed. For collaborative filtering (Kautz et al. 1997), these reviews should receive the greatest weight, since they are not reviews from strangers, but from known parties, whose tastes are also known. Separately and prominently listing reviews from friends goes a long way toward solving the trust problem associated with market information; but only for members of that social circle.

The collaborative filtering explanation, although it shows how facts can be made more trustworthy, cuts against the information value of feedback, for members outside that social circle. Given any degree of mutual back-scratching among Yelp friends, reviews by friends will pile up positive feedback; the friendly thing to do, is to vote your friends' reviews as useful, whenever encountered (especially on Yelp, where this act sends a love note to the friend). Accordingly, the more friends a reviewer has, the more feedback her reviews will receive, for social reasons alone. But consider the experience of a consumer outside the friend network: here is a review with six votes of useful, and here is another with no votes. But these counts do not signal the relative quality of the two reviews; the disparity came about because the first reviewer had lots of generous-spirited friends active on the site, while the second reviewer did not. Collaborative filtering, there-fore, to the extent that it solves the trust problem for first-order market facts, for a few, makes second-order feedback even less trustworthy, for the many who are external to the collaboration.

The dilemma is inescapable: if first-order information is trustworthy, feedback is unnecessary; conversely, if reviews are not trustworthy, feed-back can't be any more so. But collaborative filtering also emphasizes how feedback, despite its lack of economic utility, might help the review site succeed as a social formation, or even be crucial to its social functioning, as feedback socially rewards reviewers, and bonds members to one another and to the website. The presence of feedback is easy to explain from a social structure perspective, but difficult to justify in terms of supplying market facts, insofar as social motives seem likely to distort the information provided, because driven by non-economic concerns.

A Sociological Take on Trust

Enough holes have been poked into a pure market explanation to open up a space for sociology. Police power is the most straightforward form of social control. If fraudulent reviews can be detected algorithmically, then the website can maintain quality by writing software to filter out offending reviews. On the other hand, if that software filter looks only at text properties—absence of concrete words, as in sample reviews #1 and #2—it might not work. How easy is it to detect fakes by examining word choice? The question "Who is lying?" is a perennial human question, not much easier to answer than "Does he love me?"

The challenge for a web hosting site is not as simple and stark as to find fakes and jail them. It is to supply readers with reviews they find valuable. Trust in the site is built from the repeated experience of getting value from browsing reviews there. Value is judged by readers. Reviews on the site need only strike readers as interesting and insightful, even if the average review is woefully less informative, when compared to a professional review of a restaurant published in a newspaper. Preferences in a taste goods category are inherently subjective, and this sharpens the gap between objective review quality (amount of information according to economic criteria) and perceived review quality (whether I consider time spent browsing these reviews to have been time well spent). The consumer rules, in taste goods above all: websites need to host reviews that please buyer readers, not reviews that pass muster with professional restaurant critics, newspaper editors, or economists. Review quality is in the eye of the beholder.

A survey conducted early in our research drove home this point (see Box 2.7) Most of the questions focused on motives for writing reviews (Table 2.1 and Figure 2.5) but we also asked about occasions for reading reviews: "How often have you read reviews *after* dining at a new restaurant?" Only 4 percent said they never do this; 48 percent did this sometimes, and 25 percent did this often. This compares to 29 percent, 34 percent and 30 percent who sometimes, often, or almost always read reviews before dining at a restaurant for the first time. The economic model presumes that reviews are market information, obtained in advance of purchase, to aid in deciding where to dine. The survey data challenge this view, showing that reviews are consulted almost as often, after the choice has been made and the meal consumed. What is the point of acquiring market facts after purchase?

To escape this conundrum, recall that restaurants, as taste goods, are credence goods. It is hard to ascertain restaurant quality, even after purchase.

BOX 2.7   SURVEY OF YELP REVIEWERS

Data

We purchased a Qualtrics panel, with respondents screened to have written five or more Yelp reviews. A total of 357 surveys with good data were analyzed.

Measures

Motivations

We asked people to rate the importance of 13 motivations for writing reviews, using a five-point scale anchored by "not important at all" and "very important." The set of motivations (see Table 2.1) draws on published research concerning motivations for participating in online forums (Zwass 2010), and for generating word of mouth (Hennig-Thurau et al., 2004). We added new items aimed at factors that distinguish online reviews from WOM (e.g., "to get my writing published").

Dining behavior

We asked how often they dined out, how often they consulted reviews before choosing where to dine, and whether they had ever read reviews after having dined at a restaurant.

Review writing

We asked how many Yelp reviews they had authored.

Results

Table 2.1 shows the 13 motivations ranked on two criteria: (1) presence (that is, the number who said this motivation was of any importance); (2) correlation with the volume of reviews written. Motivations proved diverse, with a wide variety having at least some importance for many people. Publication motives were among the less important motives across the sample, but publication motives were also among the best predictors of volume of reviews produced. Conversely, community-spirited and self-enhancement motives tended to be among the most widely endorsed, but the least predictive of number of reviews authored.

Figure 2.5 provides another view of how specific motives relate to review production. We plot the average importance of each motive: (1) for respondents whose review production was at the 75th percentile or above; and (2) respondents whose review production was at the 25th percentile or below. Motives are sorted by the gap between the means, for high and low levels of review production. Publication motives best distinguish more from less productive reviewers. More productive reviewers also showed the greatest diversity in motivation, with virtually all motives having moderate to high importance. By contrast, less productive reviewers cited community-focused motivations as most important.

A stepwise regression on self-reported review count found that only one of the 13 motives was able to enter the regression: "to get my writing published." After its entry, no other motive was able to meet the entry criterion of $p = 0.10$.

Prolific Yelp reviewers are intrinsically motivated.

Table 2.1   Comparative importance of motivations for writing reviews

Incidence		Association with review production	
Motive	Absent for:	Motive	Correlation
To reflect on my experience	5	To have my writing published	0.29
To help Yelp be more effective	8	To improve my review count	0.26
To make my voice heard	9	To be entertaining	0.25
Give something back to the community	14	To appeal to those who follow my reviews	0.24
To show my taste	23	To generate feedback	0.23
To join the conversation	27	To build my reputation as a reviewer	0.22
To be entertaining	43	To impress others	0.21
To appeal to those who follow my reviews	46	To show my taste	0.19
To generate feedback	49	To make my voice heard	0.18
To build my reputation as a reviewer	54	To join the conversation	0.17
To improve my review count	67	Give something back to the community	0.16
To have my writing published	77	To help Yelp be more effective	0.14
To impress others	87	To reflect on my experience	0.06

Note: The 357 respondents rated a set of 13 motivations as to how important each one was with respect to their production of reviews, using a five-point scale anchored by "not important at all" and "very important." The set of motives is ranked first by incidence (any importance; average importance tracked incidence closely, see Figure 2.5), and by the correlation between each item's importance rating with the self-reported count of reviews produced. All correlations were significant at $p < 0.05$ or better, except for "reflect on my experience," where $p = 0.2$.

That's why diners consult reviews after as well as before dining: they are still trying to make sense of what they experienced. Social ratification can support that diner's tentative judgment that the restaurant was pretty good, and good in precisely the way she surmised. Or, reading pans and slams can solidify her tentative impression, that last night's meal was long on pretense and short on cuisine. A buyer of taste goods may not trust her own taste judgment, if made alone and in isolation from what other diners have to say.

But once we reach this conclusion, we are no longer dealing with

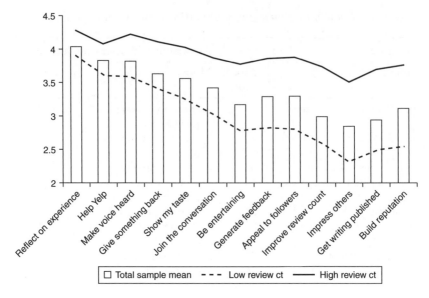

Note: The Y axis shows average importance on a scale where '5' means 'very important'. Bars show overall sample mean for the importance of each motive. Motives have been ordered on the chart from those with the least difference in importance between more and less productive reviewers to the greatest difference. More (less) productive reviewers were defined as those above the 75th percentile (below the 25th percentile) on the measure of self-reported review production.

Figure 2.5   Motivations of more (less) productive reviewers

buyers—one-dimensional market participants trying to optimize purchase decisions. These are now consumers, acting in a social context, and not autochthonous. These review readers are living their lives, not calculating purchases. As with much else in life, the meaning of consuming, the meaning of that meal still settling in my gut, is not determined individually, but socially, within the Yelp social formation. The diner's experience is not complete when she pushes back from the table. Only after reviews have been browsed, maybe right there on a smartphone, and she experiences what other diners experienced, does her meal conclude.

The review, the thing you read rather than the bite you take, is as much a taste good as the restaurant reviewed, and the quality of that review is as hard to judge, and as multiply sourced, and as much about suitability, as restaurant quality. Yes, the experience of reviews on a site will be improved, if fakes are minimized; but this doesn't take the review reader much further than the diner who assiduously avoids restaurants that fail their Health Department inspection. The challenge: the review hosting site has to minimize disappointing reviews, even if genuine, and maximize the count of pleasing reviews, however defined. These will mostly be genuine, but may be pleasing, or not, for many other reasons. Yet, judgments that a review is pleasing or disappointing are taste judgments, for which there is no algorithm. Meanwhile, the task of getting enough good enough reviews proceeds within a competitive context: other review sites are but a click away. If the good review writers, the tasteful and pleasing ones, gravitate to other hosting sites, the hosting corporation suffers financially.

To revert to a political science context: easier to control people by instilling patriotic fervor, than by putting armed thugs on every corner. Even in less totalitarian contexts, a police force is helpful, maybe even necessary, but not enough to control a population. Better if the population controls itself, by having internalized beliefs and values. Returning to review sites, it is helpful to police for fakes, and also to sequester the weak-minded or ill; but success requires a steady supply of large numbers of reviews that readers want to read, and feel good about reading. Success requires subtler forms of social control than putting handcuffs on crooks. To improve review quality, Yelp is not limited to sequestering reviews likely to disappoint. Yelp can also foreground reviews that readers will find rewarding. But achieving salience doesn't have to be as crude as listing a review at the top of the page. There are more nuanced ways to manipulate salience.

To sum up, I began the essay with a straightforward economic explanation of why online reviews exploded, and then proceeded to complicate and undermine that account at every turn. As in the siege of a castle, ladders were laid up the wall, rams hammered the gate, and catapults hurled stones and fire, even as sappers tunneled beneath, and spies inside fanned doubts. Market explanations enjoy a well-defended redoubt in Late Capitalist America. Only sustained assault could pry reviews loose from the grip of economics.

What emerges, in opposition to the economic view, is the reflexivity of reviews, their fractal and ramified character. By reflexive, I mean their doubled nature, the doubling back that occurred again and again as we inquired. Restaurants are taste goods, but reviews of these restaurants are also a taste good. Reviews supply market facts, and feedback and reviewer dossiers are market information on market information. Reviews are read before purchase and afterwards. Reviewers and review readers will be the same person on different occasions. A review hosting site needs to be concerned with quantity and quality, but quality is almost impossible to ascertain, except as suitability to an individual, whether it be quality of restaurant or quality of review. And yet, quality must be maintained on a mass basis, and not only for the few. Consumers of restaurants consume reviews as well. Everything is two-faced.

If I were a literary theorist, or even a follower of Bourdieu, I might natter on about reflexivity, and maybe elevate it to the status of a paradox, to make reviews an incomprehensible thing, or at least, something you can't latch onto without my scholarly tackle. That's more anti-Enlightenment than a consumer sociologist needs to be. It is enough if reviews emerge, not as narrowly economic, but as all too human, driven by complex motives, social to the core. That is enough to clear the way for sociology, and for understanding how social structure shapes new consumer behaviors online.

INSTITUTIONAL LOGIC AT YELP

This phrase comes out of institutional theory, a major branch within sociology (Scaraboto and Fischer 2013; Thornton 2002; Powell and DiMaggio 2012). As argued earlier, institutions are social structures. Institutional logics will refer to social structure in operation. Keep in mind that structure is a *Gesellschaft* concept not relevant to intact communities, and less relevant as we drop toward the solidarity horizon. A hard-headed sociologist, who rejects use of the noun form of "institution," whenever "organization" would do as well, might even assert the redundancy of institutions, institutional logics, and social structure. Three labels, one phenomenon.

Unlike cultural capital, which might be a theoretical term, or could be nothing more than a metaphor, institutional logic can only be a metaphor. Logic is a branch of mathematics, and organizations and other social entities can neither be nor behave as mathematicians or calculating machines. As metaphor, institutional logic suggests that institutional settings respond to people's agency in predictable ways: we can find a rationale that explains why some actions succeed even as others fail. And just as the premises within a logical argument compel the conclusion, the metaphor of institutional logic suggests that actions must either succeed or fail, depending on whether these run with the prevailing logic or cut against it. For instance, an attempt to change a decision, already made within a bureaucracy, will be less successful than the attempt to stall that decision until higher-ups get distracted and drop the matter. At the root of the metaphor lies the idea that actions, taken within or against a collectivity, lead to outcomes in a rule-based way.

However, to speak of logic may be a stretch too far. It risks giving too much agency to structure, and too little to people, even as it crams social being into a mechanical mode (Billig 2013). A better metaphor, although beyond my capacity to impose, might be institutional terrain. Water, which will play the role of individual agency in the terrain metaphor, runs downhill. No matter how rugged or eroded a terrain, if you know the slopes, the slope angles, and their juxtapositions and relative heights, then for any rain shower, at any spot on the map, you can predict the path water will follow, the speed at which it will move, where it will end up, and whether it will have enough force to blast aside a rockfall, undercut a slope, or only peter out in the sand. Nonetheless, these predictions will remain fallible and probabilistic, with unanticipated tipping points: the apparent boulder, which was actually the protrusion of a big rock, or the hidden pocket of sand.

To see the advantage of this terrain metaphor, take the point of view of a hiker dropped into a remote part of the American West, which he's never visited before and for which he has no map. It's not easy to grasp such terrain from any vantage within it. If he needs to get over a mountain range, the low point, the best pass, may not be visible from where he stands. Likewise, if he has climbed over a saddle and traipsed through a small canyon into a bigger one, there's no way to tell if this is the main canyon, that should be followed, or only a box canyon. If the canyon is dry, it may not even be clear which direction is downhill: a 2 percent slope is tough to see as a slope; the eye sees it flat. Any terrain is difficult to master from within its bounds.

Under the institutional terrain metaphor, the task of the sociologist is to draw the contour map. He or she must identify the steep pitches, find the high points that repel water, find the low points which can receive water, and compute the carrying capacity of basins. If there is a design component—review hosting sites are designed structures, not naturally occurring—then the sociologist acts as hydrologist. The goal is to site the dam to produce the best possible reservoir, or compute the flood risk for a location, based on knowledge of the terrain.

I introduce this alternative metaphor because a sociologist should distrust the rhetorical subtext to institutional logic. In logic, true premises correctly argued compel the conclusion; and to speak of institutional logics carries a whiff of determinism, of the physics envy that haunts social science. Does social structure compel outcomes? This seems a step too far. With institutional terrain, outcomes are only probabilistic. There is a chaotic element to whether a rain storm, blowing toward the mountain from the south, will or will not dislodge this boulder, triggering a landslide that does or does not block this side canyon, and turn the runoff down this path or another. The terrain metaphor better captures the probabilistic nature of encounters between individual agency and social structure. It's better suited to history.

Regardless of metaphor, what has to be uncovered are those non-market structures, apart from police power, which a Yelp can use to improve the reviews it hosts. I found two such structures in Yelp: friending and honor.

These are institutional logics under the old metaphor, or slope configurations under the new terrain metaphor, which are conducive to a positive experience of reviews, for buyer-readers, and which make author-reviewers more likely to write some types of reviews versus others. Friending and honor help a hosting site to provide a better experience to readers and reviewers, who are so much more than buyers and sellers; and these enhancements may help a Yelp to win the struggle against other hosting sites.

The conundrum: strangers can't be trusted. Even the ones that aren't dangerous may not be competent. Market mechanisms are not enough to control this problem: incentives to cheat are high, and the buyer-reader's ability to detect cheating is low. A website can ameliorate the trust problem through the exercise of police power, but police power is not enough to achieve the desired result, which is a steady flow of reviews that will be pleasing, to the wide range of buyer-readers the hosting site must attract and hold. Logics of friending and honor build on police power to move a website toward this sweet spot.

Logic of Friending

Under a market explanation, where all Yelp does is host market facts, Yelp would not need to offer a friending function. Buyers don't need to be friends with one another or with sellers. Only when we view an online review site as a social formation, and not a marketplace for information, does the logic behind friending become clear. Likewise, once you accept that the problem of trust cannot be solved by market mechanisms, the way lies open for social structure to step into that breach. And police power alone can never be enough, because the problem of trust, in the case of a taste good, with its experiential and credence aspects, has two elements: avoidance of the fake, but also approach to the suitable. As a buyer-reader, I seek reviews that speak to me, that address the suitability of this restaurant, for me, credibly. I want tasty reviews.

Friending logic serves several goals. For buyer-readers, and author-reviewers, it ameliorates the hard edge of this *Gesellschaft* formation, this loose association of strangers consuming restaurants, and reviews. Friending on Yelp takes the form of an invitation: an email to your Yelp account that says, almost literally, "Can we be friends?" This social gesture is difficult to make in adult life, under modern, mass, anonymous, urban conditions. In pure form this gesture may be unbearably awkward, even in the amorphous precincts of teenaged and college youth. After kindergarten, where young children do say this to one another ("Let's be friends"), friendship mostly just happens, through propinquity and repeated juxtaposition. Friend is a silent nomination that may never be voiced explicitly by either party, and only occasionally acknowledged, under query from somebody else in a shared social circle ("Are you friends with . . .?").

All this changed, with the advent of Facebook and its predecessor social media sites, going back past MySpace to the almost forgotten friendster. com. A study I cannot undertake, but that could be sociological in my laudatory sense, would examine how the meaning, and even the reality, of friend has changed in the Facebook era. Perhaps only an older fellow like me, who long predates Facebook, could write the preceding paragraph, with its pre-Web understanding of what a friend is and how people used that word. It seems unlikely that an online review site like Yelp could make friending logic work, make friending happen, had more generalized social media not first laid a foundation, converting friend to a web-enabled, web-sourced, virtual rather than physical relationship. Post-Facebook, friend is an explicit nomination, public for anyone to see, conveyed electronically from someone who, until that moment, might have been mentally inventoried as a stranger, someone you know of but do not know, or maybe had never heard of at all.

The more narrow focus of a consumer sociology forces me to leave Facebook behind; but it is important to acknowledge the foundational role played by earlier social media in making Yelp possible. Tracing Yelp's line of descent, to Facebook and MySpace, reiterates that in *Gesellschaft* times, technology shapes social reality. Changes in technology make possible new forms of association, in the context of new social formations.

Returning to friending on Yelp, it helps to get concrete about how the act of friending proceeds. Perhaps, after browsing reviews for a while from the outside, you decide to join Yelp. The trigger might be that you tried to respond to a review, but could not, because responding is only possible after joining Yelp (reviews may be read indefinitely, and in any quantity, without becoming a member). Once you can respond to reviews, you can also post reviews. Your first friending invite might be either sent or received. You either send a love note, or receive one. Although either might occur first, your sent friending request may be declined. You risk being rejected if you start out as a sender. Scary! Conversely, you are unlikely to receive a friending request unless you have written a review, and on the probabilities, are more likely to receive a friend request, if you write more than one. Most Yelp members use a nom de plume, and there are millions. Unless you already know someone, who has told you her nom de plume, you have no way to find a particular person, whom you may know of from outside, to befriend. Exception: a person who makes themselves visible by writing a review, in which case, Yelp makes friending easy.

Your first experience of friending will likely come on the receiving end. And that friending occurs only because you wrote a review. So you get a friending request. The only things you can know about the sender, who is identified with a live link, is the text of their reviews, plus whatever they've put into their profile. If the sender is a complete stranger, and has written no reviews, and has a minimal, bland profile, the recipient may decline ("What kind of creep . . .?"). Conversely, if the requestor has written a few reviews, maybe of restaurants you know, and has a profile with a little snap to it, then you may well say yes, even though to a stranger. To receive friending requests, you have to write reviews, and to have your friending requests accepted, you probably have to have written several. On the receiving end, a friending request is a concrete sign that you do have a public, that people do read what you write, why even, that you have a fan.

Now let's look at the institutional terrain sculpted by the technological apparatus of friending. Participation starts on the receiving end. The recipient has probably written several reviews, as these prompt friending invites. A friendship request is most likely to be accepted if it comes from someone who has also written several reviews, and put some energy into their profile. Next, count of friends is displayed, opposite each review displayed for a restaurant. The friendship capability provided by Yelp is self-promoting. Members readily learn that friending is both possible and common. The presence or absence of friends is highly visible. It forms part of the reputation of the reviewer, and gives information about whether to trust one review more than another. ("Hmmm . . . this review was written by someone who has zero friends. Nobody likes this guy.")

Furthermore, friend invitations will be experienced as rewarding, concrete evidence that you have both gained a public and are favorably regarded by that public. High friend counts will also be viewed as desirable: they feed into your reputation, and avoid a negative mark from prospective readers ("Hardly any friends, and he's reviewing a tapas bar???"). The desirability of having friends helps to overcome the risk in sending out friending requests. Whether as sender or receiver, you appreciate how friends boost a reputation. Both friender and friendee, on acceptance, see their friend count incremented by one; and the profile page of each now contains a link to each other, and to each other's friends. Reputation is not only a matter of how many friends, but who they are. ("Let's see, who has he got for friends? Oh, I've read Jollyrodger, he's a big sushi reviewer, cracks me up.")

Next, let's probe further the slope and terrain created by friending. As we've seen, friend count is most likely to be non-zero if the member is a review author. Second, friend counts will be higher for members with higher review counts. This correlation has several drivers, with reviews providing a pretext for friending, and friending motivating more review writing. Third, the norm that friend count should correlate with review count creates contrast effects. A reviewer with two reviews and no friends is a newbie, and can be accepted as such. A reviewer with 35 reviews and 17 friends is as expected. But a reviewer with 100 reviews, and only two friends, has a lot to say that few people like to hear. Might be a blowhard; maybe a crank.

Friending tends to link together, and mark out, those most engaged in Yelp: the people most engaged in review writing, the most socially integrated people with the best social skills, and the people most highly involved with dining out, with food, with cooking. An absence of friends, or disproportionately few friends, marks out the reverse: people who write reviews that nobody cares about, or whose profile is boring or offputting, or who don't have any insight to offer on restaurant dining, and, most especially, people acting as paid and unpaid shills.

Recall that a shill is someone who writes a review for compensation or for other untrustworthy motives. A shill may have been recruited on Amazon Turk by an unscrupulous business owner, or may be earning a discount coupon, or may be a paid employee. In each of these cases, the friend count is likely to be low or zero. The Turk wasn't paid to create an elaborate profile, or to send out friend requests, but only a nominal amount to dash off a review. Other kinds of shills will also have few or no friends. Shill behavior will be instrumental: write the fake review and you're done.

The presence of friends, their count, and the ratio of friends to reviews, can each signal whether a review is genuine and the reviewer credible. You can trust active reviewers with lots of friends on the site. This signal will reach both buyer-readers and software algorithms. As I'll show later, an empirical examination, of reviews filtered by Yelp, shows that the best way to predict whether a review will be judged suspect, and filtered, is low friend count.

The power of friending logic does not stop there. As well as helping buyer-readers decide whether to trust a review, friending motivates reviewers, with each friend request supplying both proof that you are reaching a public, and evidence that this public responds favorably. More reviews and better reviews are likely to result. I am also more likely to feel a sense of belonging—a powerful motivator, per self-determination theory—when Yelp becomes a place where I make friends, and where people act friendly toward me. I can't get that sense of belonging from a repository of market facts provided by public-spirited strangers. With friending logic, Yelp ceases to be a strictly *Gesellschaft* social formation, and moves toward the solidarity horizon. Moreover, these new friends are local. Yelp has a messaging facility that lets you tell friends, "Friday we're off to Rudy's Oyster

Bar, come join us." Virtual association, on Yelp, may become physical association, in a way unlikely to occur on Amazon, or epinions.com, or other
nationally focused review sites. This potential alone moves Yelp membership away from the pure *Gesellschaft* pole.

Moving toward the solidarity horizon offers another benefit: it reduces
the vitriol and barbarity for which the Internet has become infamous.
Trolling seems less likely to occur on a website where friending logic has
sculpted the terrain.[35] Truly ugly acts require anonymity and estrange-
ment: solidarity needs to approach its nadir. Even the minor ugliness of
an invective-filled rant, posted after an awful dining experience, becomes
less likely if this is going to be read preferentially by friends, for years
and years. A judicious exercise of police power by Yelp can support this
outcome. If vicious rants land quickly in jail, then they will seldom be
viewed; and their comparative scarcity sets up an expectation, and ultimately a norm, that people don't act this way on Yelp (no broken windows
here, move along, perp).

Finally, friending logic enables collaborative filtering. When I browse
reviews for a restaurant on Yelp, any reviews written by my friends are displayed first, above reviews written by strangers. If I have dozens of friends
active on the site, many of the restaurants I investigate will have already
been reviewed by one or more friends. Reading mostly reviews from friends
enhances my pleasure in browsing Yelp, and diminishes problems of trust.
Reviews from friends, who probably became friends because I liked their
reviews or they liked mine, are more likely to be written to my taste, and
to show whether some restaurant will be to my taste, than a review from a
perfect stranger. At a stroke, the problem of suitability is solved. The same
logic causes trust issues to recede. The author of the review is no longer a
stranger, but a member of my social circle. We have a track record together.
If I know that his tolerance for spicy food far exceeds mine, and he rates
that new Thai restaurant as "good, but not very spicy," I can reweight this
judgment, while trusting that he knows his Asian cuisine.

Collaborative filtering is typically lauded for the quality of information
it yields; but friending logic on Yelp confers this benefit and much more.
It supplies not only better market facts—a more accurate prediction of
whether I will like some restaurant—but also a better experience of the
Yelp site and a better experience reading and writing online reviews. With
reviews from friends foregrounded, it becomes more likely that the most
salient reviews, the ones that dominate my experience, will be good reviews,
both suitable and trustworthy. This benefit scales: the more friends I make,
the more I benefit.

Friending logic also benefits Yelp the profit-seeking firm. In the
vernacular, friending boosts the stickiness of the site. As I become a

more active participant on Yelp, with a growing file of reviews and an expanding roster of friends, the odds that any other review hosting site can provide me as pleasing an experience go down. If I start looking at reviews on Google+, I don't get the benefit of collaborative filtering. I also don't benefit from Yelp's police power (Google does not filter on a regular basis). And once Yelp has established dominance, as was true in San Jose in the 2011–2013 era, I won't see anywhere near the same quantity of reviews on Google+. As a writer-reviewer, I may receive helpful votes on Google, but the friending opportunities are minimal, and the odds of getting feedback are lower, due to the lower readership. I also can't establish as rich a dossier, and at least initially, I will lose the reputation I built up at Yelp. Why switch?

Friending logic acts as an effective marketing tool as well as a powerful social structure. Although the consumer sociologist can't contribute much to the study of Facebook, and is not a marketing scientist, a consumer sociologist readily appreciates the marketing implications of consumers' social experience. Understanding consumers can reveal why some businesses are more successful than others. Yelp succeeded due to its mastery of social formations made newly possible by the Web. Whether this mastery was inadvertent, or reflects the brilliance of its founders, I cannot say. But a consumer sociologist is happy to point to the competitive advantages that flow from a grasp of friending logic, and a savvy approach to social structure.

Honor Logic

Yelp has another social structure that shapes its terrain: honor logic. Each year Yelp nominates some members as Elite. The Elite designation, along with friend count and review count, is one of three reputational items that accompany every review displayed on Yelp. Feedback counts for each review are also displayed (browse yelp.com for examples). Together these four facts are always available, when deciding whether to trust. Yelp provides even more reputational data, such as lifetime feedback totals, but you have to go to a reviewer's profile to get more. That profile is only one click away, but it is a click away. Although easy enough to do, and although there will often be a wealth of additional relevant data within the reviewer profile, click through is less likely. Most trust judgments will rely on the text of the review and these four facts displayed with it.

Yelp does not publish the rules used to nominate a member to the Elite. During our research, we saw promotional language on the site, in the spirit of Marine recruitment: the Few, the Proud, the Brave. Yelp presents the Elite designation as a relatively exclusive honor, a mark of distinction worth the striving. But Elite membership comes only by the grace of Yelp, in a Calvinistic way. You have no way to apply and no guarantee that striving will make it so. Elite members could have been named the Elect.

In San Jose at that time, Yelp Elite had much higher scores across all reputational markers. Every Elite member in our data had more than 100 reviews, sported dozens or hundreds of friends, and recorded similarly high lifetime feedback totals. But this cross-sectional analysis cannot show the direction of causality. To be named Elite should be motivating; and in our exploratory interviews, we found non-Elite members who craved that award; and in other interviews, with those already named Elite, found ongoing high levels of engagement with Yelp. Without a longitudinal tracking study, we cannot know to what extent high scores on reputational markers cause you to be named Elite, or come about as a consequence of your being so named.

The Elite designation is a mark of honor. The sociological question is: how does the decision by Yelp programmers, to set up an honor logic, influence how reviews are experienced by ordinary buyer-readers? A more psychological account—a cruder take, I would say—would view the Elite title as a straightforward attempt to motivate reviewers to produce a greater quantity of reviews, and better reviews, to the financial benefit of the hosting site. This motivational calculus has been labeled gamification (McGonigal 2011), a coinage to make Billig (2013) shudder. The idea here, which is not wrong: to be nominated to the Elite, because of what you wrote, should appeal not so much to status envy, which I discredited in an earlier section, but to your desire to be judged competent—one of the three fundamental motives in self-determination theory. It's an earned promotion. Some other review hosting websites, such as Amazon, also have honor logic in place; others, such as Google+, do not. The presence or absence of honor logic is one of several treatment conditions in the great natural experiment under way among hosting sites. However, this motivational explanation for why Yelp has the Elite category, while apropos, also seems to me uninteresting, because purely psychological, and uncontroversial to boot. It is true as far as it goes, but it doesn't go very far in explaining the operation of honor logic as a social structure, how honor shapes institutional terrain.

Returning to the problem of trust, the presence of Elite reviewers recasts the problem. It is no longer a matter of whether I should trust this review, but of whether I can trust this reviewer. This reduces the time and effort the buyer-reader must spend. If I am active on Yelp, over some months I will investigate dozens of restaurants. I may dine at only a handful, but if I am choosy, I will look at reviews for three or four restaurants for each one I patronize. In turn, I may scan a dozen or two reviews for each of these restaurants. The upshot: I may read hundreds of reviews over several months. That's a lot of trust judgments to have to make.

BOX 2.8   PRODUCTIVE REVIEWERS DOMINATE YELP

Simple math justifies this assertion. Here is a thought experiment. Suppose the total number of reviewers is ten. Eight people contribute one review apiece, one person contributes ten reviews, and the final reviewer contributes 100. That one reviewer—10 percent of the population—accounts for 100/118 of all reviews, or almost 85 percent. For readers who visit this hypothetical review site, the probability that any randomly selected review was written by that prolific reviewer is 0.85. Expressed as odds, you are 5.66 times more likely to read a review from that prolific reviewer as any other.

In our Yelp data, we found review production to be markedly skewed, in line with this thought experiment. The 25 percent of reviewers who had produced more than 100 reviews accounted for 79 percent of the total stock produced, while the top decile of reviewers accounted for about 54 percent of reviews written.

Odds are good that any randomly encountered Yelp review was written by a highly productive reviewer. If these people are identical to the general run of Yelp participants, then this disproportion is of no consequence. But if prolific reviewers have a distinct motivational profile, as indicated by Box 2.7, then consumers' experience of Yelp will be shaped by the characteristics of prolific reviewers—for instance, their explicit desire to publish.

If instead many of these reviews come from Yelp Elite, I can decide, once, to trust the trusted reviewers. I will still have to weigh conflicting judgments (Elite members won't all agree whether that new sushi restaurant is the real thing or a commercialized pretender), but I can do so based on the text of the review, confident that reading this one, and taking the time to weigh it, is worthwhile. The institutional logic of honor solves the problem of what to trust by making it a question of whom to trust. Honor logic provides an institutional guarantee of trust at the level of the reviewer rather than the stand-alone review. True, the rich dossiers found at Yelp permit this vetting of reviewers to occur for any review; it is always possible to do a background check on a reviewer when deciding whom to believe. But to vet every reviewer individually, every time, as will occur in a pure market for information, is time-consuming and wearisome. With honor logic, the institution guarantees the trustworthiness of a reviewer, once, for every other member to see. When this person is also a productive author, then with the flop of a bit, hundreds of reviews on the website are guaranteed as credible and genuine.

To invoke a Darwinian metaphor, when Yelp designates some reviewers as Elite, it performs unnatural selection, as in breeding. Rather than leave market forces to pick out better from worse reviewers, based on naturally occurring feedback votes, or friend counts, or review counts, Yelp managers intervene and select individuals on a purposive, non-algorithmic basis.[36] In another context this would jeered as government tinkering and interference: selecting winners, as decried by libertarians. On Yelp, this purposive, unnatural selection goes a long way toward solving the problem of trust, while addressing the larger challenge of how to create a treasure trove of insightful and pleasurable reviews that will make buyer-readers return again and again.

Yelp acts as a breeder, rather than waiting for market forces to bring about natural selection. Yelp decides what kind of review and reviewer it wants to encourage. By creating an honor designation, Yelp motivates those so honored to produce more of what got them honored. Over time, with more reviews produced by those so motivated, the composition of the population of reviews will shift toward what Yelp wants to see. A newly arrived buyer-reader, not yet committed to Yelp, is more likely to have an initial good experience, rather than encountering the sort of vacuous or fraudulent review showcased earlier. As the site attracts and holds more buyer-readers, it becomes more valuable to advertisers, and more lucrative for the Yelp corporation. This is what it means to design a social system for private profit. Review hosting exemplifies how technology creates new kinds of social structure that draw on old human propensities, such as for honor.

The psychological effect of the honor designation, on those so honored, is straightforward, acting to boost motivation. The population effects, in terms of breeding better reviews, are more subtle. More subtle still is the social action of honor, and the underlying social reality of honor, which allows it to have these effects. Honor provides a good touchstone for distinguishing psychological from sociological perspectives, as done earlier against economics. Sociology isn't the nemesis of psychology; it's more like the runt of the litter, the younger brother eclipsed by his bigger, stronger, faster older brother who is better at everything, so that nobody pays any heed to the kid. Even this metaphor is misleading; sociology as an intellectual discipline is almost a century older than psychology (Nisbet 1966). But sociology's success, in academe and the world, is dwarfed by that of psychology, so that it has become almost impossible for consumer researchers, and scholars in other emerging and interdisciplinary fields, to think in sociological terms, even when the setting calls for it. To psychologize becomes a reflex.

What, then, is honor? Let's first distinguish it from related terms, which a hazy understanding of sociology might confuse. Honor is not status, defined as that to which people show deference. Nobody in America defers to some stranger because his review has "Elite 2014" next to it. Somewhat closer is distinction, as I have used it in this book (which may not be the same as Bourdieu's 1984 usage, assuming one could even pin down such a prolix author). But distinction is still too much under the command of the individual, connoting effort, ability, accomplishment, outcomes that can be individually achieved rather than bestowed by a group. Review count earns you distinction; honor is not yours to compel. Prestige may be a synonym of honor, but its connotations are not quite right, being too bound up in historical usage with status rooted in tradition. Likewise, reputation is both too neutral a term, able to take on either a positive or negative meaning, and has too much to do with favorability in the beholder, a psychological disposition rather than a social fact.

A sociological perspective will tie honor to the social tendency, found in most human groups, whether above or below the solidarity horizon, to treat differences among people as pertinent to judgments about those people, and to link some of these differences to more favorable judgments. Which differences will be honored varies: hunting prowess in a tribal band, or copious publication in an academic setting. But the impulse to honor appears widespread. The judgments shaped by honored differences will also vary; nonetheless, those honored will have their actions judged to be good, and expected to be good, known in advance and without additional evidence, to be good. You can, and should, trust the honored. And it is this trust response, the built-in tendency to accept at face value and treat as credible the actions of honored ones, which makes honor logic so powerful when designing an online review site.

Honor is a social reality because you do not have to decide: the honored are trusted, automatically and without deliberation. The Achilles heel of economics, when under attack from psychology, is its overemphasis on decision-making, deliberation, as a characteristic and necessary feature of ongoing, daily, moment-by-moment human action. *Homo economicus* is modeled on the careful shopper, standing there at the shelf, scrutinizing the unit price, organizing the set of breakfast cereals in order from highest to lowest quality, and maybe plotting them on an orthogonal axis by brand reputation, and then identifying the optimum cereal for purchase based on the price–quality trade-off. But from a psychological perspective, decisions are costly, as recognized in later attempts to adapt classical economic reasoning to psychological facts (Williamson 2005). There is neither time nor energy to make decisions every minute; much of daily life, especially in consuming, has to be placed on autopilot, setting a course, once, and then withdrawing from further decisions.

It is the same with reading online reviews, the more so with a taste good like restaurants, where rational, utilitarian decision-making is not likely to occur. There's no time to judge the credibility of each reviewer, nor any desire to work that hard; dining out is supposed to be fun. Honor serves as a heuristic: trust the trusted reviewers. Give greater weight to the judgments of the honored versus the obscure. The human terrain is preshaped to direct judgments in favor of those honored; going with the honored is as automatic as water flowing downhill.

Summary: Institutional Terrain and Socio-Technical Design

With friending and honor logics in hand, we recognize and grasp the gap that separates reviewers and review readers, as they really are, from one-dimensional buyers and sellers exchanging money for goods at the market clearing price. But we also see and accept that the institutional terrain that shapes individual agency on Yelp is designed: it is software, written code, and not a natural thing. A tribal band, pre-*sapiens*, may be a natural phenomenon, no more and no less than a baboon troop, obeying scientific laws no different in kind from those that govern the assembly of proteins under the control of DNA. But honor logic, as put in place on Yelp, is something a programmer dreamed up. It may draw on a pre-existing, and perhaps pan-human response, to make vertical distinctions among people; but on Yelp it is a constructed social structure, made possible by technology, that shifts probabilities on the margin.

The new consumer behaviors seen on the Web are fascinating: we see social structures that did not exist before, which are directly enabled—midwifed—by technology. A major conceptual shortcoming of Tonnies's account of *Gemeinschaft* and *Gesellschaft* was its static character: one, two, and done. Paradise and then Fall, with no Resurrection to close out the story.[37] Once we accept that technology drives social change, it follows, from the inherently dynamic character of technological innovation, that social change must be ongoing. *Gesellschaft* is not an end state, a dull neutron star of collapsed sociability, but a new beginning, which is not a renewed stasis, but a rich petri dish, colonized by new kinds of social life, in an unfolding that is not yet, and may never be, complete.

Psychologists, and economists mostly, are committed to a concept of human nature. In philosophy of science terms, their commitment to human nature is a commitment to naturalism. Humans are organisms in the one, and buying units in the other, and these assumptions are necessary for there to be scientific laws that determine how people act, in the same way as the laws of kinetics determine how bodies move. Given a human nature, there can never be anything new; or rather, everything is equally new, and nothing is really new: humans are humans doing their human thing, now as before, always the same in their changes, which are only fluctuations, and not displacement along a trajectory.

The consumer sociologist, whose parent discipline of sociology couldn't exist before the *Gesellschaft* transition, and whose focus on consumers is newer still, can never believe in an enduring human nature: an absence of fundamental change. Sociology is a historical rather than a natural science; and if historical science be a contradiction in terms, if there can be no scientific knowledge of history, then the sociologist, regretfully, will resign his scientific credentials, happy at least to escape from physics envy. History is primary. Social reality changes, and even that possibility of change is itself historically located, in *Gesellschaft* times, and not a permanent condition, from the beginning, nor necessarily everlasting, later on, after our era. But today, and for some centuries now, social change has been real. Social formations are exactly that: not eternally subsisting Platonic forms, but things formed in and shaped by history, formations that became that way, that developed, and that are different now than before, newborn, mortal.

Transition to Data Analysis

As this essay proceeds to its denouement, here is a recap of its long argument. To begin, I presented economic and psychological explanations for online reviews, intended as a foil for sociological explanations. Online reviews were described as market information, an unalloyed good and an imperative, something produced for buyers by other buyers motivated by some mix of community spirit and status envy. These initial explanations foundered on the rock of unexamined assumptions about collectivity and real human needs. Yelp was redescribed as a machine for making publics, after public was introduced as a *Gesellschaft* social formation made available anew by the technology of the Web. I presented the desire for a public as an enduring intrinsic motivation. The economist rallied, noting that the Yelp corporation was a market participant, and that the quality of reviews could be guaranteed by either a competitive hosting market, or the two-level marketplace set up by Yelp, in which second-order market information solved the problem of trust in first-order market information. These fallbacks were in turn found wanting, dismissed as incapable of ensuring quality information. Market explanations, in terms of buyers, were further routed once we saw that review reading occurred almost as often after dining as before, casting doubt on a theory of reviews as information designed to help buyers choose. I concluded by discussing the institutional terrain set up by friending and honor logics, social structures designed to supply enough good enough reviews.

What remains is to add empirical data. These data are presented in a humble spirit, not as proof or even evidence for the argument, which extends far beyond any imaginable empirical foundation, but only as a set of interesting and pertinent facts, which may prove relevant to future studies of online reviews. As most of the data do not come from interviews, nor surveys, nor lab experiments—which account for the bulk of consumer data collected by academics today—the nature of the data, and the treat-ment applied, show how a sociologist might approach empirical work differently from a social psychologist.

DATA

Descriptions of empirical method are inevitably technical, and of interest to only a few. Hence, I have placed the truncated method sections for these studies in the Appendices. Statistical results are likewise technical and have also been exported to the Appendices. This frees the main text to set up the questions the data were gathered to answer, and summarize the answers obtained. A survey of Yelp reviewers was presented earlier in the essay, as Box 2.7. The data discussed next are archival, extracted from the Yelp site, and pertain to selected restaurants and reviewers in San Jose, California. These data reflect events and actions, not self-reporting, as in more con-ventional interview and survey data.

Feedback Studies

Question: Does feedback motivate reviewers to write more, and to keep writing?
All hosting sites are designed to enable feedback. In a simple psychological account, feedback is the carrot that keeps the donkey moving: recognition and reward. In the crudest account, feedback does for reviewers what food pellets do for pigeons: acts as a Skinnerian reinforcement to bend behavior as desired. In terms of data, this suggests a straightforward linear relation-ship: + feedback → + reviews. The more feedback I receive, the more motivated I will be to write more reviews.

In a more subtle formulation, feedback acts not in Skinnerian terms, as a reinforcement, but provides a gate or go-ahead signal: "Yes, I am being read; yes, I do have a public; therefore I shall continue to write, because I have succeeded in gaining a public, which is what I want." In this formula, to write a review for Yelp, for the first time, is to test the waters: "Anybody out there?" Feedback completes the circuit, confirming that the signal sent was received, and that a connection has been established. This metaphor places the review writer within a cybernetic system, rather than treating him like a pigeon.

The second formula predicts a different relationship than a simple linear association. It suggests that feedback may be more important, even only important, for new writers who have not yet established themselves as reviewers. The predicted relationship between feedback and reviewing should be non-linear. There is first a binary outcome: whether review writing continues, or not, based on whether any feedback is received, or not. Second, after some feedback has been received, review writing will continue, to whatever degree suits the life choices, and the centrality of gaining a public, for that reviewer. People who make it a practice to write reviews will receive varying amounts of feedback, but these variations will have no linear association with output, once reviewing becomes established. Once the initial work of feedback is done, variation thereafter in the amount received is only noise. The purpose of feedback is to help novices sustain the practice of reviewing, not to boost the count of reviews produced by established reviewers. In terms of a data equation: if new reviewer and + feedback → reviews continue; if old and + feedback → no information on continuance.

However intuitive these two possibilities, the null hypothesis also remains potent: amount of feedback might have no detectable effect on whether reviewing is sustained, or whether reviews are written in volume, for any set of reviewers. There are two ways that feedback could prove unrelated to review count. First, feedback might have a different purpose than to sustain reviewing. As discussed earlier, feedback may be intended as second-order market information, a device for ensuring trust rather than a motivational aid. Second, feedback may be essentially random, responding to a chaotic mix of reviewer traits, reader traits, restaurant traits, and who knows what else.

Of note is the field experiment on feedback conducted by Muchnik et al. (2013). These researchers, working with a news site that allows its readers to give feedback on the posts of others, manipulated the site software to randomly give or withhold extra feedback votes to posts. They found that a post that got (positive) feedback, tended to get more feedback, independent of the quality or other characteristics of the post. In short, they found a bandwagon or pile-on effect: positive feedback begets more, independently of whether the post is any good. If this bandwagon effect were to occur on Yelp, it would tend to destroy or confuse any relationship between feedback received and reviews produced.

Findings for feedback
In San Jose, with Yelp restaurant data, we found a strong linear association between feedback votes and review counts (Appendix A). Prolific reviewers had high lifetime totals of feedback received, while infrequent or new reviewers had low counts of feedback. We also found positive feedback to be common on Yelp: all reviewers in the sample who had written more than ten reviews had received positive feedback.

This cross-sectional analysis, which takes a snapshot at one point, cannot answer the question of whether feedback causes review writing to be sustained or boosted. Hence, we went back to Yelp one year later and collected follow-up data: who continued to write reviews? How many more reviews did they write?

We found that overall, feedback did not act as a reward: people who had received more feedback by Fall 2011, did not write more reviews during the next year; there was no boost to productivity (Appendix A). However, we did find a difference between novice reviewers, who had written ten or fewer reviews, and established reviewers who had already written 11 or more. For novices, but not for established reviewers, the presence or absence of feedback did predict whether review writing would be sustained. If no feedback had ever been received, the person tended to stop writing reviews for Yelp. Conversely, if any feedback was received, a novice was more likely both to continue, and to write more.

To write reviews, to seek after a public, is intrinsically motivated. Thousands of ordinary consumers enjoy the opportunity to be writers, to reach a public, which Yelp affords. Once these people learn that they can reach a public on Yelp, as evidenced by the receipt of feedback, they continue to write, at whatever pace fits their lifestyle and life goals. Getting at least some feedback early on is important, but after that, the amount ceases to matter. Feedback is not the reward sought by review writers. They seek the opportunity to gain a public.

Feedback systems may also operate as an institutional logic. To not get any feedback causes wannabe reviewers to drop out and stop writing. From Yelp's perspective, people who write reviews that no one likes, get weeded out. Reviewers who have good taste, who know how to please readers, get roped in. The population of reviews and reviewers on Yelp undergoes unnatural selection. Feedback systems shape the institutional terrain to breed better reviews, by selectively retaining better reviewers.

Trust Studies

Question: Does feedback signal that a review can be trusted?
Although we found that feedback can be explained as a means to encourage novice reviewers, feedback could still supply second-order market information, to aid buyer-readers to pick out better from worse reviews, and decide which ones to trust. Or, despite its incentive effects on novices, feedback could still be pure noise in this second context, and useless as a heuristic for evaluating a review. That is the empirical question: noise or signal?

The difficulty with testing this question: where to find a place to stand, to determine review quality. What criteria to use? We solved that problem by working with our research assistants (see Appendix B). In contrast to the study described in Appendix A, feedback here means feedback per review, and not a reviewer's lifetime total count, of feedback received across reviews. Review feedback is shown beneath each review on the Yelp display, next to the buttons that let you give feedback. For many reviews, these counts are zero. Although all productive reviewers get some feedback on Yelp, less than half of the reviews we collected had received any feedback. Although the receipt of feedback does not mark out motivational differences among established reviewers, it may mark out a review as special.

Findings: reviews that receive feedback

We found that better reviews were slightly more likely to get positive feedback, even after controlling for number of friends, restaurant expense, and extremity of rating (Appendix B). A review that got feedback is a better review, *ceteris paribus*. But the effect is small, too small to justify the weight that some invisible hand explanations might want to place on second-order market information, as a heuristic for deciding whether to trust.

Question: What signals does Yelp use to pick out untrustworthy reviews?

Trust judgments by individual consumers are invisible, and made on the fly. However, Yelp's trust judgments are on the record, and visible to all. As noted in the main body of the essay, Yelp exercises police power on its site, by filtering out some reviews posted by members and throwing them in jail. Because jailing is done by algorithm, we thought to reverse-engineer Yelp's filter, to see what criteria Yelp uses to jail reviews.

Neither we, nor Yelp, nor any reader, can know for sure which reviews are fake. Nor can we know how many criteria, other than falsity, might be used by Yelp to filter reviews. It goes without saying (but has to be said, because some journal reviewers failed to grasp this point), that Yelp would never knowingly disclose, to ourselves or any outsider, the criteria used by its filtering algorithms. The more potent Yelp reviews become, in determining the success of local businesses, the greater the incentive to game Yelp's system. Gaming Yelp's system means figuring out how to avoid the filter, which means the filter has to work in the dark to work at all. Police power, exercised in the dark, plays no role in free market explanations.

Even on the outside, however, we can gather a sample of filtered reviews, and compare these filtered reviews to others not filtered. Any differences that emerge will provide clues about the criteria used by Yelp to filter out reviews: the signals that cause Yelp to distrust a review.

Findings: reviews that get filtered
The best predictor of filtering was whether a reviewer had no friends, followed by whether the reviewer was a novice, followed by whether the review was short (Appendix C). It appears that Yelp is institutionally distrustful of novice reviewers who have no friends and write short reviews. Intuitively, this sounds like a pretty good description of a possible shill. Yelp actively exercises its police power, and channels this power along the institutional terrain set up by logics of friending and honor. None of the filtered reviews had been written by Elite members.

A final question of interest is whether the metrics of review quality, discussed under the previous question, bear any relation to filtering. Are poor-quality reviews, independent of length, friends, and word count, more likely to be filtered? We found this to be true, but again, the effect was small: better reviews were slightly less likely to be filtered.

Implications of the trust studies
Beyond easily parsed metrics such as friend count and review count, Yelp must also run reviews through some kind of natural language algorithm, tuned to detect linguistic characteristics of vacuous reviews. For instance, our first perusal of a set of filtered reviews flagged "amazing" as a word that can get a review filtered on Yelp. But to further explore this point would take me away from sociology proper, toward sociolinguistics. An enormous research opportunity beckons, to those so inclined: millions of public texts about public objects, waiting to be analyzed.

Sociologically speaking, Yelp actively exercises a police power. In political terms, Yelp is committed to government interference in the free market of review production. Yelp does not trust that every review posted is worthwhile, and this distrustful stance incrementally improves the value of the market information Yelp provides. Yelp, institutionally speaking, is congenitally distrustful, willing to assume the worst about a new member, and throw their reviews in jail. This is risky. Every filtered review is a slap in the face, especially for a new reviewer only tentatively engaged; the equivalent, at a bar, of turning toward a person who sits down next to you, and stating in a flat voice: "You liar." In everyday life, "Screw you" would be a mild reply. On Yelp, the equivalent would be "Get somebody else to write your blankety-blank reviews." Yelp takes a risk when it filters a review. Yelp risks throwing its seed corn into the garbage. How can it build a lucrative review hosting site by driving away would-be reviewers, during their most vulnerable hour?

Yelp must judge the trade-off to be worthwhile. Yelp willingly risks crimping growth in its stable of reviewers, and curtailing its wealth of market information, if that leads to a better experience for review readers; better, because vacuous and fraudulent reviews are suppressed. Yelp distrusts market forces.

A final question: what kind of reviews might we find on a hosting site that did not exercise police power?

Comparative Study

Question: Does the exercise of police power make a difference to the type of reviews available on a hosting site?

Yelp filters out short reviews from less-established reviewers. By comparison, a site that does not actively filter reviews, like Google+, should reveal a review population somewhere in-between regular Yelp reviews, and filtered Yelp reviews. The question of interest is the exact location of Google+ reviews, within the gap that separates filtered and non-filtered Yelp reviews. If Google+ reviews are closer to filtered Yelp reviews, on a metric such as word count, then the absence of police power on Google+ makes a large difference in the quality of the reviews posted there. Conversely, if Google+ reviews are located closer to regular Yelp reviews, then Yelp's exercise of police power represents an improvement only at the margin, a matter of touching up rather than sculpting the population of available reviews.

Any such comparison is handicapped in two respects. First, there is only a small overlap in the metrics that can be gathered from Google+ versus Yelp (Box 2.9). Second, even if we find on Google+ a dramatic shift toward the filtered end of Yelp reviews, the attribution to police power can never be secure; these two hosting sites differ in many other respects. Hence, even more so than before, these data are presented only in the spirit of, "for what it's worth."

We found Google+ reviews to be much fewer in number, with fewer than 200 accumulated across these 12 restaurants, as compared to more than 800 posted for the same restaurants on Yelp, during about the same period in 2012. We also found Google+ reviews to be much shorter on average, about 40 words. Even Yelp filtered reviews were almost twice as long, averaging 88 words, while regular Yelp reviews were almost four times as long (Appendix B). We conclude that the different social formation created at Google+, with its absence of social controls, attracts a different review than does Yelp. You can't say much about a dining experience in 40 words.

BOX 2.9   YELP COMPARED TO GOOGLE+ REVIEWS

After our initial data collection from Yelp began, Google overhauled its review hosting site and rebranded it under the Google+ name. Google's prior version had not gained much traction, and might have gone the way of Citysearch and Yahoo Local, absent this intervention (these two, which had become moribund by the beginning of our Yelp research, are discussed in Wang 2010). The new version includes some collaborative filtering, if the review reader had joined Google circles (a competitor to Facebook), and if other members of their circle had written reviews. In other respects, Google+, like its predecessor, continues to follow a relatively pure free market model, in which anyone with a Google account (tens of millions) can post a review.

Toward the end of 2012, as we worked with filtered and non-filtered Yelp reviews, we decided that Google+ reviews might offer an interesting third point of comparison. We first confirmed that the 12 San Jose restaurants that we were studying on Yelp also had reviews posted on Google+. Next, our research assistants gathered each of these reviews and scored them. We found only two metrics in common: word count and review count. Since the second of these is inherently biased in Yelp's favor, because Yelp has been in existence much longer, we were limited to comparing word count.

Findings

At first we thought we had 1000 or more Google reviews to compare. Unfortunately, most of these turned out to be either anonymous reviews from before the Google+ overhaul, or Zagat questionnaire responses (Google had purchased Zagat), not reviews. That left only 176 named reviews from 2012. These were so short that word count appeared to be the only reportable metric: 40 words on average. For the record, the 200 earlier, anonymous postings on Google were even shorter, averaging less than 30 words.

LIMITATIONS

I did not discuss or analyze any review texts in this essay, except for fictitious examples. I focused on reviewing as a social practice, rather than on individual reviewers and what they wrote. Review texts belong to linguistics, or rhetoric. A sociologist can't go there, although a sociolinguist might.

A very different inquiry would have started with individual consumers, proceeded to analyze each one's oeuvre of reviews, compiled information on their background and social location, perhaps interviewed a sample. Had I done so, an ethnography would probably have been the result, not a sociology.

Still another very different inquiry would have manipulated review texts, and randomly assigned these as treatment conditions. A simple example would be to create rants and raves, accompanied by ratings of 1 or 5, and examine audience response, to see which reviews were judged more credible, or had more power to change perceptions. This would have produced a social psychology, and a laboratory exercise. Who cares what college sophomores think about reviews of a French restaurant, one they can't afford to patronize? Who believes that the responses of students, sheltered in a classroom, whose professors have a duty of care, can predict trust decisions in the field, where hundreds of dollars are at stake, and the risk is a ruined date?

Relative to these two foils, sociology is both more distant, and more real. It does not focus on individuals, and it does not manipulate within the confines of a laboratory. It is not warm, and does not promise control. Sociology will not be to everyone's taste.

Another limitation: the n-dimensional model of social formations, in Figure 2.4, was only sketched; developed just enough, to suggest how the variety of *Gesellschaft* forms might be structured. To make room for the idea of a public it was only necessary to cut back the undergrowth. Future research will have to identify the major rays—the key dimensions along which social formations vary—and position these relative to one another. The model in Figure 2.4 stands as an alternative to stale polarities, pedestrian 2 x 2 quadrant models, and arid Cartesian grids, when the goal is to capture the diversity of evolved social structures.

CONCLUSION

Morozov (2012) decries the techno-utopian view that characterizes many treatments of the Web and its impact on society. Keen (2008) similarly mocks the cult of the amateur, disparaging the idea that online reviews can substitute for the insights of a knowledgeable professional (cf. van Dijck 2009), or the rationalized products of a Weberian bureaucracy. But these critics portray reviews as not-so-good market information, failed attempts to help buyers choose. I took a more radical stance, and challenged the claim that reviews are market information, arguing instead that reviews represent something more, and something less.

Yelp, and online review sites generally, emerge as a new type of Web-based social formation. On the one hand, Yelp commands a vast volunteer workforce, while on the other this volunteer workforce comprises a large part of its user base (Moon and Sproull 2008). Unlike conventional ad-supported media businesses, Yelp users produce most of what they consume there. This unusual structure is shared across many online review sites (for example, TripAdvisor), but not all (for example, Amazon, where reviews are an adjunct to a more conventional retail business that sells products produced and promoted by professionals). The items produced on Yelp are intangible but influential, trivial but permanent, only words but having the power of speech, an extraordinary opportunity for the ordinary person to write for strangers.

Yelp is something new: a machine for creating publics. Yelp is a privately owned and maintained, ersatz social formation, organized for profit, that throws off benefits to consumers as an ancillary to its main line of business, which is to sell audiences to advertisers. The benefit, which is the opportunity to publish, is valuable enough, to enough millions of ordinary people, in the United States and around the globe, to give Yelp a stock market capitalization in the billions, starting from nothing.

Old problems of trust recur in these new social forms, and the difficulties of determining who can be trusted, and what to trust, grow ever more pressing. The advent of online review sites represents another turn in the cycle of modernity, which in the West has proceeded as a movement toward looser forms of association among comparative strangers lacking any long-term intimate bond. Modernity, as Tonnies and the early sociologists argued, has meant the end of community, narrowly defined as a set of intimately bound known parties, each with a set role based on long tradition (Nisbet 1966). Online review sites turn the ratchet another step, as it becomes possible for millions of complete strangers to share taste judgments with one another, concerning such intimate experiences as dining, at any spatial remove and without expiration date. This new form of sociability requires new mechanisms for securing trust, such as friending and honor logics, which attempt to restore the more traditional forms of association which modernity, operating now through the Web, tore apart. Yelp presumes the death of community. A yearning to recover solidarity fuels Yelp.

NOTES

1. This halcyon era predates Watergate, cries of liberal bias in the media, and the decline of trust in elites and institutions, now so characteristic of the age. And this is not to say that reviews were never controversial, or that authors and chefs never howled about the flagrant bias and epic incompetence of some professional reviewer. But earlier in my life, the picture sketched in the paragraph was once accurate.
2. Six efforts in all, ending with a desk reject from a third-tier journal; I can be obstinate. Later, Shelby spoiled this story, by getting a much revised version of the feedback studies accepted at a special issue of the *Journal of Strategic Marketing*.
3. As young scholars in business academia will already have heard repeated ad infinitum, good research, research worthy of the most prestigious journals, research to get tenure, must be theory research. In practice this means psychological or economic theory, or in

some small precincts, ethnographic theory. Since the theory must already exist for the work at hand to be perceived as theory research, this creates an innate conservatism in journals, which favors extensions (I dare not say tweaks) of existing theory, and disfavors research focused on new things. Caveat, young scholar: pursuing a consumer sociology grounded in the phenomena may be hazardous to your publishing success.

4. The extent and richness of this dossier varies across review sites, but the possibility of a dossier is inherent.

5. The original heading was "massification," but Billig (2013) knocked that out of me.

6. I do not want to get caught up in a debate concerning Structuralist versus Functionalist accounts in sociology; but the consumer sociologist needs to be aware of why both terms have a presence in the literature, and that each has partisans.

7. Although market information is a term of art, it is also six syllables, and what Lanham (2006b) calls a "-*shun*" word. I'll use shorter synonyms when I can.

8. In fact, as Box 2.2 shows, both the number of people writing reviews, and the number of reviews written by some people, far exceed the values in this thought experiment. But this was not recognized when economic explanations for online reviews were first offered early in the millennium.

9. I don't currently have a Facebook account; the first person singular in this sentence is a rhetorical maneuver.

10. *Ceteris paribus* in terms of journal quality, of course; and do read Billig's (2013) mournful and piquant reflections on scholars' much greater access to citation counts here in the Internet era, and what our proclivity to check these counts might reveal.

11. Whether that small fraction of humanity that attends an elite school, and goes on to get tenure as a publishing academic, might have an unusually deep and enduring need for status enhancement, would be a different question.

12. Alternatively, tenured academics like Deci and Ryan, who are among the most comfortable and fulfilled people on the planet, may underestimate what motives predominate among the ordinary sort of person, which is to say the moderately miserable person, who falls close to the mean for life satisfaction here in Late Capitalist times.

13. I am not sure Billig (2013) would agree; see his take-down of the supposed virtues of technical vocabulary, with its purportedly greater precision.

14. Whether this celebration of marketplace communities makes consumer culture theorists the "useful idiots" of neoliberal ideology is a question considered in Askegaard (2014).

15. In principle, sociology could study community, same as ethnography. But historically, in the narrow sphere of consumer research, ethnography got there first. As a marginalized perspective, still on probation, I think it wise for consumer sociologists to focus on relations with strangers which remain virgin territory.

16. Cultural productions may sometimes be called texts in contemporary Humanities scholarship, as in Warner (2002), but I'm wary of this usage, and its ideological baggage, left over from the days of deconstruction. True, "text" is a much shorter word, but terms like visual texts, musical texts, and cinematic texts will always be a stretch for those not initiated into literary theory, and I aim to reach people whose brows would furrow upon hearing that "everything is a text."

17. Unlike massification, I didn't need Billig (2013) to warn me off "mediatization." Yucch.

18. In a few other cases, such as Athenian democracy, there was a public sphere with many participants who were not officials or rulers: a polis; but this was an arena for extemporaneous oral speech.

19. If you prefer the psychological terminology of self-determination theory (Deci and Ryan 2002), to gain a public yields a heady mix of competence, autonomy, and even belonging.

20. Arguably, there can be no such thing as a modern self without the possibility of a public, as Campbell (1987) appears to argue, but that is a byway I have not the time to pursue.

21. Cue Lou Reed: "Little Joe never once gave it away. Everybody had to pay and pay."

22. And said fie to Pinker's (2014) fatwa against the use of "level."

23. I've merged a label from William James with the substance of a quote from

F. Scott Fitzgerald. In consumer research, there was a big tussle over these matters in the early 1990s. The easy-minded resolution was to live and let live, and publish papers by both those espousing science, and those who had given up on science altogether. What makes the agnostic position tough to hold, is the acceptance that there really are sciences, having the glorious success attributed to physics in triumphalist accounts; but that what we do, here in sociology, may not qualify. Easier to go all in, either for or against the possibility of science.

24. Doctrinaire Marxists do not feel this strain: Zwick et al. (2008) assert that the new consumer behavior seen on the Web is the old alienation of labor under a new guise, so that ordinary consumers are duped by the million, as they labor for the capitalist owners of Yelp, who appropriate and alienate that labor, same as it ever was.

25. In this section, I speak as a marketing professor, despite my protestations that this book is about consumers. I did spend 30 years teaching marketing to MBAs.

26. This assumes that the competition sets up a natural experiment, as opposed to producing random and one-off results. That assumption may be in error; I have been haunted for many years by a guest speaker at Santa Clara, I think it may have been Ernst Boyer, who mocked "that triumph of modern casuistry, the Harvard case method." The case method tends to assume that what happened, had to happen, and that business outcomes are necessarily the result of a natural experiment. Maybe.

27. I should probably have said, in the mainstream print publications that I read: the *Wall Street Journal*, the *New York Times*, the *Washington Post*, to name those most likely to be recognized, should this note be read decades hence.

28. You could rebut the meaningfulness of this baseline by arguing for path-dependence and a random walk: (a) Jeff Bezos had some idiosyncratic ideas when he designed the early Amazon review capability in the 1990s; (b) it is easier to emulate existing database software than to design new software from scratch; (c) therefore, Bezos's design, which is only one among uncounted workable possibilities, persists across most review sites, which copied it rather than take a chance on something different. The universality of the baseline design would then offer no insight into features of the social formation it supports.

29. To the anonymous journal reviewer, who argued that this sentence should begin with "whom": Steven Pinker makes fun of you (Pinker 2014, p. 241, "stuffiest prig"). But, Nathan Haller derides Pinker (*New Yorker*, 11 March, 2014). Who to believe? Or whom?

30. Although after reading McCloskey (2010) rail against "Max U," perhaps I am too generous.

31. Of course, poking holes in the market explanation does not support any particular alternative explanation, such as social structure. But the dominance of economic explanations, especially for this sort of technological innovation, requires that these be beat back, before a space can be carved out for alternatives.

32. And if caution were heritable, then over time, the population would contain only people who had a knack for avoiding predators as children. In this sense, both Darwinian natural selection and free market explanations rely on an invisible hand. Whether the one provides ideological succor to the other, and which way the support runs, or whether the resemblance is merely accidental, would be interesting to explore in an intellectual history.

33. It has to be software because across the Yelp system, thousands of reviews are posted every day, so that filtering has to be automated to be viable. The application of police power by algorithm is one of many novelties seen in the online review space.

34. The numbers and proportions are different on Amazon and some other review sites. I've shopped for books where there were not many reviews, but where several had received 100 or more feedback votes. This may reflect a difference in the size of the potential audience: national or global for a book but only local for a restaurant. Sites also differ in what kind of feedback can be offered. A rich menu of future research opportunities beckons, once the veil is lifted and scholars stop viewing feedback as a market mechanism with an obvious function.

35. Trolling, in 2014 when I first encountered it, required an urban dictionary or similar source to define. Troll, if you've ever read *Three Billy Goats Gruff* to children, is an apt metaphor for the ugliness of the Internet behaviors described.

36. Because of the numbers involved, I imagine that Yelp proceeds in two phases: an algorithm first picks out 100 or 200 local candidates, based on simple metrics like review count, friend count, and lifetime totals of feedback. Yelp city managers then cull this initial list for the best candidates on more subjective grounds, such as panache, insight, style, caliber of the profile, and so forth. If the managers who do the culling have a good sense for what styles of review will provide a positive experience for buyer-readers—if these managers have good taste in reviews—the result will be to select productive reviewers whose writing will typically be experienced as valuable, all without a great expenditure of management time. An interesting task for a management scholar would be to identify the traits and skills required to be a successful Yelp city manager, and how these may be identified in hiring. Not much is written about how to hire good taste.

37. Marx hewed more closely to the Biblical template, adding the socialist paradise at the end of history, to complete the three-part tale characteristic of Judeo-Christian eschatology.

Interlude: From gaining a public to going public

The final essay examines Pinterest, a website that postdates even Yelp, just as Yelp postdates fashion blogs, which in turn appeared more recently than personal Web pages, which in turn postdated discussion boards—the first online behaviors investigated in consumer research. Pinterest is really new.

This final essay is the shortest, and the least focused on alternative explanations from competitor fields such as economics and psychology. Here I do not have to prune away misunderstandings, as with cultural capital, or beat back the imperialistic overreach of economics and psychology, as with Yelp. Essay three may be the least sociological as well, as it invokes psychological concepts such as daydreaming: an intra-psychic event. It fits, nonetheless, because with Pinterest, daydreaming ceases to be an invisible private act and becomes a public, shareable event, socially visible, which opens it to sociology. Pinterest enables dreaming out loud. It offers a final opportunity to explore the meaning of public.

Even so, this essay might not have made the final cut, had not Campbell (1987) made daydreaming central to modern consumption. That fact, along with the sheer newness of the behaviors that Pinterest has made possible, earns the attention of a consumer sociology.

Another argument for inclusion: Pinterest shows how technology creates new forms of social being. Pinterest advances one of the master themes of the book: that in a *Gesellschaft* world, social change is occasioned by, and premised on, technological change. Human nature—that fiction of a deracinated academic psychology—does not change. But the space of social possibilities, once technological innovation became dynamic in the 18th century, has been changing and continues to change. New technologies make new social formations possible.

To attribute social causation to technology is to risk being labeled Marxist. Karl Marx was the first and the greatest modern materialist, and to attribute social force to technology is materialist. One of the pioneers in thinking about the sociocultural impact of technology was Walter Benjamin, whose famous book will haunt this last essay, and who was an avowed Marxist. But it is wrong to conflate Marx, materialism, and the hypothesis that technology has social force. Precedence in time, and habits of mental association, do not an explanation make. To accept the formative influence of technology on sociability does not require us to pledge allegiance to a Marxian economics. We do, however, have to set Hegel aside, and accept a fundamental uncertainty about where society is headed. Future technological change is unknowable, and with it, the direction of future social change. Social being became malleable when the solidarity horizon began to drop away, with the emergence of the first cities thousands of years ago. It has become more malleable as the solidarity horizon has retreated further during the Industrial / Scientific / Technological / Capitalist (I/S/T/C) Revolutions. The more malleable social being becomes, through technological advance, the greater the role of technology, in shaping new social formations, and driving their emergence.

The larger project, then, is to accept technology as socially creative, and powerfully influential, without being dragged back into old arguments about Marx, and without getting trapped in stale dualisms that oppose matter to spirit. To understand the social impact of technological innovation, we must strip off these blinders.

Essay Three: Pinterest—to make public the private

with Barbara J. Phillips[1]

ORIGINS AND PREDECESSORS—KEY FEATURES OF PINTEREST—
Pinterest Behaviors—First Analogue: Photo Album and Scrapbook—
Second Analogue: Women's Magazines—What is New—Taste Goods, Styles,
and Fashion—The Problem of Fashion and the Uncertainty of Taste—
PRODUCTION OF THE CONSUMER IN HISTORY—To Consume, to
Daydream—Make the Interior Exterior, Make Public Your Dreams—Costless
and Riskless—Pleasures of Immateriality—Taste and Identity—Why Possess
an Image?—CONCLUDING COMMENTS

In Pinterest, the newly possible centers on how images are consumed.
These words are crucial: it is images that are consumed, and on Pinterest
images are consumed. To view images, or collect images, or paint images, is
not new. And to consume—to shop, to desire, to possess, to consume as the
stomach does food or the palate does wine—is not new. But what Pinterest
allows the ordinary person to do with images is new.

It has never before been so easy to find and view images, nor has it ever
been so simple to create and share complex images, nor has it ever been
so inexpensive to amass large numbers of images. This new capacity, to
possess imagery, presumes a transformed image, dematerialized, virtual:
phosphors evanescent on a screen, electrons coursing through a diode. The
image has ceased to be ink on a page or paint on a canvas and has been
rendered insubstantial. Both your means to acquire, and the nature of
what you possess, have changed.

The price of image abundance: physicality disappears and uniqueness
drains away. For art theory (Benjamin 1936; Lanham 2006a; Scott 1994),
all Web images are simultaneously copies and fakes: digital code masquerading as color, shape, and line. A digital image can have no aura, in Walter
Benjamin's terms. For images created in Photoshop, there can no longer
even be an original. Non-digital copies can be printed on paper, but these

are no more original than the image drawn on screen by the image-maker, who is naught but a software user. Digital imagery has no original.

A digital image may generate physical copies that can be touched, held, hung on a wall. But these are only copies, just as every image on a screen is only a copy. The unoriginal image does not exist in any one place. It is reproduced as needed on the device at hand, and can exist in any number of locations, equally itself in all, and truly present in none.

The digital image is always a fake. It never is a picture and always is a string of numbers. These binary numbers, long long long strings of 1s and 0s, with the aid of technology, can fake it, can make a picture appear without using any pictorial material. Dematerialization is complete.

And yet, it was matter that made the image immaterial, technological matters, the hard physics of phosphor excitation and photon emission, the electrodynamics of magnetic impulse, the laser burning a pit. Trees fall only in the inhabited forest, never otherwise, as Bishop Berkeley achieves his apotheosis. The image doesn't exist until it is called for, and disappears when not in use. Material means have idealized the image, and dematerialized it altogether. Near-magical science has disenchanted the image. Images are no longer art, but consumer goods, stocked on a shelf and available for sale, one at a time or in batches by the million.

Because every image is faked, and there is no longer an original, the boundary that marks out some images as art dissolves. Copy ceases to be a term of opprobrium. Art has to be found somewhere else apart from imagery. Once no image can be marked out as special, as Art, then every image shows some art, and every viewer becomes an aesthete. Images pass into the demotic, and aesthetic judgment spreads wide.

With the Web, it becomes possible to consume immaterial goods, digital images. Immaterial goods occupy an uneasy middle ground: between tangible goods, such as normally come to mind when the phrase consumer goods is used; and private dream images, which are intangible to all, including the dreamer. On Pinterest you can consume the immaterial, and Pinterest is but an early signpost, on a way laid by the Web, to be followed by other formations as yet unseen.

ORIGINS AND PREDECESSORS

This is not the first time that technology has altered the imagery seen by ordinary people (Schroeder 2002). Just as the printing press made a public possible, a possibility that exploded anew after the Web, so also photography preceded the Web, in transforming images and how consumers relate to imagery.

Ewen (1988) calls attention to a 19th-century essay by Oliver Wendell

---

BOX 3.1   MORRIS, MARX, AND LEFTIST NOSTALGIA

Ensconced in my white, male, first-born self, enjoying my respected, tenured, lucrative business school position, I have been insulated from the scornful, Leftist strain of elitism. It sounds like this:

> Style is a process of creating commodity images for people to emulate and believe in. As frozen, photogenic images . . . become models from which people design their living spaces, or themselves, extreme alienation sets in . . . The marketing engines of style depend on anomic subjects seeking to become splendid objects. The extent to which objects seem so promising may be but an index of the extent to which the human subject is in jeopardy; destined only to be defined as a *consumer*. (Ewen 1988, p.91)

Although infused with hand-me-down Marxism, the roots of this particular scorn, directed onto consumers of mass-marketed adornments of self and home, lie with William Morris, one of the founders of the Arts and Crafts movement in 19th-century Britain. For Morris and his many contemporary descendants among the cultured, if an object isn't handmade, lovingly crafted with the devoted labor of an artisan, it is dreck. Consumers of manufactured goods are poor wretches, who lose themselves in Scrooge-like avarice for cheap and shoddy goods, bedazzled and befuddled by the crafty images of the master manipulator, that spawn of Hell, the advertiser.

Pinterest and what is new about it cannot be glimpsed from behind the veil of this ideology. The consumer of immaterial goods on Pinterest, the connoisseur of images, has first to be respected, before her actions can be understood. Contempt is not a theory.

Holmes (1980 [1859]) that speculates on the cultural impact of the new technology of analog photography. As interpreted by Ewen, Holmes argued that the spread of photography must separate surface from substance, and lead people to value appearance over reality. With photography, and mechanical reproduction generally, the idea of the copy, and the withering of the authenticity and aura of the art object, entered cultural discourse (Benjamin 1936). Before photography, images were rare, material, and embodied (Joy and Sherry 2003). Images were art, requiring skill and effort to craft, and of the elite. With photography and supporting technologies, such as color lithography, it became possible to consume an image without consuming art. You did not need to travel to the imaged object: it came to you. Photographic images could be acquired, possessed, and consumed at leisure, with little effort or expense; visual pleasure spread out, and was no longer confined to particular times, such as church ritual, or places, such as museums.

Photography was the original demotic turn (Turner 2010). Once leveraged by the Eastman Kodak company, photos profoundly democratized image making and image viewing. Pinterest is a second turn on a cycle that started here, just as the Web, as opportunity to publish, is a second turn on the printing press.

Ewen's gloss on Holmes shows that insubstantial images began to proliferate long before the Web. A first take would be that Web imagery is Benjamin's mechanical reproduction, perfected and multiplied many-fold. But with the Web, the change in quantity is so extreme as to induce a qualitative change in the experience of imagery, just as physical laws change, once the sphere of interest becomes small enough, as in quantum physics, or large enough, as in cosmology. The Web transforms image relations. It continues the action of photography, but goes beyond what analog photos could do.

KEY FEATURES OF PINTEREST

Nonetheless, this was all true in 2010, just before Pinterest was launched. I have only described what the Web made possible, rather than what was realized, in Pinterest. To see exactly what is new with Pinterest, let's first study what a user can do there.

Here you can acquire any digital image, anywhere on the Web or off, and make it your own by pinning it to a location that you control. A click of the mouse suffices to place an image in a digital album, the pinboard, after which, you possess it, and can view it at will. The key elements that come together on Pinterest are:

1. Any image, from any source, can be stored in a personally controlled collection bin.
    - If the image began as a physical photo or drawing, it can be scanned and uploaded; hence, any image.
    - If it was initially a percept of an object or scene, that percept can now be digitally captured and uploaded: just raise your smartphone and click; hence, any image
2. Once on the pinboard, the image can be accessed anywhere, any time, and viewed any number of times.
    - Even ten years ago, the urge to include a qualification or caveat would have been irresistible: "any time . . . that one has access to a computing device with a Web connection." But in an always-on smartphone era, that caveat becomes otiose, and drops away.
3. The number of images available to the ordinary person, that she might choose to possess, is huge, inexhaustible. Even if she spends all day every day browsing the Web, and pins every image she sees, her fingers

a blur on the mouse or screen, there will always be uncountable additional images she has not yet seen.

- Strictly speaking, this describes the context in which Pinterest arose, rather than calling out a distinctive feature of Pinterest. Pinterest might never have been conceived, or might have been stillborn, if the Web had not already madly proliferated imagery.

4. The cost to possess is vanishingly small. No matter how many images have been gathered, there is no dollar cost; and the cost to acquire anew, in terms of effort expended, remains minimal. Old guys like me, who remember when we downloaded an image over a modem, and navigated the Windows file tree to find a place to store it, while hoping there was still space on the 10 meg hard drive, can only marvel at the ease of the "Pin it!" screen button, and the unlimited storage offered in the cloud.

- And yet, the cost in terms of effort cannot be zero, because the effort to possess, which is strictly speaking unnecessary, must still be made. Pinning an image is mostly not needed, because that image could be found again; the Internet never forgets. One can always go on the Web tomorrow, either to find new images, or locate and re-view an image seen before. Pinterest, and the opportunity to possess, is an unnecessary add-on to what the Web does intrinsically: provide an abundance of images stored in perpetuity. Because Pinterest is unnecessary, what consumers do there becomes all the more interesting: why do consumers want to possess images, rather than simply view them?

5. The cost to consume is likewise vanishingly small, zero in dollar terms (one already owns a smartphone and pays for Web access for other reasons). And the pinboard software, especially with a touchscreen device, renders nominal the effort to find any possessed image.

- If you have never used Pinterest—and especially if you are old like me—find a Pinterest user with several well-populated pinboards, set her up on a touchscreen device, and ask something like, "Show me your best chocolate cake recipe." Then watch them zoom to it. After that, go back to your non-touchscreen Windows desktop and use the file directory to find the first Word file you saved there (good luck).

6. In sum, Pinterest gives universal free access to all images everywhere, any time. And that's to exaggerate only a bit.

Pinterest has one more notable aspect: pinboards are public. These can be kept private, or some can be made private while others are kept public—many users have multiple pinboards. Yet the default, for most early users,

---

BOX 3.2   PINTEREST DATA

For the research that underlies this essay, we analyzed 20 Pinterest pinboards that contained 2291 separate images. Our analysis of these images differs from net-nography in that it is not intended to be an ethnography of the pinners (Kozinets 2009). It is modeled instead on the analysis of historical archives, literary texts, and aesthetic objects (e.g., Sewell 2005; Scott 1994; Schroeder 2002). We supported the analysis of images by reading widely in the trade and popular press on Pinterest, and conducting informal interviews with Pinterest users personally known to us. We also joined Pinterest.

We sampled pinboards from female pinners in three product categories associated with the female sphere: kitchens, weddings, and kids, and added another, more loosely bounded category of "miscellaneous." We included boards that contained between 70 and 200 images, having determined in a pretest that boards with only a few images (20 to 40) did not provide enough information for a meaningful visual analysis, while boards with more than 250 images made it difficult to discern thematic patterns. One of my co-authors randomly selected the first five boards that met our criteria in each of the four topic categories and then she along with my other co-author analyzed these boards.

The findings and a more complete discussion of the methodology can be found in Phillips et al. (2014). I touch only lightly on the results in this essay.

---

was to leave pinboards visible to other Pinterest members. That visibility was not just potential: in its early days, the Pinterest home page would stream, in real time, images as they were pinned to pinboards by members. Any appealing image could be re-pinned to one's own board; and, with or without re-pinning, each streamed image gave access to its pinner, and all her other images, for the price of a click or swipe. Box 3.2 details the research that underlies this essay.

Summarizing, Pinterest has two key properties: it allows you to possess, and then consume, images, free of limits and costs. Here Pinterest reflects the overall trend on the Web, which has increased the plenty and decreased the cost of so many things. Second, with Pinterest those images you possess are made public and displayed to strangers. This too reflects an intrinsic feature of the Web, what Turner (2010) called the demotic turn, in which ordinary citizens become visible to one another, and available to one another, en masse. My twist on Turner's insight: it is tastes that become visible and available. In a fashion blog I can show my taste in clothes to a mass of strangers. With a Yelp review I can publish my restaurant tastes. On Pinterest I can display my taste in kitchen cabinets for all to see. Tastes, ordinary tastes, consumer tastes, are set free to circulate. With these features of Pinterest in hand, let's look next at what people do with this new-found capacity.

Pinterest Behaviors

First, Pinterest offers the standard social media functions: you can follow another member, to stay abreast of their new pins. Your count of followers is public, similar to how Yelp makes public your list of friends. On Pinterest you can also create a profile, as on Yelp, but during our research in 2011–2013, these profiles seemed less robust than on Yelp, more often left skeletal or minimal; as if not very important.

Second, each pinned image carries along a mini-dossier, which shows the count of times it has been repinned, along with a live link to its source. This link gives access to the entire catalog from which the image came, if it was not a one-off. If the image has a commercial source, the link may convey brand identity. A picture of a handbag might have link text reading "dolce&gabbana/ luxe/floral_237428," making that brand visible, while providing the same connectivity as any banner ad; that is, click and go there, to see what other beautiful images Dolce & Gabbana might offer. Link text and image tag information can be searched on Pinterest. Search makes actual, the potential for any image to be public.

Next, site software permits a gradient of engagement, ranging from passive to very active. This usage gradient is important to lay out, because its range may not be obvious. When discussing Yelp, I could rely for tens of pages on the shared assumption that "people read reviews to decide what to buy." Everyone knows that! That assumption ran so deep that I could later hit the reader over the head, by showing that Yelp users also read reviews after dining; which at a stroke, unfroze many assumptions about Yelp (market information, not so much).

That gambit is not possible in this essay on Pinterest, because the usage model is not apparent to all. Legend has it, that in Pinterest's earliest days, many venture capitalists were perplexed when the founders pitched the site as an investment opportunity: what the heck would you do with that? Legend further has it that all the perplexed were male, while the early and most enthusiastic users of Pinterest were female. Not legend at all is that early scuttlebutt had members referring to Pinterest as "digital crack for women" (Dvorak 2012). Whatever the early usage model was, it was engrossing, even addictive—for some female users. I mention this upfront, to impress on you that Pinterest has a female sign, is a gendered thing.

Cashing out that gendered insight will take a long time, so let's return to sizing up the activity gradient. The verb consume applies across the entire gradient, and the object is always imagery, but there are differences:

1. At the most passive level, you can log on to the Pinterest home page from time to time to look at images pinned by others since your last

visit. By 2012, you could hit "Refresh" after ten minutes of browsing down to the bottom of the home page, and find more new images to browse up at the top; and this refreshment could continue, until you were ready to stop and do something else.

- Does this remind you of those old experiments, where rats had electrodes inserted into the pleasure centers of their brain, and could get a jolt of pleasure by pressing a lever, which they were wont to do over and over, even to the neglect of eating? Me too.

2. At a somewhat more active level, you might be browsing elsewhere on the Web, reading, looking, searching, or shopping, and in the course of this off-Pinterest activity, decide to pin the image in view. You were not looking for images, or necessarily looking for anything, but if on encounter, an image stimulates your desire to possess, the Pin it! button is always there, and to acquire that image takes but a click or a tap.

- You don't have to put aside the focal activity to pin; you might not engage the Pinterest site itself, in one of the more active modes described below, for hours, days.

3. In a more active mode, you might go on the Web with the express purpose of adding to a pinboard. Here you actively search for images to add to your collection. You may search on Pinterest itself, look at the pinboards of people you follow, search on some other specific website, use a search engine to search widely on the Web, or move back and forth between all of these during the session. Your goal that day is to acquire more images, typically in accordance with some theme: holiday recipes, kitchen countertops, bridegroom dresses, or kids' bunk beds, to name just a few seen in our research.

4. In an equally active but less acquisitive mode, you may rearrange images on an existing pinboard, move an image between pinboard locations, clean up pinboards by deleting images no longer of interest, or establish new pinboards to prepare for future collections.

5. In still another active mode, you may engage with other members: choosing to follow them, checking out their latest pins, sending queries or exchanging messages, or responding to any of these.

- Again, we found this sort of dyadic interaction to be less common on Pinterest than on Yelp or on blogs. Overall, Pinterest users appeared remarkably unsocial.

Finally, let's reverse the question: what do we not see on Pinterest, relative to what might have been expected? First, personal photos were rare; we saw not one in our dataset of more than 2000 images. Pinterest is quite unlike what Instagram had become by the time of writing. Users were not posting photos of family, pets, friends, and home; they collected images of other things, made by other people, located somewhere else. Pinterest users also did not collect other people's home-made images of pets or kids. Most images posted on Pinterest were professionally made and commercial in origin. The image stock on Pinterest consists of things you can buy.

Second, fine art images were rare. Not a single one of the images on the kitchen, wedding, or kids boards reproduced a museum-quality piece of art. There were no Vermeer still-lifes on the kitchen pinboards, no Impressionist water lilies on the wedding boards, and no Rousseau lions on the kids boards. Instead, we found consumers playing with immaterial images of ordinary consumer goods. To consume images, to get pleasure from the visual, no longer requires art. The most superficial image, scorned by elites as kitsch, may please the demotic consumer. Pinterest did not turn consumers into museum curators. They remain ordinary people, consuming now immaterial goods, images, dreams made visible—not art.

Yet another rarity, as touched on above, was ongoing interaction with other Pinterest users. Likewise, there seemed to be little concern with how many followers one had, or with constructing and showing a persona to the Pinterest *Gesellschaft*. What we saw on Pinterest was public being—visibility to and availability for a mass of strangers—without social interaction. There was not even the distant, hands-off interaction of writing to be read by strangers. The product of your efforts is visible, the product of everybody else is visible, but that is all: image sharing without interaction. There was no movement toward a solidarity horizon with selected others, as on Yelp, and little concern with elevation and distinction, as in fashion blogging. But as I'll later show, taste remains central, in Pinterest as in Yelp and fashion blogs.

With this abstract of Pinterest elements and behaviors in hand, let's look next at pre-Web analogues, to sharpen and focus the novelty of what occurs on Pinterest. Photography, while it is the technological predecessor of Web imagery, is too vast an undertaking to serve as an analogue for Pinterest, being a technology and not a specific activity. Rather, we need to examine what ordinary people did with photographic imagery before the Web came along, and made both immaterial imagery, and its possession on Pinterest, possible, easy, and fun.

First Analogue: Photo Album and Scrapbook

The mechanical reproduction of images begins with the daguerreotype in the 19th century. Art prints go back before the printing press, but these were the province of a specialized guild, produced only by professional artists. The daguerreotype freed the image from art, and then the Kodak camera pried it loose from the grasp of professionals. The amateur snap-shot, from about the turn of the 20th century, provides one line of descent for Pinterest.

With the advent of the Kodak, ordinary people began to do two things with their photos: compile albums and assemble scrapbooks (Christensen 2011; Helfand 2008; Katriel and Farrell 1991; Tucker et al. 2006), with the first of these more widespread, and the second less common and also more gendered. A large proportion of camera owners compiled albums, while a smaller number, mostly women, assembled scrapbooks. Of the two, the direct line of descent for Pinterest runs from scrapbooks. A photo album contains mostly one thing: my photos of my family and what we did and where we went. A scrapbook might contain: (1) photos of my family; (2) commercial photography, whether torn from a magazine or otherwise obtained; (3) other sorts of printed or mechanically reproduced items, such as trade cards, ticket stubs, a playbill, or a menu; and (4) a larger, vaguer category, best described as physical tokens: a scrap of the quilt my baby slept under, or a piece of wallpaper from before the kitchen remodel.

A scrapbook, although it may be just as personal and familial as a photo album, is sourced differently and may have a broader subject matter: not just me and my family, but also where I've lived, and where I might like to go, and who I might someday be. While a photo album will be strictly focused on aids to memory, a scrapbook may also contain aids to fantasy. It might contain a photo of the kind of wallpaper I'd like to put in the living room, or a magazine photo of a crib in which to rock my baby, should I ever conceive. The diverse content and future orientation seen in scrapbooks makes them a better analogue for what became possible with Pinterest.

Second Analogue: Women's Magazines

The photo album and the scrapbook provide analogues for the active usage of Pinterest. The use of women's magazines, especially in the fashion and home categories, provides an analogue for the passive use of Pinterest, the pure browsing of imagery. What we see in a *Vogue* or a *Better Homes and Gardens* are pictures: page after page of photos large and small. Even the advertisements often consist of nothing but a picture, a brand, and maybe a brief remark: no body copy, no verbally stated claims (although a completely text-free ad is more common in fashion than home magazines; see Phillips and McQuarrie 2010). This contrasts with academic research on advertising, which mostly manipulates the wording of ads. The disjunc-tion between the two, the real pictorial ad and the scholarly focus on words in ads, has long been a puzzle.[2]

The rapid diffusion of Pinterest may explain why magazine ads directed at women are so pictorial: women have long been consumers of imagery *qua* imagery. That's why women's magazines are full of pictures: to look at photographs of people wearing nice clothing, living in skillfully decorated homes, whipping up scrumptious desserts, is pleasurable. Again, if the images collected on Pinterest were art images, we'd all say, "Of course: everyone knows that to view art is an end in itself." Art requires no instrumental purpose. Art supports autonomous pleasure-seeking. But the images in women's magazines are not art. They are pictures of consumer goods. And yet, women, as they view these magazine images, are often not shopping. The photos are not clear windows onto product objects, which enable an inspection of quality and suitability (Phillips and McQuarrie 2010). It can be darn hard to see clothing details in a fashion ad; and more often than you might think, the clothes in the ads can't be purchased, but were created expressly for the photo shoot that made the ad. The ad isn't about the clothes. It's not a shopping aid. The ad tells a story about the brand. These magazine ads, these branding efforts, are pretty pictures, and can be enjoyed as such apart from any instrumental purpose. Looking need not be shopping.

Scholars have not faced the fact of passive image viewing. Wider neglect leads to the incomprehension of Pinterest, seen among some male venture capitalists: what good is software for gathering and looking at pictures, of things you don't plan to buy? Answer: the same good as provided by a copy of *Vogue* in the doctor's waiting room. To view images of things that are merely consumer goods, even though you are not shopping, is nonetheless pleasurable, in the way that art is pleasing. It does not have to be a picture of a magnificent redwood tree. It does not have to be a painting by Monet. It does not have to be a photo of a kitten or puppy. It can be a picture of a kitchen countertop with a bowl, or a kid's bunk bed, or a wedding favor; anything about which a consumer might daydream.

What Is New

What's new in Pinterest is new relative to these analogues. Consumers have been "just looking" for decades, and the success of picture magazines was built on this proclivity. Consumers have been compiling photo albums and scrapbooks for a long time. But in these analogues, images were physical, tangible, and costly: material things. Less obvious, and only partly a function of cost: these older forms of imagery were limited, scarce, and could not be summoned at will. Every issue of *Better Homes and Gardens* will contain some pictures of kitchens, but there can be no guarantee that this month's issue will depict a country kitchen, or show how a stainless steel dishwasher looks, placed under a butcher block counter. In the old physical days, prior to Pinterest, images were titrated out by institutionalized taste-makers, the magazine editors and ad agency creatives, who controlled which images would be published and made available to ordinary people. Pinterest is new because it abolishes cost and limit.

With Pinterest, images can be had for free: free of costs and free of old limits. There are still constraints. Only images that someone else put up on the Web are free; posting your own images to Pinterest, from some location off the Web, costs effort. Even this constraint is slipping away, as smartphones take over, but the point remains: some types of images are more likely to appear on the Web. Limits reappear as constraints at the source, even as limits on finding and collecting disappear.

The images most likely to appear on the Web are commercial images: images of goods for sale. There is a financial incentive to post such images, just as magazine advertisers have a financial incentive to spend large sums on good photography, and make the resulting images available to magazine publishers without charge (or, for a negative charge, since the advertiser has to pay for the privilege, of providing that magazine's readers with pretty pictures to view). The new limit on image freedom: the easiest images to find, and most likely to be of high caliber, are commercial images. The freedom conferred by Pinterest is a freedom to browse and collect images of goods for sale.

New, with Pinterest: consumers can dream out loud about consuming. A consumer can dream in public about the kind of kitchen she might like to have, or the wedding she might stage, or how her child's bedroom would be decorated, if she were ever to have a child. And consumers can eavesdrop on the daydreams of one another, and act as bricoleurs, assembling and reassembling their own daydreams from bits and pieces of the fantasies of others, including commercial fantasies, dreams for hire.

It's as if, in the old world of physical photo albums locked away in private homes, you could steal out in the night, an unseen ghost flowing through the keyhole of any house up and down the street all across town, and turn the pages of every photo album, bearing away on your bosom an impress of any image you fancied, to be placed in your own album back home. Meanwhile other ghosts are stealing up and down the same street, silent and unhailed, slipping into neighbors' houses and home again, bearing images of their own choosing. No trace is left of these visits, except that a small counter by each image ticks up, to bear witness that this image has once again impressed another, and been acquired. This metaphor captures the public availability and crowdsourcing that occurs on Pinterest, but also the paucity of social interaction.

Taste Goods, Styles, and Fashion

It is not only commercial images that dominate Pinterest: it's imagery within taste good categories. I earlier identified clothing, food, and home décor as prominent examples of taste goods. Pinterest allows more to be learned about how ordinary people consume taste goods. The sociological paternity of what follows runs from Simmel (1957 [1904]), as interpreted in Gronow (1997), through Campbell (1987). Time to define fashion, taste, and style, in a way useful for illuminating Pinterest and what is new there.

Taste is aesthetic preference within a fashion context: what looks good to your eye and what does not. In turn, fashion is to be understood in the sense of Simmel (1957 [1904]; cf. Campbell 1987). Fashion pertains to any category of consumer goods where multiple aesthetic options are present at any one point, but also change over time. Fashion extends beyond clothing and personal adornment. Here I follow Gronow's (1997) gloss on Simmel: a category is subject to fashion when: (1) the goods in it have non-functional elements; (2) these come in multiple versions; and (3) some people like any one version while others dislike it. Each such option can be termed a style.[3] A style is any one of the aesthetic options available in a particular taste good category. Style occurs at multiple levels. We can identify a style of cabinet door, but also the country style in kitchen design, or at an even more macro level, the minimalist style in home décor. Some writers use "a fashion" in the same, singular noun sense, as in the fashion for frills and tassels, or the fashion for ostentatious house façades. However, I think it best to reserve "fashion" for the fact of multiplicity and change, and "style" for the singular options that are multiply present and that change over time.

Taste goods are inherently subject to fashion: they are categories where goods are offered in multiple styles that vary over time. All styles of cabinet door function as doors, but there are many possible styles of kitchen cabinets, and the set of all possible styles is unbounded; new styles may come into being. If we zero in on cabinet door knobs, we can argue about whether one style is more or less functional (some may be harder to grip by the elderly), but in fashion categories, the variability in style dwarfs the variability in function across the multiple options on offer. We see many styles, all of which are functional. And although there may be no functional difference between a door of knotty alder with a round mushroom knob of brass, and a maple door with silver handles shaped like a parenthesis, a consumer may have a preference for the one or the other that is visceral, as in "Yucch!" or "I love it." It is a style that one likes or dislikes, and it is fashion categories that offer multiple styles to like and dislike. Taste is manifest as liking one style versus another. Taste is not a preference based on functional utility. Taste doesn't deliberate. Taste comes from the gut.

A mutable plethora of styles is found wherever consumer taste operates; there are countless styles of kitchen cabinet, countertop, or faucet, innumerable options for decorating a child's room, and any number of wedding themes. But Simmelian taste and fashion can deploy only within a mass consumer society, that is, in modern or Late Capitalist culture. There are not countless styles of dress in a traditional society: there is only the one correct style, and it does not change. Tradition prohibits fashion, and only static forms of taste, such as the class tastes of the early Bourdieu (1984; cf. Gronow's critique), can be exercised in a traditional society.

To talk about a cabinet style, or country-style kitchens, or the minimalist style, is only to switch levels, from item, to repertoire, to regime. Accordingly, when working at the level of minimalist style, Victorian style, Craftsman style, some authors prefer to speak of taste regimes (Arsel and Bean 2013; derived from Foucault's work on discourse regimes). A taste regime governs preference at a general level; a regime rules in, or out, uncountable individual items. A taste for minimalist design in home décor drives choice of furniture, use of textiles, acceptable color schemes, and more. Whether at the level of item or regime, taste remains visceral: if you have a taste for Victorian style, minimalist décor will feel ugly and barren; if your taste runs to the minimalist style, Victorian décor will seem garish and overdone; you might even retch. The terms of invective change, but the vitriol never ceases: styles are espoused or shunned, celebrated or scorned. Taste for, is also disgust against.

Taste regimes and particular social groups need not align (although often, people will go there: taste lends itself to restrictive practices, at the level of regimes as elsewhere). But taste regimes do draw individuals together as like-tasted. Unlike tastes repel; my distaste for your possessions impels dislike of you. But, contrary to the ethnographic view, and apart from small oppositional and marginalized groups, taste regimes are not subcultures which organize and identify people. Adhering to a regime is a loose form of association. Rather, taste regimes separate and organize consumer goods in product categories where fashion reigns. Regimes can be pressed into the service of identity projects but need not be. For the consumer, that *Gesellschaft* creature, living amidst abundance in Late Capitalist times, regimes solve the problem of fashion in an economical way, by organizing item styles into larger sets. And fashion is a problem, because abundance poses difficulties. Abundance produces vertigo of choice.

The Problem of Fashion and the Uncertainty of Taste

Campbell (1987) may have been the first to recognize how a Simmelian analysis of fashion challenges classical economics, and undermines economic history guided by the classic view. Fashion means multiplicity and ceaseless variation, novelty and impermanence. Style—that which multiplies and changes anew—implies non-functional variation. Therefore, stylistic variation must be independent of functional utility. The problem: how do consumers develop any preference, in the absence of differences in utility? And how can consumer preferences change, again in the absence of any change in utility? Campbell (1987) stated this problem historically: how could the modern consumer, the being enmeshed in the modern fashion pattern, have ever come into being?

Soon I will need to lay out Campbell's (1987) historical analysis, the better to explain Pinterest, just as it was necessary in Essay One to lay out Bourdieu's ideas about cultural capital, its evolution and vicissitudes, before I could explain the success of some fashion bloggers. Pinterest enables a weightless and accelerated commercial dreaming. What happens, once consumers can dream this way? Before reviewing Campbell's analysis, and returning to Pinterest with fresh eyes, I want to put Campbell's historical treatment in context, via a few ahistorical claims.

Uncertainty is constitutive of fashion categories. Consumer uncertainty is the native context for the exercise of taste, for choosing among styles that have no functional difference. Taste discovery must occur, before the consumer can consume; or maybe taste refinement, when uncertainty is somewhat less. Consumer taste permits of education, per its Latin root *educere*, to bring forth what was latent within. Pinterest, it will emerge, is software conducive to taste discovery, taste refinement, and taste education. The taste educated on Pinterest is consumer taste, taste for one style or another of goods within fashion categories. Taste discovery, refinement, and education are possible, and also necessary, because consumers, *qua* consumers, are uncertain of their preferences. I don't know, yet, what I like best. This fundamental uncertainty throws a road block in front of economic analyses that would tie consumer preference to utility.

It shames me that I spent decades reading and doing consumer scholarship without encountering Campbell's argument. That may reflect poorly only on me. Still, to recapitulate Campbell's argument, and showcase his conceptual apparatus, may be time well spent, if there are others like me. Although it will be a long detour, Campbell will help us to grasp what happens on Pinterest.

PRODUCTION OF THE CONSUMER IN HISTORY

Campbell argues that the everyday activity of daydreaming is not human nature. Rather, to daydream is characteristic of moderns. Daydreaming seeds modern consumer behavior, which is inconceivable without it. The medieval shepherd did not daydream while tending his flock; that behavior was not possible then. An aristocratic youth in 1640 did not daydream about hunting foxes; that is to project our psyche back in time. But for a character in a Jane Austen novel to daydream, about where she might live, and how she might dress, once she meets her soul mate, is perfectly apropos. Daydreaming is a peculiarly modern sensibility, deeply bound up with the birth of the consumer, the person who seeks pleasure from purchases that are not necessary, the person who has wants as well as needs.

I can't do justice to Campbell's thesis here; it is a beautiful and subtle argument pursued over hundreds of pages and across centuries. But we need it to appreciate what is new in Pinterest. Campbell self-consciously modeled his essay on Weber's *The Protestant Ethic and the Spirit of Capitalism*. The conceit: that Weber succeeded in explaining how capitalists, those who produce the wealth of goods we now enjoy, developed out of Calvinist beliefs; but that Weber, and the scholars who followed, neglected to explain how the consumers of those goods came into being. If Protestantism created capitalists, then who or what created consumers, those who spend rather than save, and then spend again, and again? Campbell eviscerates past attempts to explain where these spenders came from, including those advanced by Veblen and classical economists. Consumers didn't exist before the 18th century, and their advent has to be explained, just as capitalism didn't always exist, but requires a historical explanation, whether in Weber's terms or some other.

What is the modern consumer pattern, then? It rests on wants rather than needs, and pursues fashion rather than cleaving to tradition. Consumers experience incessant, unslaked and unslakeable, wanting, hankering, seeking. Only because there are consumers who want to buy, and cast aside, and then buy more, can there be modern capitalism. Can't sell except to a buyer; can't keep selling unless the buyer keeps buying. Campbell pinpoints the unceasing purchase of the new, seen most clearly in fashion categories, as the conundrum to be explained. Seeking until satisfied, and then stopping seeking, is easy to understand. Seeking, getting, and remaining unsatisfied, leading to seeking, getting, but still unsatisfied, and on and on, is fundamental to consuming, and the foundation of capitalist profits. Campbell puts a firm foot down: supply does not explain demand.

Stating what Campbell wanted to explain is the easy part; conveying his book-length historical explanation in a few paragraphs is harder.

To gloss: consumerism has an intellectual history. A new habit of mind emerged in the 18th century. Campbell, lapsing alas into sociology-speak, labels this mental practice "autonomous self-illusory hedonism." That wretched phrase limns what daydreaming does. To explain the origins of daydreaming is to explain the modern consumer. Briefly:

1. Calvin's religious doctrine of predestination created a problem: to be one of the Elect was a terrible, awesome, wonderful state, calling forth the most intense desire; yet nothing could be done to achieve it. Only God's grace availed.

2. This led to the doctrine of signs: that one could recognize the Elect, and one's own salvation as one of the Elect, by certain signs. Weber showed how thrift and sobriety and deferral of gratification, leading to capitalist prosperity, became signs.

3. Campbell (1987) picks up the theme about a century later, in England, as the harshness of Calvinist dogma, and the grimness of predestination, made salient the problem of theodicy: how could a just God have designed such a cruel world?

4. The solution, for some intellectuals, was to know God as above all good. They reasoned that if the Godhead is ground and ultimate expression of the Good, then benevolence must be central to the Godhead. This led to a new twist on the doctrine of signs: the Elect were now those who showed forth benevolence in everyday word and deed.

5. To demonstrate and enact benevolence, one had to feel such emotions as pity and agapic love. And for the behavior to be benevolent, rather than crassly instrumental, these emotions had to be patent, visible, and exhibit the signs of an intense inner experience consistent with a state of grace.

6. This marked the first step toward an autonomous, self-illusory hedonism: emotions were internalized to become the focus of experience. Devout Protestants learned to devote themselves to experiencing emotions appropriate to the benevolent—which could include a horror of sin and a terror of wickedness—and to experiencing these emotions, even those conventionally thought today to be negative, as pleasurable, and pleasurable because signs of grace. Emotional control, which had begun as suppression of feeling, morphed into a positive form of control, an ability to summon emotions at will; to feel, and thus enact, benevolence, with all its outward signs.

7. To experience emotions as pleasurable required the devout to engage in fantasy, where emotions could best be experienced at will, and more perfectly realized. The emotional man or woman, whose

emotions were obvious to all, and whose deliverance to emotion was unreserved, as seen by their reactions to the miserable unfortunates encountered in the daily round, and the cruel fate seen everywhere in the world, were now signed as the Elect.

8. The habit of fantasy was further fueled by Gothic and romantic novels. The initial flush of prosperity from the Columbian exchange, the growth of world trade, and the dawn of the Industrial Revolution had launched a middle class with the leisure and prosperity to fantasize. The spread of imaginative literature helped to diffuse the new habit of fantasy outside select circles of devout intellectuals, and more broadly within the rising middle class.

   - I see this as one of two weak hinges in the argument. Campbell's intellectual history, of what intellectuals were doing, appears tight and sound; how the new habit of mind spread to the masses is more difficult to grasp.

9. Daydreams always lead to disappointment; fantasy is intrinsically more perfect than real experience in the world. Disappointment provides an emotional experience; emotional experience is good, holy, and righteous. It is pleasing to have emotions inasmuch as these are a sign of grace.

10. But pleasure, whether in emotion or for its own sake, requires novelty, to be sustained. Campbell highlights the changing role of pleasure. Pleasure had not been a life goal, or a very important goal, certainly not an esteemed goal, prior to the modern era. The search for pleasure, and its pursuit in emotion, which is most autonomously obtained in fantasy, which can be varied at will, and thus provide the novelty that is central to pleasure, defines a modern sensibility.

   - A second weak hinge in the argument is how the habit of fantasy got directed onto goods for sale, since that supplies the crucial link to the modern consumer, rather than simply to the modern sensibility.

11. With this plank the argument falls into place and stands foursquare. The great religious impulse of Protestantism led along one branch to capitalists, per Weber, and on the other to consumers, per Campbell. Individuals had to learn to focus on pleasure. They learned to derive pleasure from emotions in pursuit of signs of grace. Once settled into the pursuit of pleasure they were committed to fantasy and daydreams. Once daydreaming spread beyond the intellectual and spiritual elites to the mass, it was readily focused on goods for sale, as the most accessible targets for fantasy. Having been first fantasized, actual goods are always a disappointment. And from here, the cycle of incessant wanting cranks up, the sleeve is caught in the gear, and

there is no longer any escape from consuming. Moderns are broken to that wheel.

To Consume, To Daydream

To be a modern consumer requires daydreaming. The modern consumer must daydream so that she may be inculcated with the habit of wanting new things. She must learn how to dream a delightful fantasy of idealized pleasure. She must get a taste of the perfect, perfection never possible in the real material world, but easily conjured in fantasy. Once she has gotten a taste of perfection, and learned to pleasure herself with dreams of the joys that money can buy, she will become and remain a motivated buyer. She will stay motivated, because she will always be disappointed. Because she is always disappointed, she learns to hanker after the new, the not-yet-a-disappointment-unlike-so-many-before. And because her fantasies require novelty, the modern fashion system appears. And because new looks, new surfaces, new appearances, new images are demanded, the modern capitalist system of supply can thrive, and the Industrial / Scientific / Technological / Capitalist (I/S/T/C) Revolutions gain traction.

Campbell (1987) locates the consumer in history. He makes the modern consumer a historical being, and a creature of her 18th-century beginnings. Now the Web, with Pinterest, turns the wheel of history once more. What happens, now that we have universal costless daydreaming, acquisition without purchase: the "zipless buy," as Erica Jong might put it?

To answer this question, we have to answer two more specific questions: (1) What happens once a dream can be made visible, pinned like a butterfly, and reanimated on command? (2) What happens, once we enjoy freedom of image, no limits, abundance beyond imagining, acquisition without payment? These two developments are linked, but they are not the same. Nor are they separate; both work together to shape the new consuming that Pinterest enables. With Campbell's argument mostly in hand—I have not yet considered the problems it poses for the utility explanations favored in economics—let's draw out the implications, of dreams for free while dreaming out loud.

Make the Interior Exterior, Make Public Your Dreams

What happens to a dream that is made public? Dreamer separates from dream. It is not psychologically possible, to engage fully in your daydream, while standing aside to assess it. But once a dream has become an external image, it can be revisited later, and scrutinized as a thing apart. As external image, it can be compared, both to the internal and ongoing dream from which it was drawn, and to any other external image, from any other dream occurring before or after. Dreams can now be lined up, sorted, ordered, graded . . . even deleted. What was subject is now object. You can inspect your dreams.

The dreams in question are not night dreams, lived narratives, but consumer dreams, daydreams, wish fulfillments: "That would give me pleasure to own, I would be pleased to possess such a _____." And in the zipless buy that Pinterest enables, I can possess an image of it, right away, right now, for free, for nothing. And I do, I acquire it. And then I acquire one of those, and one of these, and another, and another. And then eventually I get tired or distracted, and move on to do something else, not because I ran out of money, but because I ran out of desire.

There you have a straightforward, blow-by-blow envisioning, of what a Pinterest user does in active mode. I left implicit, but need now to expose, this important constraint: the consumer does not daydream in a scattershot manner. Today she may be dreaming about kitchens, tomorrow weddings, but most days she dreams upon a theme. What are the implications of thematic Pinterest dreaming? Let's examine more closely cases where the consumer's dream theme is of taste goods, and then layer on Campbell's insight: that dreams are always more perfect in the dreaming, than they can ever be, when realized in the world.

I dream, I make a zipless buy, I wake up; and later I look at that image in the cold light of another day. I have realized my dream, and accordingly, what I possess, the image I inspect, does not seem quite so perfect. It no longer takes me to the acme of pleasure. Sigh. Granite counters are a bit tired now, don't you think? And does anyone dress her bridesmaids in pink any more?

After experiencing this dynamic, the Pinterest user could proceed along either of two paths. Our empirical data resolves the ambiguity (see Box 3.2). One possibility, parallel to what Campbell hypothesized for the early modern consumer, is that disappointment with the acquired image fuels the search for more images. The consumer will cycle through pleasure dream → zipless buy → disappointment → new pleasure dream, and go through this cycle endlessly, as occurs for fashion clothing in Campbell's analysis. Under this hypothesis, pinboards over time will show a random walk among images, as the consumer cycles through different colors of granite counters, looks at marble for a while, gives caesarstone a try, takes a spin with limestone, returns to granite, and eventually moves on to some other theme in some other purchase category, abandoning the kitchen counter pinboard altogether.

But in taste good categories another path might be taken. Like this: pleasure dream → zipless buy → disappointment → adaptation → second pleasure dream, now an adjustment of the first rather than a replacement → zipless buy → disappointment, but not so much, needing less adaptation → third pleasure, a finer adjustment to the second → zipless buy → no disappointment; at least, with the immaterial image, and for a time. Yes, this one really is to my taste! Or, omitting for simplicity the buy and disappointment steps, the dream cycle might proceed: this one is nice → but I like this one too → this one is different still, but also nice → this is like the first, but I like it rather better → now I see it! This is the One. It has everything I liked in #2 and #3, and more.

The buy–disappoint cycle for taste goods might look more like range-finding artillery practice, than a random walk among discarded choices. That's what we found when we examined the time course of pinboards (see Phillips et al. 2014 for more details). We saw the dreamer hone in on what she really liked, in a cybernetic, Test–Operate–Test–Exit process. Taste goods are hyper-credence goods: even I cannot be sure that this kitchen cabinet design is or is not to my taste. I may not know, in the initial dreaming, what I really like or would like best; I may not have dreamed that one yet. To make my dream exterior, promotes distance, and makes space for a new and better dream to replace it. The export of dream to image provides the means to educate my taste. On Pinterest, I can know myself better, which is also to be better, to have better taste. And when dreams can be dreamed and distanced, over and over, almost for free, the process is speeded up, and becomes visible, as a new thing consumers do: taste refinement.

Taste discovery serves as a second example of a dream cycle for taste goods, which leads to the same end, by a different route. Taste refinement was serial: the artillery fire one at a time, adjusting after each blast. I dream, I buy, and, disappointed, I dream a little better. Taste discovery proceeds in parallel. I kinda like all three of these wallpaper designs from yesterday, but none of them quite grabs me. Oh here's another one, very different, but maybe better. This next one is bold, maybe too much. Ah, here we go, that's the One, even though it's far from where I started.

When dreams were held only internally, as in the world before Pinterest, it was hard to compare. Only when dreams are acquired as images, which can be placed side by side, and revisited on another day, is it possible to get the necessary distance, and discover a new dream that is even more to my taste. In taste discovery, my taste need not be a fixed static thing that I approach more and more closely through range finding, but a mutable and contingent thing, that changes over time, in the way that an education changes how a person thinks, going down unexpected paths. The governing metaphor is not artillery range-finding, but house-hunting, where there will be visits to many houses, on multiple jaunts, with choice suspended, until finally, having a much better idea of what they'd really like, the couple settle on the one property where they make an offer. This may be a house first visited weeks earlier, that didn't rise to the top at that time, because the couple did not yet know their own tastes, and could not gain this knowledge except by seeing more houses. And if you have ever bought a house as part of a couple, then the notion that taste—yours, hers, his—is not settled, or known in advance, should resonate.

Costless and Riskless

Having established the effects of dreaming in public, it is time to explore the second essential element of Pinterest: the zipless buy, seamless acquisition. "Images for nothing, and your dreams are free," to warp that Dire Straits song. To develop the effects of public dreaming, I applied Campbell's insight: dream → pleasure, reality → disappointment. He wanted to explain the origin of the Western European fashion pattern and material purchases, while I'm trying to explain the effects of acquiring immaterial goods on Pinterest. The next thesis: the costless, riskless, zipless element in Pinterest, both supports the effects of being public to oneself, and leverages its result.

The seamless acquisition process, applied to images conceived as immaterial goods, enormously speeds up Campbell's pleasure–disappointment cycle, producing a fantastic increase in the pace of acquisition. Only the wealthiest and most profligate, heiress or trophy wife, could acquire this fast this many material objects; but she'd be weighed down by past purchases, and their disposal. Even here, it's easier to imagine a rapid material cycle for clothing (women's shoes, to use a staple of comic strips), than for whole kitchens. The costless aspect of acquiring immaterial goods leverages the Campbellian cycle, the way cheap debt leverages investment: it leads to ever so much more.

Because immaterial goods are free, hundreds can be acquired over a short interval. Rapidity makes taste refinement and taste discovery viable, in a way that could not occur with either material goods, or material images meted out by magazine editors and advertisers. Was taste refinement or taste discovery even possible for ordinary citizens prior to the Web? Rapid image acquisition presumes an abundance of Web imagery, which implies the absence of editorial limits or cost constraints. But in a further turn, the Web did not produce an abundance of still-life paintings with fruit, or family portraits, or diagrams of photosynthesis. The Web hosts images of things you can buy. On Pinterest consumers acquire and possess images, rather than collect or compile images.

The flip side of costless is riskless. Absence of cost reduces risk. But risk encompasses more than financial risk. We can speak of taste risk, the danger of making an error, of buying something you don't really like, that isn't really you. And we can point to social risk, the risk of buying something you thought would please others whom you wish to please, but which instead causes them to judge you harshly, and conclude you are a person who lacks taste, or maybe, has bad taste. These risks are pressing when you acquire material goods visible to your immediate social circle. As we will see, to consume immaterial goods on Pinterest is much less risky. Reduced risk makes Pinterest new, and very, very engaging.

Just as free is opposed to costly, taste play opposes taste risk. Taste play maps onto taste discovery, the play of taste. But taste refinement might sound like work, labor, drudgery; and that is not my intent. So let's unpack taste refinement first, to develop the impact of costless and riskless images. Immaterial goods liberate the consumer—then what?

Recall that a radical uncertainty lies at the heart of consuming. Ordinary consumers are keenly subject to this uncertainty across all purchases, but uncertainty is greatest in taste good categories. That's why, on Yelp, people read reviews after dining: did I have a good experience, and how good was that restaurant really? Uncertainty shapes the modern consumption pattern described by Campbell. We can delve further into this uncertainty by revisiting Campbell's contrast between utility and pleasure. It again saddens me that I spent decades in business and marketing academia, before discovering Campbell's insightful contrast between the two. Separating the two perspectives, to the embarrassment of conventional economic accounts, is one of Campbell's several contributions. The consumer sociologist must grasp it.

Utility comes from satisfying needs: to get food when hungry, and water when thirsty, are type cases. If you are hungry, food also tends to supply pleasure, but the pleasure is an incidental concomitant of satisfying need. If you are not hungry, or not hungry enough, many kinds of food—boiled potatoes without salt or butter come to mind—fail to give pleasure. Conversely, consider wine, which exemplifies what you can place in your mouth, roll on your tongue, swallow, and gain pleasure from, even though it is not correct to say that you satisfy a need for wine. It is incorrect, a category error and bumptious, to speak of the utility you get from sipping wine, but appropriate and fitting to speak of the pleasure you experience, while sipping a good Cabernet.

On first take, pleasure and utility line up with wants versus needs. Campbell's deeper insight was that pleasure differs from utility in requiring novelty. If I'm hungry enough, a prisoner in a dungeon fed rarely, those boiled potatoes will provide utility every single time, because they satisfy a need which recurs. But if I sip the same $100 Cabernet, today, yesterday, the day before, and all week long, it will gradually cease to provide pleasure, until I take a break from it, and come back to it fresh.

However, novelty poses a paradox for the consumer. Pleasure requires the new, but not every new taste provides pleasure. I can't tell you how many times I've bought a new Cabernet (I had better tell you that I'm at $25 for everyday wine), and not been pleased. Novelty entails uncertainty. The new taste won't always taste good.

Uncertainty can't be reconciled with the idea of a utility function, which is economist-speak for the different preferences seen across segments. In discussing Yelp, I explained that utility was circularly defined, and thus had no content: since it is axiomatic that consumers are utility maximizers, if an expenditure of time, money, or effort was made, then its object must have provided some utility, and more utility than any available alternative. This circularity is fine for purposes of the mathematical equations in which individual consumer utility provides a term. The trouble starts when we move on to locutions such as utility function. This phrase slips content into utility. We give different content to the utility sought by different people, to explain their different choices. But utility has no content. It is a placeholder term for "that which the consumer always seeks to maximize."

If utility functions had content, then taste preferences would pre-exist, and not be uncertain. For example: suppose, in furnishing a kitchen, the consumer's utility function specifies distressed hickory for cabinetry. This exemplifies contentful utility: distressed hickory satisfies her more than cherry or quarter-sawn oak. When she finally encounters a hickory door, she automatically prefers it over the other door designs in the display, and if the price is right, she proceeds to purchase. In this story, hickory fits her utility function like key to lock. After contact, no uncertainty remains, except for whether the price requested matches the utility provided.

Campbell adroitly skewers the heroic assumptions required to assert that preferences pre-exist and taste is certain. Novelty cannot be possible under this scenario. All the skirts that can ever be—hem high or hem low, thick bustle or sheer fabric, pleated or flat, pink or blue, frilly or plain, tight or loose—would have to be keys cut to some pre-existing lock. These locks, the utility function that corresponds to each skirt design, would have to precede the skirts that unlock them. Every consumer would have to carry an enormous vector of preferences, one set for skirts, one for tops, one for shoes, one for purses, and . . . is that believable? Nonsense! Next year's skirt fashion does not exist, nor does a corresponding utility function. Consumers don't know their taste in advance of opportunities to exercise it.

Numbers like N^k quickly grow large, as the N of alternatives and the k of skirt attributes increase. But in a world of Big Data, an economist might not be too perturbed by these heroic assumptions. If we switch from skirts back to kitchen cabinets, there may only be 49 types of wood used, seven distinct molding styles, and seven kinds of raised surface, for 2401 combinations in all; surely not beyond the wondrous human brain (still no good explanation for novelty, but we are giving the economist the benefit of the doubt here). Ah, but now let us return to Pinterest, and to consuming images, immaterial goods. What the consumer pins is not a door design from a catalog page, but a complete kitchen, photographed from one angle, with this lighting scheme and that color palette. The number of possible kitchen images is, literally, infinite. And yet, the consumer likes some, doesn't like others, and in our empirical work, we found a convergent pattern over time to the images pinned.

Taste is emergent. It does not precede exposure. Pinterest is revolutionary, because the elimination of cost plus the abundance of the Web accelerates taste emergence, making it visible. We can see ordinary consumers learn, and grow, as they consume images over time. We can watch consumers hone their dreams. Taste refinement is self-education, made possible when dreams exit our minds as images. It is highly engaging, not wearisome or laborious.

Taste discovery is slightly different, and more obviously playful (Huizinga 1949). Taste refinement supposes that the consumer has a particular taste, but doesn't yet know it exactly. In refinement, the object of knowledge, her own true taste, has emerged, but the consumer only hazily glimpses it. Taste refinement rests on a build-up model, in which the rudiments of a system of preferences have coalesced (oak looks so dark and heavy in a cabinet door, and cherry just seems sterile), which the consumer might further refine (I like the knots in pine, but pine is too yellow), before finally settling on an enduring preference (knotty alder, that's the One, plenty of texture with a ruddiness that fits my color scheme). Taste discovery goes deeper, and presumes greater uncertainty: do I even want cabinet doors, or would open shelving look better in this modern style house? Would glass doors work? I dunno. Keep looking.

Pinterest accelerates taste emergence, from a slow, grudging process, invisible even to the consumer herself, to a rapidly unfolding journey of discovery. Speed changes things. Free changes things. And immateriality reduces risk, which makes bold.

Pleasures of Immateriality

Given a mutable plethora of styles, and some degree of product involvement, taste discovery becomes an imperative for modern consumers. If you are a taste leader, like the fashion bloggers in Essay One, you may discover tastes for others, and be followed for that reason.[4] If you are an ordinary consumer, as most pinners on Pinterest must be, taste refinement is more likely. You refine by aligning with a taste regime (Arsel and Bean 2013), and then exploring how that taste regime applies. There are countless ways to style a dwelling. But as a rule, ordinary consumers do not seek to be unique in their décor, and do not decorate piecemeal. Rather, to bring order, consumers seek an overall style, a taste regime, from among a small number on offer in their cultural context at that time. The minimalist aesthetic provides an example. Minimalism governs the taste regime advanced in the *Apartment Therapy* blog studied by Arsel and Bean (2013). This aesthetic abhors clutter in home décor.

In a fashion category, there must always be other, contending taste regimes, such as the Arts and Crafts aesthetic, or, less common today, a Victorian aesthetic. Once a consumer aligns with a taste regime—only the rare fashion leader or artist can pioneer new taste regimes—she proceeds to develop her understanding of that taste regime by applying it to life projects. Arsel and Bean (2013) give examples of how a taste regime gets fleshed out within the life world of an individual, who must ultimately buy one chair rather than another, pair it with this style of table, and put these on top of, or only adjacent to, this rug. Or, leave out the rug. That sounds like work.

Relative to material objects and physical imagery, the immaterial images circulating on the Web are easier to find, costless to acquire, available in profusion, more diverse in provenance, and, with the aid of Pinterest, may be helpfully curated by demotic consumers just like you. Ease and wealth encourage play and pleasure.

By contrast, to consume, at considerable cost, a material good, burdens the consumer. The home décor website examined by Arsel and Bean (2013) is titled *Apartment Therapy* (*AT*); a serious business, and a title that situates home décor as a remedy for some malady. Likewise, the consumer behaviors discerned among the consumers of the *AT* site by Arsel and Bean are work behaviors, actions designed to constrain uncertainty: problematization, implementation, ritualization.[5]

These behaviors are appropriate responses to a choice domain experienced as risky. Under the traditional meanings of taste, in which taste judgments classify the consumer socially (Bourdieu 1984), to decorate and furnish a dwelling is socially dangerous. It can cost limitless amounts, and expose you to unlimited contempt, should your taste in décor be found wanting. To stage a wedding, and to make purchases that establish you as a nurturing mother, are similarly risky, in social as well as financial terms. By contrast, to pin a picture of a kitchen, or to gather ten images of bridal bouquets, is not risky. It is fun: you possess without permanence, you make a zipless buy. The pictures may never be viewed by anyone in your social circle; and if viewed by a stranger, as most pins must be, you are unlikely to hear that stranger's judgment on your taste. Acquiring and displaying immaterial images comes free of cost and risk. Pinterest returns a measure of carefree pleasure to female domains, where material consumption may be burdened with social anxiety and deep doubt. Pinterest ameliorates taste risk, and that may explain its intense attraction to women ("digital crack").

Taste and Identity

To describe behavior on Pinterest as taste play, invokes a contrast with identity work, as described in the ethnographic tradition (Arsel and Thompson 2011; Thompson 2014). A consumer identity, Arsel and Thompson argue, is a culturally articulated construct built up from long-term engagement in a set of aesthetic practices for consuming. Such an identity "Is not a cultural entity that one can shed—in the manner of a T-shirt or a bracelet—because [it is] integrated into the practices through which consumers materially, affectively, aesthetically, and intellectually relate to the social world." In contrast to self-schemas, where consumers have latitude to add or drop elements, and elaborate or set aside part of the schema, "aesthetic tastes and consumption practices that have been established in a more embodied manner are not so easily abandoned" (Arsel and Thompson 2011, p. 804).[6] Identity confines, like ball and chain.

Taste play on Pinterest emerges as the opposite of the embodied, costly, effortful construction of identity. An immaterial image can be pinned, and later deleted, even more easily than a T-shirt or bracelet can be donned or taken off. You can pin an image of a bride's dress without having to try it on, be seen in it, purchase it, or commit to its material possession. Tomorrow a dress in a different style, reflecting some other taste, and different associations, can be pinned next to it. This playfulness differs starkly from the weighty investments in identity, and the sunk costs that constrain identity choice, seen in Arsel and Thompson's (2011) account of hipsters struggling against a devaluing myth.

Pinterest is not a site for identity work. It is something new. Pinterest supports taste play, taste discovery, taste refinement. Taste need not be a route to identity, or an identity trap. Taste can be a quest for what pleases.

Why Possess an Image?

Why bother to pin a Web image? There is no need to take possession of an image on the Web, by placing it in a personally owned digital vault; in most cases, the image can be bookmarked and viewed again any time. You don't need a virtual scrapbook to view desirable images at will; new images appear on the Web every day. The question, again: why take personal ownership of selected Web imagery?

The answer: ownership, even immaterial possession, implies commitment. To pin is to own, and to take possession declares, "It is me, or might be." Commitment powers taste refinement and taste discovery. Psychologists have learned that feelings are information (Cho et al. 2008). Behavior also sends information, a signal to me, from me: my action, what I choose to own, tells me about my taste, what I like. If I only view an image on the Web, then no matter how favorable my momentary response, if I do not act, do not take possession when I easily could, then it is not clear whether I really like it. Unpossessed images pose the same problem as private dreams: I can't assess my dream until I export it, and I can't know how much I like an image, if I have not taken the trouble to possess it. "You're not serious," as the saying goes. Possession is always serious; possession matters, even for immaterial goods.

To take possession of a kitchen image, by pinning it to a public board, is to declare, to self and others, "me." The declaration is enough to launch the Campbellian cycle of pleasure dream → real disappointment. Possession entails some commitment. But pinning is still orders of magnitude less costly and risky than building a material kitchen, even as it remains commitment enough to kick-start taste refinement and discovery. By driving down the cost and risk to acquire and possess taste goods, Pinterest gives ordinary consumers a new opportunity: to pursue the education of taste.

Taste education on Pinterest has another analogue, different from the scrapbooks and picture-heavy magazines discussed earlier. Historically, taste education was expected of a cultivated individual, if they aimed to inhabit the sphere of high culture, high art, the canon. The notion that great art provides great pleasure is a commonplace, but it applies to only those whose taste has been educated. Everyone knows that frequent exposure to the canon can school and refine taste (Arnold 1869). Lacking exposure to great art and literature, you'd remain a bumpkin. We call on these old notions today, when pressed to give a rationale for liberal arts education. But in the past, this pleasure and refinement was reserved for an educated few, those rare individuals who had got enough cultural capital to take pleasure from Marcel Duchamp's exhibition of a urinal, no less than Rembrandt's *The Night Watch*. What gets missed, in the high art account of visual pleasure, is the delight that an ordinary consumer may take in the most kitsch sort of teddy bear picture. We didn't find much art on Pinterest, but we found consumers taking aesthetic pleasure from immaterial images, kitsch or no, low and popular though these may be.

Within the sphere of elite cultural objects, it is conventional to suppose that taste must be educated, and that regular immersion in paintings, and efforts at comparison and contrast of selected images, is necessary if artworks are to yield their full measure of pleasure. The novice consumer of art is not expected to know what she likes, or even to appreciate what is worth liking and what is only kitsch. The novelty on Pinterest: demotic female consumers are now similarly engaged in educating their visual taste. The textbooks for this learning are images of mundane consumer goods in fashion categories. Each category of taste good offers an unending variety of looks and styles. Consumers do not know what they like until they look at it. The more they look, the more they learn. With each zipless buy, the more their taste develops.

Viewed sociologically, taste uncertainty has been an abiding feature of consumer society, most marked in fashion domains. Its neglect, in consumer theory, reflects the disinterest in and disrespect for female categories and female experiences decried by Maclaran et al. (2004), Thornton (1996), and others. Stop short, next time you hear derisory remarks about fashion ("slave to fashion," "fashion victim"). These are rooted in dismissal, and ignorance, of a consumer experience that, although universal, is felt most keenly by women in contemporary Western culture: uncertainty about what looks good. Aesthetic theory, in focusing on elite consumption, has failed to see that taste for mundane consumer goods is no less subject to discovery and education, than taste for elite art objects.

Any fashion domain—any product category where taste operates because styles proliferate—will evoke consumer uncertainty. Consumer desire in fashion categories is nascent and inchoate, the more so in the case of major, one-time events: planning a wedding or redecorating a kitchen. To align with a taste regime helps the consumer cope with this uncertainty; at a stroke, the kaleidoscope of fashion freezes. For example, once you commit to the minimalist aesthetic in home décor, you will never again have to choose among antimacassars. But any taste regime worthy of the name can be interpreted in countless ways without deviating from that regime. Alignment with a taste regime is only a beginning; the consumer must still discover how she will interpret that regime. On Pinterest consumers can align themselves with a taste regime, while developing and educating their personal aesthetic under its sheltering umbrella. You may even discover a compatible taste regime initially unknown to you.

To consume images on Pinterest is to play. Keep in mind the root meanings of taste, as in "this is to my taste," and "mmm, tasty." Visual images pleasure ordinary consumers. To come upon a new image that is to one's taste can, in the extreme, yield aesthetic delight. To possess that delightful image, to pin it to your board, gives the same pleasure as to acquire a desired physical object. Taste education on Pinterest means to pursue pleasure, which is to resolve uncertainty about what I like. I make ongoing acts of discovery: I learn that I like that kitchen cabinet paired with that countertop displaying those spoons arranged that way. But to take off, to absorb the consumer, this play, this pleasure of discovery, requires that images proliferate, cost almost nothing, and be easy to find. Pinterest realizes what the Web made possible.

Seen against this theory of taste play and pleasure, economic theory, with its known utility function, emerges as an unduly masculine take: a firm projection of self into the world, key into lock. Taste uncertainty is a feminine idea: an opening of the unformed self to the world. In a fashion category, taste cannot be fully known in advance. I only learn what I like, when I see it; to be sure that I like it, I have to buy it, make it mine.

Taste uncertainty, and the pleasure of taste play, motivate the unceasing browsing of images on Pinterest, and their selective acquisition. I don't know what I like to look at, until I go looking; but when I do find something I like, it is pleasurable to look at it, and then to look at it again.

Taste discovery is not laborious or dutiful: it is free play. To resolve taste uncertainty is inherently pleasurable, as Berlyne (1974) argued: arousal → release. To go looking for images, confident of finding new ones to like, is fun. To know that I can immediately possess any image I find, is exciting. To enjoy rights of ownership over these images, is comforting.

CONCLUDING COMMENTS

Pinterest reveals a neglected aspect of how taste operates. In keeping with Bourdieu (1984), consumer researchers have mostly studied the social functions of taste (Arsel and Thompson 2011; Holt 1998). In Essay One, I distinguished between the vertical and the horizontal operation of taste. In its horizontal operation (Lamont 1992), taste judgments group together like-minded consumers, and separate unlike consumers. Consumers affiliate with one or another taste regime and social group to further their identity projects. I called this the ethnographic perspective on taste. In the more traditional vertical operation of taste, consumers are grouped as better or worse, and placed in a higher or lower social position, in accordance with their taste judgments. Here taste serves as a restrictive practice, designed to out and exclude social inferiors (Goffman 1951). In either case, taste displays can be a risky, disconcerting, and sometimes morose affair. Taste determines whether a consumer will be accepted as a peer, or as a member in good standing of some desired group. Taste determines whether I will be rejected as inferior, or cast out as foreign.

Pinterest reveals a third dimension of taste, one which is private rather than social. The third dimension focuses on how a consumer relates to specific objects, rather than to other consumers, or to social collectives. In addition to taste as up versus down, or in-group versus out, taste has a third dimension: near versus distant, me versus not-me, approach or avoid. Here taste becomes tropism, not classification: inclination, not membership or position. In its private, selective aspect, taste acts as a compass: it guides the consumer as she pursues pleasure. I like that, I don't like to look at that, that's to my taste, that's not very tasty. The consumer life project, on Pinterest, is not to show good taste, but to find what tastes good.

NOTES

1. An earlier version of some of these thoughts appeared in Phillips et al. (2014).
2. Actually, it doesn't seem to bother most of my fellow consumer psychologists, who have gone right on studying advertising by manipulating words long after historical research had documented that, decade after decade, ads contain ever fewer words with an ever greater focus on pictures (Pollay 1985). The overemphasis on studying verbal persuasion in the one sphere, advertising, where it is less and less common, and where the frontiers of visual persuasion are constantly being pushed out in highly innovative ways, is a scandal.
3. For these definitions to work, style must be used only as a singular noun, "a style." Stylish, styled, and similar adjective and adverb forms will only confuse the issue and have to be set aside.
4. Pinterest, since the time of our research, appears to have moved toward the fashion blog process, with Pinterest advertisers working with Pinterest "influentials," pinners with larger followings, to promote selected images.
5. The authors do not cite Michael Billig's (2013) enigmaticization of the excessivization of nominalization seen in the social sciences.
6. Arsel and Thompson, in their discussion, are pursuing an argument with earlier research on the self. See their references, which should be read in conjunction, if you find yourself puzzled at how two common words, self and identity, easily interchanged, could provoke such a dispute.

Epilogue: The Borg Redux

Now that we have explored fashion blogs, Yelp reviews, and Pinterest boards, it is time to step back and consider what it means to do consumer sociology. Here I must part company with Billig (2013), who decries the thing-ification seen in modern day social science: the paucity of human actors, and the surfeit of things, when discussing social being. Billig objects to the way that processes take over, and human agency disappears. Here the literary figure of the Borg can be revelatory. Billig's advice, to focus on people and what they do, and to stop talking so much about social things and how they impinge upon people, is spot on—for psychologists. But it cannot take the sociologist very far.

The psychologist studies human beings: individual agents. He or she needs to be aware of the effects of social structure, as one kind of environment, on human action; but a psychologist rightly emphasizes individual agents, and how they respond to their environment, social and otherwise. The sociologist is not so fortunate. He or she has to invest social structure—inhuman collectivity—with agency, else fail the test of doing sociology, which is to recognize the separate reality of collectivity, a reality that includes autonomy of action. Sometimes social structure, as institutional terrain, bounds human agency in a maze. Sometimes technology makes it possible for people to do things they could not do before; in which case, where does agency lie: with the people doing, or the technology that enabled?

The Borg give a vivid picture of structure taking over human beings, replacing the agency of individuals with the imperatives of an anonymous collectivity. It hurts. The Borg disfigure those they assimilate. The awful truth behind Billig's denunciation of scholarly writing in the social sciences: scholars write about processes and things, make these the actors who occupy center stage, and slight the role of human beings, because that is the true state of affairs in Late Capitalist times. We walk around with machines grafted onto our skulls, drilled into us, moving our limbs with a clumsiness alien rather than human. How could it be otherwise, when we interact with machines all day every day: in the morning, Sonicare toothbrush, refrigerator, microwave, stove, phone, car, computer; and returning home, dishwasher, clothes washer, dryer, hairdryer, TV, Sonicare. A *Gesellschaft* world is Borg. As a literary figure the Borg only exaggerate, render visible, a true description of these times.

The Borg would be a false metaphor if we were talking about humans before civilization, who lived within a communal band. These early humans did not have technology drilled into them, and their agency was unsullied. Except, in this pre-*Gesellschaft* time, before the modern self was formed, although human agency remained intact, and had not yet been Borged, it was also dispersed. The animism common among early peoples dispersed individual human agency out onto the natural world, investing it into rocks and trees and wind.

The paradox: an individual human, possessed of agency, is a Western and modern project, and did not exist thousands of years ago; but risks being false, a lie to itself, because such agency is not conceivable, except in a *Gesellschaft* world, where its demise is always threatened by an assault of social things. That kind of social structure, hostile to individual agency, was blessedly absent in early times, before the Agricultural Revolution; but then, there were no modern selves, no individuals as we use that word in the West, to grab hold of agency, and gather it back into themselves, from the rocks, trees, and ambient spirits who laid claim to it.

The Borg is one of several metaphors I wove through the book. In rough order, the clotted prose of sociologists was compared to the hot congealment of lava, which petrifies what it touches. Turner's (2010) demotic turn was recast as a megaphone, and Bourdieu's work compared to a beautiful garden gone rank from neglect. The Web was represented as a new printing press, and Yelp a modern soapbox. The market was rejected as a false metaphor for Yelp. Publication was depicted as spark striking tinder. Institutional structure was compared to terrain and individual agency to water. Pinterest was compared to a ghostly adventure, and its effects explained as a zipless buy.

All of these devices can be dismissed as mere metaphor, as affectation or useless ornament; even, as not scholarly. Yet, I seem to ask you to take them seriously, as knowledge—not as representation, but as substance. How can mere metaphor be knowledge? Foucault can help us here.

Foucault is like Bourdieu. Everyone knows the name, and knows that this fellow is supposed to have said something important, or at least interesting; but few are certain exactly what.[1] And they were both French, which in an Anglo-Saxon context, may excite either a healthy skepticism, or an unhealthy idolatry. This Epilogue builds on the Foucault who wrote the *Order of Things* (1970) and *The Archaeology of Knowledge* (1972), works mostly eclipsed in the scholarly consciousness today, by his earlier studies of madness, and later studies of sexuality. Foucault did seem to change his mind a lot, with every book and pronouncement, to the point of mocking himself for it, front-running his critics, in the Preface to the *Archaeology of Knowledge*. Hence, what follows won't be any kind of intellectual history, any more than Essay One was a careful history of Bourdieu's thinking on cultural capital. For my purposes, Foucault is good to think with, which only means that these thoughts started while reading him.

The key insight from the *Order of Things*: our way of thinking—our fundamental conceptual stance toward the world—is historically situated, and temporary. A deep and maybe unbridgeable gap separates how we think today, in our era, from how people a few centuries ago thought, even though they might speak the same language, and use many of the same words. Of course, this insight drives any intellectual history: to show that people used to think differently than we do today, and to bring alive both the internal coherence and the necessary conflicts, of those now vanished ways of making sense of the world. What's profound in Foucault is the idea that the gap that separates is profound: so gaping as to call into question how we could both be right, those of us thinking now, versus our predecessors thinking then; or whether either of us could possibly get it right, now, then, or later. Foucault notes wryly that our predecessors were sure they were right, just as Richard Dawkins, and Stephen Hawking, are convinced they have the right of it now. Dawkins knows that religious and supernatural accounts of life, anything but the blindest natural selection, are purest bunk. He doesn't believe; he knows. Hawking knows that physicists have obsolesced philosophy. He doesn't just think that to be the case; he has proof. So also, medieval thinkers knew that walnuts had to be good food for the brain, because walnuts and brains looked the same, had the same convolutions. Long ago, similarity had to be meaningful, it could not be accidental; as well, ask Dawkins today to believe the reverse, that life was not accidental, but had some purpose; he knows that not to be true. We knew differently, once, and we may know differently still, on some later day.

Here I need to inoculate you against a misunderstanding of Foucault that is widespread in some corners of academia (he's been dead for 30 years, and can't defend himself). The conventional trope: Foucault was an aggressive relativist, who denied the possibility of objective knowledge. Foucault was adopted to that end, by scholars in the Humanities, unhappy with the growing dominance of the sciences within American universities in the 1980s and 1990s, as elsewhere in Late Capitalist times. Personally, I have never, in my adult thinking, found relativism to be a defensible philosophical position, and reading Shelby Hunt cemented that reluctance. So the first step in making Foucault useful to consumer sociology is to spare him conviction on that charge.

In "Truth and Power," part of a collection of essays translated as *Power / Knowledge*, Foucault (1980) discusses how he came to study the epistemological claims of medicine and psychiatry, rather than physics. I infer from this essay that Foucault was quite happy to let physics escape from history, and to accept $E = mc^2$ as knowledge, as truth, now, then, and later;[2] likewise with DNA replication, or the kinetics of motion. It was claimants to scientific status, as in psychiatry, whose claims were open to doubt, on whom he focused. A quick check now, especially any of you with quantitative training, who have stuck with me this far: do you think of psychiatry today as a successful science, successful at least on the order of genetics, if not chemistry and physics? No? Me neither. How about . . . social psychology, political science, and the other social sciences? Not sure? Neither was Foucault.

Let's approach Foucault as someone who made distinctions among claimants to scientific status, and who separated out weaker claimants, tied to more suspect methodologies, with scanty evidence of success in the form of technological achievement. It is these claimant disciplines, and only these, that he subjected to a searching historical critique, and in so doing, called the scientific project of the social sciences into question. This is how we may escape the now stale science wars of my youth: yes, physics is knowledge, and chemistry is real, and genes govern, but social things, our being together: do we have, can we have, scientific knowledge of collectivities, with the word knowledge used in the exact same sense as in physics? I remain agnostic.

Hewing to an agnostic frame of mind, we can extract, from Foucault, ideas important to any nascent discipline aimed at social knowledge, such as my project here of a consumer sociology. The Borg metaphor provides a focus. The question of interest: can referring to a literary device, such as the Borg in the *Star Trek* series, provide, contain—yea, discover—knowledge? Can a redescription of social structure, as Borg, state knowledge? The dominant answer in the West, since the Scientific Revolution (Shapin 1996), and the Death of Rhetoric (Bender and Wellbery 1990; Lanham 2006a), has been a firm "No."

Let's be clear: most scientists accept that metaphor can be helpful to a popularizer—oh, term of scorn, here in scholar world—and that a metaphor can translate actual scientific knowledge, can serve as a useful teaching device to convey the gist of a scientific finding to an audience unable to follow the science itself. But a metaphor cannot produce knowledge, it can only express knowledge in a form more palatable to a junior, novice, undereducated, dare I say subaltern, audience. Metaphor belongs to style

(Sword 2012), and has no truck with content. Any scientist knows that to be the case.

A sociologist does well to contest this settled wisdom. Consider the kind of expression that has been accepted, since the Scientific Revolution, as itself consisting of knowledge, as directly providing knowledge, real knowledge, truly scientific knowledge. For example:

$$X = V_0 t + \tfrac{1}{2} a t^2$$

In words: the distance travelled, by a body made to accelerate, will equal its initial velocity, plus one-half its acceleration multiplied by the square of the time elapsed, subject to the use of common units to measure distance, velocity, and acceleration.

Such equations, which abound in kinetics and the physics of heat, are accepted by scholars, in claimant disciplines outside the physical sciences, to contain true knowledge. That's the root of physics envy: if you know velocity, acceleration, and time, you know distance; if you know mass, volume, and initial temperature, of ice cube and water, you know how much you can cool 100 milliliters of water by dropping in one ice cube weighing ten grams.

Look closely at that physics equation. With it, we can diagnose the terrible writing style, common in social science, which so vexes Billig (2013; cf. Lanham 2006b). The canonical form of social science style:

[long noun phrase] → [is] → [longer noun phrase] → [preposition] → [noun phrase] . . . [repeat].

In simple outline:

$$X = Y + Z.$$

Sentences, in social science, ape, in words, the mathematics of physics equations. Physics envy in action.

To misquote Isaiah: "Mathematics is the Lord of Knowledge and there is no Other, no true Knowledge, apart from Mathematics, but only Pretenders, and Falsity." I poke a little fun by describing the devotion to quantification, common across the social sciences, in religious terms. But it is a serious point. Today large numbers of college-educated and graduate-trained individuals in America—scholars, but also business people and journalists, almost everyone not a committed practitioner of a Humanities discipline—know, really know, that that mangled quote from the Bible, however sarcastic my intent, states the truth. If something can't be quantified, expressed in a mathematical formula, it isn't real knowledge. Can't be. There is only one kind of true knowledge, and it is scientific knowledge, which is mathematically formulated knowledge. All else is opinion, surmise, or mere rhetoric, a poetic gloss on the real.

Foucault helps: he explains how, in the era before the Scientific Revolution, eminent thinkers knew, really knew, that similarity in appearance meant connection in being, connection at the root, real connection. There could be no accidental similarity. If the Borg resemble the automatons into which social structure can turn individuals, then the Borg, and stories of the Borg, must state some truth about social structure, reveal structure as it really is, convey knowledge that may not be captured, any better any other way.

To embroider the theme with which I began the book: it is hard to overstate the distaste that quantitatively trained scholars feel, toward the claim that math falls short, that there is a place math can't go, that is also a place of knowledge. Nothing I write here will change the mind of any established scholar who feels that way. The Borg have got him. The play again is for the PhD student, who will sit in seminars, and see math lauded above all, by almost every instructor, for everything, everywhere, all the time, as the one and only true path to knowledge. If, using Foucault's historical perspective, I can plant a seed of doubt, lift the spell, render uncertain these heady claims for math, for a few students, then, someday, things may change. You might be our Captain Picard, who escapes.

NOTES

1. That is, everyone who took a degree in literature or any of the social sciences, from about 1980 through the present. It was, of course, possible to study economics, or take a more behavioral path in psychology, and remain blissfully ignorant of either man.
2. Recently Unger and Smolin (2015) question whether physics itself must be seen historically, destroying at a stroke the laudatory comparison of physics to lesser disciplines, on which physics envy rests; and messing up my agnostic positioning of sociology as maybe, maybe not a science like physics. However, remembering the streams of nonsense written in the 1980s and 1990s, when Humanists attempted to press quantum physics into service, to allow a little freedom into the world, I would advise the consumer sociologist not to rely too heavily on Unger and Smolin. But do read them, if these questions about science hold appeal.

Appendix A: Effects of feedback

DATA

In fall of 2011 we[1] collected the most recent 160 reviews from eight San Jose restaurants in diverse categories (steakhouses, sushi, French, barbecue), selecting in each two restaurants from among those with the highest volume of reviews. These restaurants had accumulated between 300 and 1600 reviews apiece. Collecting their 160 most recent got us reviews produced in the past six months to two years, depending on restaurant. All sampled reviewers had been active within that period. A research assistant tabulated reviewer data by consulting reviewer profiles. Only the reviewers who could also be located a year later, during the follow-up, are reported here.

MEASURES

We obtained reviewers' total count of useful votes, funny votes, and cool votes from their profile pages. As these proved to be correlated at 0.98 or greater, these three were summed to create a count of total feedback received. Next, the review count, as displayed opposite each review, was tabulated. Because these variables had a strong positive skew, for statistical analyses, the natural log of each was used (first adding 1 to feedback counts, since these can take values of zero). One year later, we collected these variables again, using a script.

INITIAL FINDINGS, 2011

We found a very strong linear association between the logs of feedback count and review production, with $r = 0.91$. Also, every reviewer in the sample who had produced more than ten reviews had also received at least one feedback vote.

The median count was 27 reviews produced; 70 percent had produced a dozen or more reviews; to be in the top quartile required production of 100 or more reviews; and to be in the top decile required almost 250 reviews. Next we consider the effects of feedback over time.

MEASURES

We subtracted review count in 2011 from review count as of 2012 to get the dependent variables: whether review production was sustained, and at what volume. To measure whether reviewing was sustained, the count was dichotomized; for volume, we took the natural log to address the skew.

A dummy variable was created to identify novices, defined as those with ten or fewer reviews, as these were the only review count levels where feedback was not universally received. Only for these people, where there was sometimes an absence of feedback, could we test for the rewarding effect, of receiving any feedback at all.

ANALYSIS

Data were analyzed in keeping with the two-part model commonly used in public health and ecological research (for example, when analyzing how many patients were hospitalized, but also how much was spent in the event hospitalization occurred; or whether a species was present in a biome, and if so, with how many organisms; see Afifi et al. 2007).

FINDINGS, 2012

In the ensuing year, about 77 percent of these reviewers produced one or more additional reviews, 38 percent produced ten or more new reviews, and 5 percent produced more than 100 additional reviews. However, only 54 percent of the novices sustained review production, as compared to 86 percent of established reviewers, and 94 percent of reviewers who had accumulated 100 or more reviews.

We found no evidence that amount of feedback received gave a boost to future review production (Table A.1). The beta coefficient for the natural log of feedback, after first entering the log of review production as of t_1, was slightly negative but not significantly different from zero (B = −0.057, $t = -1.32$, $p = 0.18$). The bias-corrected, bootstrapped, 95 percent confidence interval, per Hayes's (2013) procedure, on the product of the beta coefficients, from review production to feedback, and from feedback to subsequent review production, was computed as − 0.176 to + 0.04.

Table A.1   Effect of feedback on reviewer productivity

	B	SE	t
Log review count at t_1 → log of subsequent review production, if any	0.770	0.06	13.0***
Log review count at t_1 → log of feedback at t_1[a]	1.247	0.016	76.7***
Log of feedback at t_1 → log of subsequent review production, if any	−0.057	0.043	−1.32
Indirect effect (1.247 x −0.057)	−0.071		
95% Confidence interval on indirect effect[b]	−0.176 to +0.040		

Notes:
These tests were performed on the subsample that produced one or more subsequent reviews ($n = 900$), and the coefficient reported is the unstandardized B from an OLS regression.
a   Feedback count was incremented by 1 prior to taking the log, inasmuch as some feedback counts were zero.
b   This is the bias-corrected bootstrapped confidence interval computed using the INDIRECT macro for SPSS developed by Hayes (2013). As it includes zero, the total indirect effect of reviews as mediated by feedback is taken to be not significantly different from zero.
* $p < 0.05$** $p < 0.01$*** $p < 0.001$.
SE = standard error.

Because this confidence interval includes zero, we concluded that feedback neither has a direct effect on subsequent review production, nor does it participate in an indirect effect of past review production on subsequent production. Among continuing reviewers, there is no evidence that feedback functions as a reward.[2]

Next, reviews at t_1, feedback at t_1, and a dummy variable indicating novice status (review count ≤ 10), were regressed on the dichotomous measure indicating whether review production had been sustained (Table A.2). The test of interest is whether the interaction term, formed by multiplying feedback by novice status, has a positive and significant coefficient. This proved to be the case: for individuals whose review production was not well established, amount of feedback did have a positive coefficient of 0.042 (Wald's statistic = 6.7, $p = 0.01$). Also, low review count per se was associated with a reduced probability that review production would be sustained. Among more established reviewers, feedback had no significant impact on this likelihood (Table A.2). The significant interaction indicates that

Table A.2   Effect of feedback on whether reviewing is sustained

	B	SE	Wald's statistic
Review count at t_1 → probability of any subsequent review production	0.010	0.002	18.9***
Dummy variable for novice reviewer → probability of any subsequent review production	−1.20	0.196	37.4***
Feedback at t_1 → probability of any subsequent review production	0.001	0.001	0.01
Interaction term → probability of any subsequent review production (effect of feedback for novices)	0.042	0.016	6.7**

Notes:
For these tests a logistic regression on the entire sample ($n = 1110$) was used.
* $p < 0.05$ ** $p < 0.01$ *** $p < 0.001$.
SE = standard error.

receiving greater amounts of feedback does increase the probability that review writing will be sustained, but only for less well-established reviewers. To probe further the effects of feedback on novice reviewers, we examined a cross-tabulation of the 331 reviewers with ten or fewer reviews authored as of t_1 (Table A.3). The odds of receiving no feedback decline rapidly as reviews accumulate. In a log-linear analysis, we tested a 10 (level of review production at t_1) x 2 (presence or absence of feedback at t_1) x 2 (no / any subsequent review production) design (see Table A.3 for cross-tabulation). Backwards elimination was used to determine which interactions were significant. This analysis showed a significant three-way interaction ($\chi^2 (9) = 22.9, p < 0.01$). Even within this group of novice reviewers, it is at the lowest levels of review count that the presence or absence of feedback makes the greatest difference. Looking at the 183 individuals with initial review counts of five or fewer, the odds that they would sustain review production were more than twice as high if they got feedback. Among these minimally productive reviewers, 70 percent of those who got feedback produced additional reviews, as opposed to 33 percent of those who got no feedback.

Receiving feedback does increase the probability that review production will be sustained, and in volume; but only for the least well-established reviewers. Feedback makes no difference once reviewing gets established as a regular practice, if only because all these reviewers get feedback.

Table A.3   Feedback and novice reviewers

Review count at t_1	Any feedback at t_1	No subsequent review	Any subsequent review	Totals	% receiving feedback
1	No	20	7	27	
	Yes	–*	–	–	0.0
2	No	21	11	32	
	Yes	–	5	5	13.5
3	No	12	4	16	
	Yes	–	11	11	40.7
4	No	6	3	9	
	Yes	19	17	36	80.0
5	No	2	5	7	
	Yes	9	31	40	85.1
6	No	1	2	3	
	Yes	16	15	31	91.2
7	No	1	1	2	
	Yes	14	15	29	93.5
8	No	2	1	3	
	Yes	9	17	26	89.7
9	No	3	0	3	
	Yes	8	18	26	89.7
10	No	–	1	1	
	Yes	8	16	24	96.0

Notes:
Novice reviewers were defined as the 331 individuals who had accumulated ten or fewer reviews as of the initial data collection.
* Indicates empty cell; i.e., for this first occurrence, none of the individuals with exactly one review at t_1 had received any feedback as of t_1.

NOTES

1. In these Appendices, 'we' refers to me and my co-authors, Shelby McIntyre and Ravi Shanmugam. We conducted this research jointly.
2. Because reviewers in the sample have different tenures, we repeated the test substituting rate of feedback (# feedback votes / # reviews). This also produced a negative but non-significant B coefficient ($p > 0.20$). Note that rate of feedback itself is significantly correlated with level of review production ($p < 0.001$). Among established reviewers, more productive reviewers receive feedback at a higher rate.

Appendix B: Predicting feedback

We collected three datasets of Yelp reviews from mid-2011 through mid-2012: (1) the feedback sample described in Appendix A, which for this study was reused to develop content analysis codes ($n = 640$ review texts); (2) a set of filtered reviews ($n = 522$); and (3) a new test set of reviews ($n = 865$). For the filtered dataset we sampled up to 80 filtered reviews from each of the eight restaurants in the developmental sample. For the test dataset, we added four new restaurants, yielding a sample of six expensive and six inexpensive restaurants that had the highest review counts in their respective categories. We then gathered reviews from the most recent eight months, capping the number of reviews per restaurant at 100.

With our two MBA research assistants, we read widely in the sample of reviews, to identify text properties that seemed to be associated with better reviews. For example, some reviews described specific menu items, and those reviews seemed to be of better quality. The coded properties that survived a series of pretests are given in Table B.1. For validation, the table shows that the codes that, in our opinion, marked out better reviews, were also significantly more common in reviews written by Yelp Elite. These properties also distinguish filtered from regular from Elite reviews; see Table B.2. Better-quality reviews were less common among the filtered reviews, and more common in reviews from Elite, honored reviewers. This means that Yelp's filter is good at weeding out weak reviews, and that Yelp is effective in nominating as Elite people who can write better reviews.

Next, we tried to predict the amount of feedback received by a review. This differs from the feedback study in Appendix A, where the focus was on lifetime total feedback received by reviewers. Here the test is whether review feedback is just noise, or whether better reviews, as judged by the content analysis, are more likely to receive positive feedback from Yelp members. We test the binary case (any feedback at all), and test for quantity (larger or smaller amounts of positive feedback).

For these tests, we controlled for how expensive the restaurant was (reviews of more expensive restaurants offer more dollar value, and may get more feedback), and how negative or positive was the rating given (extreme ratings carry more information, in the Shannon and Weaver

Table B.1   Properties that mark out better from worse reviews

Type/property	Rationale for association with review merit	Contingency coefficient (Elite)	χ^2	Reliabilities (Krippendorf's α)[b]	
				Test sample	Filtered sample
Specificity					
Menu item(s) described	Useful to have evaluation of items and not just restaurant	0.20	28.1***	0.68	0.79
Concrete details	More informative with respect to total dining experience	0.12	9.3**	0.38	0.31
Contextualization	"Took client for business meal" provides context	0.08	3.6[a]	0.69	0.76
Audience awareness					
Story form	Stories are easy to read and persuasive	0.07	3.4[a]	0.42	0.37
Cross-referenced	A review that references other reviews can be more easily integrated	0.07	2.9[a]	0.57	0.72
Explanation of rating	Provides context for numerical rating given	0.10	6.5**	0.81	0.84

Notes:
Contingency coefficients are from the initial sample ($n = 640$) on which the codes were developed. Columns show strength of the association between the text property and Elite status (1/4 the initial sample were Elite), followed by the reliability of the codes in the test and filtered samples. Reliabilities in the initial sample were lower, inasmuch as coders trained on that set, and are not shown.
* $p < 0.05$; ** $p < 0.01$; *** $p < 0.001$.
a $p < 0.10$ two-tailed
b   See Krippendorf (2004) for problems with more conventional measures of reliability, such as % agreement and Cohen's κ.

Table B.2 *Better reviews are less likely to be filtered*

Type / Property		Filtered reviews	Ordinary reviews	Elite reviews	Test of linearity (χ^2)	Somers' d
Menu item(s) described	No	278	218	46		
	Yes	244 (46.7%)	433 (66.5%)	168 (78.5%)	78.4***	0.20***
Concrete details	No	384	395	100		
	Yes	138 (26.4%)	256 (39.3%)	114 (53.3%)	50.9***	0.16***
Contextualization	No	399	452	121		
	Yes	123 (23.6%)	199 (30.6%)	93 (43.5%)	27.6***	0.11***
Story form	No	511	628	184		
	Yes	11 (2.1%)	23 (3.5%)	30 (14.0%)	37.5***	0.06***
Cross-referenced	No	488	596	179		
	Yes	34 (6.5%)	55 (8.4%)	35 (16.4%)	15.0***	0.05***
Explanation of rating[a]	No	488	575	191		
	Yes	34 (6.5%)	76 (11.7%)	23 (10.7%)	5.9*	0.04**

Notes:
Results are for the combined test (n = 865) and filtered (n = 522) samples. The χ^2 test is the Mantel–Haenszel test for linearity in SPSS and Somers'
d is a measure of how well each code predicts classification of a review as filtered, ordinary, or Elite.
a Although this code satisfies the statistical test for linearity, its proportion of incidence was not monotonically increasing across the three groups
   and it was not used in subsequent regressions.
* $p < 0.05$** $p < 0.01$*** $p < 0.001$.

1949 sense), and how many friends the reviewer had (we assumed that Yelp members are more likely to give feedback to reviews written by friends).

The tests reported are hierarchical regressions, in which control variables are entered first, and text properties last. This teases out the unique contribution of better-quality review text, to answer the question: after controlling for extraneous factors, do better reviews get more positive feedback, or not? If so, then Yelp members can and should place more trust in reviews that get positive feedback; these votes are signal, not noise.

The regressions showed that the more friends a reviewer had, the more feedback his or her reviews got (Table B.3). Feedback is a biased signal: it doesn't always mean a review is good, but sometimes just means the writer had a lot of friends.

Restaurant expense was strongly associated with feedback. Expensive restaurants are risky, so that a review can be more valuable, which translates into greater odds of that review receiving feedback. Rating discrepancy—unusually negative or positive numbers—also predicted whether a review would garner feedback. As predicted by information theory, reviews that come to an unusual judgment of a restaurant—especially negative ratings—get more positive feedback.

Based on these tests, at best, feedback is a noisy signal of review quality. But it is nonetheless a signal, and not just noise: adding the five properties that mark out better reviews provided a significant increment in prediction. For the logistic regression, for entry of the block χ^2 (5) = 11.1, $p < 0.05$, and for the regression on log feedback, R^2 change = 0.039, F (5, 342) = 3.9, $p < 0.005$).

Despite its many distortions, on Yelp feedback sends a signal, albeit noisy, that picks out better from worse reviews. Some trust can be placed in feedback.

Table B.3 Predicting whether a review will receive feedback

Variable(s)	Logistic regression on any feedback (n = 865)				OLS regression on log of feedback if any (n = 352)		
	(1) Zero-order association (r)	(2) Wald	(3) χ^2	(4) ΔR^2	(5) b	(6) F (change)	(7) ΔR^2
Social factor							
Count friends (log)	0.53**	48.1***	52.7***	0.059	0.36***	50.8***	0.127
Information theory factors							
Expensive restaurant	0.23**	36.4***	52.9***	0.056	.24***	42.7***	0.095
Rating			23.4***	0.023		13.5***	0.056
Discrepancy	0.07*	9.9**			0.24***		
Positivity	0.08*	1.2			0.31***		
Text properties			11.1*	0.011		3.9**	0.039
4a. Menu item(s)	0.08*	1.8			-0.01		
4b. Concrete details	0.15**	0.3			0.09		
4c. Contextualization	0.11**	0.2			0.03		
4d. Story form	0.26**	3.2			0.10*		
4e. Cross-referenced	0.08*	1.6			0.11*		

Notes:
The columns give: (1) the correlation coefficient, on the entire sample, for each predictor, with the untransformed count of feedback votes; (2) the Wald statistic, in the complete logistic regression, for each individual predictor; (3) the χ^2 test of whether a predictor or block of predictors provided a significant increment in prediction when entered in the order shown; (4) the increase in Cox–Snell R^2 produced by entering that predictor or block; (5) for the regression on logs, for the subsample that got any feedback, the standardized beta for each predictor in the complete regression; (6) the F statistic for the change in R^2 produced by adding a predictor or set of predictors in the order shown; and (7) the increase in R^2 at each step.

* $p < 0.05$ ** $p < 0.01$ *** $p < 0.001$.

Appendix C: Reviews that get filtered

DATA AND ANALYSIS

We combined the filtered and test datasets, and used a binary logistic regression to examine properties that distinguish filtered reviews.

VARIABLES

Prior literature has identified low review count, low word count, and rating extremity as correlates of reviews likely to be fake or otherwise untrustworthy (Luca and Zervas 2013; Mayzlin et al. 2012; Pan and Zhang 2011). Intuitively, a short review from a consumer with no history that gives an extreme rating is more likely to be dishonest or incompetent, and hence, untrustworthy. Here extremity was measured by two dummy variables, picking out ratings of '1' and '5' respectively.

We also tested friend count and lifetime totals of feedback. Because the zero level may be meaningful in its own right (that is, the difference between having one friend versus none may matter more, than the difference between having ten and 20 friends), both friend count and lifetime feedback were split into zero/any, and both the binary and intact counts (as logs) were tested.

FINDINGS

Word counts, and the reviewer's count of reviews, were good predictors of filtered status (Table C.1). About 55 percent of filtered reviews came from reviewers with five or fewer reviews posted (versus about 13 percent for non-filtered), while the mean word count for filtered versus non-filtered reviews was 88 and 158, respectively. New or inactive reviewers were more likely to have a review filtered, and short reviews were also more likely to be filtered. Contrary to prior work, rating extremity—a possible rant or rave—was not a unique predictor of whether a review would be filtered.

Table C.1 *Predicting which reviews will get filtered*

Factor	(1) Zero-order associations	(2) Non-social factors		(3) Increment for social factors		(4) Stepwise analysis (order of entry)	
	(Score to enter)	B	Wald	B	Wald	B	Wald
Previously Investigated:							
Review count (log)	426.0***	−0.94	269.5***			(2) −0.78	117.6***
Word count (log)	103.9***	−0.39	33.1***			(3) −0.39	30.2***
Extremity-negative	9.5**	0.25	0.6				
Extremity-positive	3.6	−0.15	1.1				
Social factors							
Any friends	448.9***			−1.46	38.8***	(1) −1.7	122.5***
Friend count (log)	406.8***			−0.09	1.0		
Any lifetime feedback	116.7***			0.73	9.1**	(4) 0.53	6.7**
Lifetime feedback count (log)	369.6***			−0.15	2.4		
Total R² (Cox and Snell)		0.325		0.389		0.386	
Filtered reviews correctly classified		354 (67.8%)		391 (74.9%)		379 (72.6%)	
False positives		150 (10.8%)		130 (9.4%)		127 (9.2%)	
False negatives		168 (12.1%)		131 (9.4%)		143 (10.3%)	

Notes:
Table shows results for a series of logistic regressions run to predict membership in the filtered versus the test sample. Columns show: (1) Rao's score to enter the regression for all variables; (2) results of a logistic regression with just the four non-social factors previously investigated in the literature; (3) coefficients and test statistics for the four social variables when these are added to the regression containing the non-social factors; and (4) a stepwise analysis in which non-social and social factors compete for entry into the regression, and numbers in parentheses indicate order of entry. Note the positive sign on the coefficient for any lifetime feedback (e.g., reviewers who had received at least some feedback over their reviewing history), and see text for interpretation.

The third column in Table C.1 evaluates the contribution of adding the four social variables to the regression. The binary measures of friends and feedback supplied a highly significant increment in prediction, while the intact counts did not. Collectively, the social variables improve the Cox—Snell R^2 from 0.325 to 0.389, and with their addition, the procedure is able to correctly classify 74 percent of the filtered cases, as compared to 68 percent for the factors taken from prior literature. False positives and negatives are now notably fewer than correctly classified filtered cases (261, versus 391 mistaken classifications when social variables are excluded). Reviews from people with no friends, who have never received any positive feedback, are very likely to be filtered by Yelp.

There was one disconcerting finding: filtered reviews—which for the most part are short reviews from newcomers—were more likely to be authored by individuals with non-zero lifetime feedback. Inspection of the data shows that among non-filtered reviews, all authors with counts of one review, two reviews, or three reviews showed zero lifetime totals for second-order feedback. New reviewers typically don't get feedback at first. Conversely, of the filtered reviews from reviewers with counts of 1, 2, or 3, almost half these authors had received some second-order feedback despite this short history; and several of these had piled up dozens of feedback votes.

This finding may reflect the insight of Kornish (2009): that individuals whose first-order feedback—the review itself—reflects bad intentions, will probably try to game second-order feedback as well. We surmise that the Yelp algorithm is tuned to spot whether reviews that are otherwise suspect—short, from newcomers, who have no friends—are even more suspicious, because the authors show unduly high levels of lifetime feedback. If second-order feedback tends to come from friends, and if friends are made by writing good reviews in volume, then the presence of second-order feedback in the absence of friends, and without much of a review history, serves as a signal that the reviewer is suspect. He cheated. Paradoxically, the fact that second-order feedback is susceptible to being gamed, and hence, a weak signal of trust for the unaided buyer-reader, makes it a useful signal, in reverse, at the institutional level of Yelp.

Overall, absence of friends was the single best predictor of ending up in the filter, followed by review count, word count, and any feedback (Table C.1, right column). By itself, absence of friends was able to correctly classify 71.6 percent of filtered reviews.

Next we tested the text properties, examined in Appendix B as markers of review quality, to determine whether they could incrementally predict Yelp's filtering of reviews. These text properties did provide a modest increment in prediction of filtered status (for entry of the block, χ^2 (5) = 13.3, $p < 0.05$). Weak and uninformative reviews are also more likely to be filtered. This suggests that Yelp algorithmically scores review texts for linguistic content, and not just for word count and for reviewer properties, in making decisions about which reviews are not trustworthy.

References

Afifi, Abdelmonem A., Jenny B. Kotlerman, Susan L. Ettner, and Mary Cowan (2007), "Methods for Improving Regression Analysis for Skewed Continuous or Counted Responses," *Annual Review of Public Health*, 28, 95–111.

Anderson, Chris (2006), *The Long Tail: Why the Future of Business Is Selling Less of More*, Berkeley, CA: Hyperion Books.

Anderson, Michael and Jeremy Magruder (2012), "Learning from the Crowd: Regression Discontinuity Estimates of the Effects of an Online Review Database," *Economic Journal*, 122 (563), 957–89.

Andreoni, James (2007), "Giving Gifts to Groups: How Altruism Depends on the Number of Recipients," *Journal of Public Economics*, 91 (9), 1731–49.

Angyal, Andras (1973), *Neurosis and Treatment: A Holistic Theory*, New York: Viking Press.

Arndt, Johan (1967), "Role of Product-Related Conversations in the Diffusion of a New Product," *Journal of Marketing Research*, 4 (3), 291.

Arnold, Matthew (1869), *Culture and Anarchy*, London: Smith, Elder.

Arnould, Eric J. and Linda L. Price (2003), "Authenticating Acts and Authoritative Performances: Questing for Self and Community," in S. Ratneshwar, David G. Mick and Cynthia Huffman (eds), *The Why of Consumption: Contemporary Perspectives on Consumer Motives, Goals and Desires*, London: Routledge Press, pp. 140–63.

Arnould, Eric J. and Craig J. Thompson (2005), "Consumer Culture Theory (CCT): Twenty Years of Research," *Journal of Consumer Research*, 31 (March), 868–82.

Arsel, Zeynep and Jonathan Bean (2013), "Taste Regimes and Market-Mediated Practice," *Journal of Consumer Research*, 39 (February), 899–917.

Arsel, Zeynep and Craig Thompson (2011), "Demythologizing Consumption Practices: How Consumers Protect Their Field-Dependent Identity Investments from Devaluing Marketplace Myths," *Journal of Consumer Research*, 37 (February), 791–806.

Arvidsson, Adam E. (2013), "The Potential of Consumer Publics," *Ephemera*, 13 (2), 367–91.

Askegaard, Søren (2014), "Consumer Culture Theory–Neo-liberalism's 'Useful Idiots'?," *Marketing Theory*, 14 (December), 501–4.

Baron, Stephen, John Field and Thomas Schuller (2000), *Social Capital: Critical Perspectives*, New York: Oxford University Press.

Bayley, Stephen (1991), *Taste: The Secret Meaning of Things*, New York: Pantheon.

Becker, Gary Stanley (1993), *Human Capital: A Theoretical and Empirical Analysis, With Special Reference to Education*, Chicago, IL: University of Chicago Press.

Beer, David and Roger Burrows (2010), "Consumption, Prosumption, and Participatory Web Cultures: An Introduction," *Journal of Consumer Culture*, 10 (1), 3–12.

Belk, Russell W. (1988), "Possessions and the Extended Self," *Journal of Consumer Research*, 15 (September), 139–68.

Belk, Russell W. (2010), "Sharing," *Journal of Consumer Research*, 36 (February), 715–34.

Bender, John B. and David E. Wellbery (1990), *The Ends of Rhetoric: History, Theory, Practice*, Palo Alto, CA: Stanford University Press.

Benjamin, Walter (1936), *The Work of Art in the Age of Mechanical Reproduction*, Andy Blunden (trans.), UCLA School of Theatre, Film and Television, www.lib.unc.edu.

Berger, Jonah (2012), "Word-of-Mouth and Interpersonal Communication: An Organizing Framework and Directions for Future Research," working paper.

Berger, Jonah and Morgan Ward (2010), "Subtle Signals of Inconspicuous Consumption," *Journal of Consumer Research*, 37 (4), 555–69.

Bergstrom, Theodore, Lawrence Blume, and Hal Varian (1986), "On the Private Provision of Public Goods," *Journal of Public Economics*, 29 (1), 25.

Berlyne, Daniel E. (1974), *Studies in the New Experimental Aesthetics: Steps Toward an Objective Psychology of Aesthetic Appreciation*, New York: Hemisphere.

Bernthal, Matthew J., David Crockett, and Randall L. Rose (2005), "Credit Cards as Lifestyle Facilitators," *Journal of Consumer Research*, 32 (1), 130–45.

Beverland, Michael B. and Francis J. Farrelly (2009), "The Quest for Authenticity in Consumption: Cues to Shape Experience," *Journal of Consumer Research*, 36 (February), 838–56.

Billig, Michael (2013), *Learn to Write Badly: How to Succeed in the Social Sciences*, Cambridge: University of Cambridge Press.

Bolton, Gary E. and Axel Ockenfels (2000), "ERC: A Theory of Equity,

Reciprocity, and Competition," *American Economic Review*, 90 (1), 166–93.

Bourdieu, Pierre (1980), *The Logic of Practice*, Stanford, CA: Stanford University Press.

Bourdieu, Pierre (1984), *Distinction: A Social Critique of the Judgment of Taste*, Cambridge, MA: Harvard University Press.

Bourdieu, Pierre (1986 [1983]), "The Forms of Capital," in John G. Richardson (ed.), *Handbook of Theory and Research for the Sociology of Education*, London: Greenwood, pp. 241–58.

Bourdieu, Pierre (1990), *In Other Words: Essays Toward a Reflexive Sociology*, Stanford, CA: Stanford University Press.

Bourdieu, Pierre (1991), *Language and Symbolic Power*, Cambridge, MA: Harvard University Press.

Bourdieu, Pierre (1996), *The State Nobility: Elite Schools in the Field of Power*, Stanford, CA: Stanford University Press.

Bourdieu, Pierre (1998), *Practical Reason: On the Theory of Action*, Stanford, CA: Stanford University Press.

Bourdieu, Pierre (1999), *On Television*, New York: New Press.

Bourdieu, Pierre (2005), *The Social Structures of the Economy*, Boston, MA: Polity.

Bourdieu, Pierre (2008), *Sketch for a Self-Analysis*, Chicago, IL: University of Chicago Press.

Bourdieu, Pierre and Jean-Claude Passeron (1977), *Reproduction in Education, Society and Culture*, London: Sage.

Bourdieu, Pierre and Loïc J.D. Wacquant (1992), *An Invitation to Reflexive Sociology*, Chicago, IL: University of Chicago Press.

Campbell, Colin (1987), *The Romantic Ethic and the Spirit of Modern Consumerism*, Oxford: Basil Blackwell.

Campbell, Colin (2005), "The Craft Consumer: Culture, Craft and Consumption in a Postmodern Society," *Journal of Consumer Culture*, 5 (1), 23–42.

Chevalier, Judith A. and Dina Mayzlin (2006), "The Effect of Word of Mouth on Sales: Online Book Reviews," *Journal of Marketing Research*, 43 (3), 345–54.

Chittenden, Tara (2010), "Digital Dressing Up: Modelling Female Teen Identity in the Discursive Spaces of the Fashion Blogosphere," *Journal of Youth Studies*, 13 (4), 505–20.

Cho, Hyeyeung, Norbert Schwarz, and Hyunjin Song (2008), "Images as Preferences: A Feelings-as-Information Analysis," in Michel Wedel and Rik Pieters (eds), *Visual Marketing*, New York: Lawrence Erlbaum Associates, pp. 225–58.

Christensen, Danielle Elise (2011), "'Look At Us Now!' Scrapbooking,

Regimes of Value, and the Risks of (Auto)Ethnography," *Journal of American Folklore*, 124 (493), 175–210.

Clark, Gregory (2014), *The Son Also Rises: Surnames and the History of Social Mobility*, Princeton, NJ: Princeton University Press.

Cova, Bernard and Daniele Dalli (2009), "Working Consumers: The Next Step in Marketing Theory?" *Marketing Theory*, 9 (3), 315–39.

Cova, Bernard and Veronique Cova (2002), "Tribal Marketing, the Tribalization of Society and Its Impact on the Conduct of Marketing," *European Journal of Marketing*, 36 (5–6), 595–629.

Crane, Diana and Laura Bovone (2006), "Approaches to Material Culture: The Sociology of Fashion and Clothing," *Poetics*, 34, 319–33.

Darby, M.R. and E. Karni (1973), "Free Competition and the Optimal Amount of Fraud," *Journal of Law and Economics*, 16 (April), 67–88.

Davis, Fred (1992), *Fashion, Culture, and Identity*, Chicago, IL: University of Chicago Press.

Deci, Edward L. and Richard M. Ryan (2002), *Handbook of Self-Determination Research*, Rochester, NY: University of Rochester Press.

Deighton, John (1992), "The Consumption of Performance," *Journal of Consumer Research*, 19 (December), 362–72.

Dellarocas, Chrysanthos (2011), "Designing Reputation Systems for the Web," in Hassan Masum and Mark Tovey (eds), *The Reputation Society*, Cambridge, MA: MIT Press, pp. 3–12.

Dichter, Ernst (1966), "How Word-of-Mouth Advertising Works," *Harvard Business Review*, 44 (November–December), 147–66.

DiMaggio, Paul (1979), "Review Essay: On Pierre Bourdieu," *American Journal of Sociology*, 84 (6), 1460–74.

Durrer, Victoria and Steven Miles (2009), "New Perspectives on the Role of Cultural Intermediaries in Social Inclusion in the UK," *Consumption Markets and Culture*, 12(3), 225–41.

Dvorak, Petula (2012), "Addicted to a Web Site Called Pinterest: Digital Crack for Women," *Washington Post*, February 20.

Elliott, Richard and Andrea Davies (2006), "Symbolic Brands and Authenticity of Identity Performance," in Jonathan E. Schroeder and Miriam Salzer-Morling (eds), *Brand Culture*, London: Routledge, pp. 155–70.

Entwistle, Joanne (2000), *The Fashioned Body: Fashion, Dress, and Modern Social Theory*, Cambridge: Polity Press.

Erdem, Tulin and Joffre Swait (2004), "Brand Credibility, Brand Consideration, and Choice," *Journal of Consumer Research*, 31 (1), 191–8.

Erickson, Barbara H. (1996), "Culture, Class, and Connections," *American Journal of Sociology*, 102 (1), 217–51.

Ewen, Stuart (1988), *All Consuming Images*, New York: Basic Books.

Falk, Pasi (1994), *The Consuming Body*, London: Sage Publications.

Fantasia, Rick (2010), "Cooking the Books of the French Gastronomic Field," in Elizabeth Silva and Alan Warde (eds), *Cultural Analysis and Bourdieu's Legacy*, London: Routledge, pp. 28–44.

Feick, Lawrence F. and Linda L. Price (1987), "The Market Maven: A Diffuser of Marketplace Information," *Journal of Marketing*, 51 (1), 83–97.

Ferdows, Kasra, Michael A. Lewis, and Jose A.D. Machuca (2004), "Rapid Fire Fulfillment," *Harvard Business Review*, November, reprint.

Firat, A. Fuat and Nikhilesh Dholakia (2006), "Theoretical and Philosophical Implications of Postmodern Debate: Some Challenges to Modern Marketing," *Marketing Theory*, 6 (2), 123–62.

Foucault, Michel (1970), *The Order of Things*, New York: Random House.

Foucault, Michel (1972), *The Archaeology of Knowledge*, New York: Vintage Books.

Foucault, Michel (1980), *Power / Knowledge*, New York: Pantheon.

Gans, Herbert J. (1999), *Popular Culture and High Culture: An Analysis and Evaluation of Taste*, New York: Basic Books.

Giesler, Markus (2006), "Consumer Gift Systems," *Journal of Consumer Research*, 33 (September), 283–90.

Giffin, Kim (1967), "The Contribution of Studies of Source Credibility to a Theory of Interpersonal Trust in the Communication Process," *Psychological Bulletin*, 68 (2), 104–19.

Goffman, Erving (1951), "Symbols of Class Status," *British Journal of Sociology*, 2 (December), 294–304.

Goffman, Erving (1959), *The Presentation of Self in Everyday Life*, New York: Anchor Books.

Goldthorpe, John H. (2007), "Cultural Capital: Some Critical Observations," *Sociologica*, 2, 1–22.

Gonchar, Michael (2013), "How Much Do You Trust Online Reviews?" *New York Times*, September 24.

Gopnik, Adam (2012), *The Table Comes First: Family, France, and the Meaning of Food*, New York: Knopf.

Goulding, Christina, Avi Shankar, and Richard Elliott (2002), "Working Weeks, Rave Weekends: Identity Fragmentation and the Emergence of New Communities," *Consumption Markets & Culture*, 5 (4), 261–84.

Granovetter, Mark S. (1973), "The Strength of Weak Ties," *American Journal of Sociology*, 78 (May), 1360–80.

Gronow, Jukka (1997), *The Sociology of Taste*, Routledge: London.

Gutting, Gary (2011), *Thinking the Impossible: French Philosophy since 1960*, New York: Oxford University Press.

Habermas, Jurgen (1991), *The Structural Transformation of the Public Sphere: An Inquiry into a Category of Bourgeois Society*, Cambridge, MA: MIT Press.

Halle, David (1993), *Inside Culture: Art and Class in the American Home*, Chicago, IL: University of Chicago Press.

Hayes, Andrew F. (2013), *Introduction to Mediation, Moderation, and Conditional Process Analysis*, New York: Guilford Press.

Helfand, Jessica (2008), *Scrapbooks: An American History*, New Haven, CT: Yale University Press.

Hennig-Thurau, Thorsten, Kevin P. Gwinner, Gianfranco Walsh, and Dwayne D. Gremler (2004), "Electronic Word-Of-Mouth Via Consumer-Opinion Platforms: What Motivates Consumers to Articulate Themselves on the Internet?," *Journal of Interactive Marketing*, 18 (1), 38–52.

Hennion, Antoine (2010), "The Price of the People: Sociology, Performance, and Reflexivity," in Elizabeth Silva and Alan Warde (eds), *Cultural Analysis and Bourdieu's Legacy*, London: Routledge, pp. 117–27.

Henry, Paul C. (2005), "Social Class, Market Situation, and Consumers' Metaphors of (Dis)Empowerment," *Journal of Consumer Research*, 31 (4), 766–78.

Herbst, Kenneth C., Eli J. Finkel, David Allan, and Grainne M. Fitzsimmons (2012), "On the Dangers of Pulling a Fast One: Advertisement Disclaimer Speed, Brand Trust, and Purchase Intention," *Journal of Consumer Research*, 38 (February), 909–20.

Hodkinson, Paul (2007), "Interactive Online Journals and Individualization," *New Media and Society*, 9 (4), 625–50.

Holmes, Oliver Wendell (1980 [1859]), "The Stereoscope and the Stereograph," in Beaumont Newhall (ed.), *Photography: Essays and Images*, New York: Museum of Modern Art, pp. 53–62.

Holt, Douglas (1998), "Does Cultural Capital Structure American Consumption?" *Journal of Consumer Research*, 25 (June), 1–25.

Holt, Douglas (2002), "Why Do Brands Cause Trouble? A Dialectical Theory of Consumer Culture and Branding," *Journal of Consumer Research*, 29 (June), 70–90.

Hovland, Carl I., Irving K. Janis, and Harold H. Kelley (1953), *Communication and Persuasion*, New Haven, CT: Yale University Press.

Hovland, Carl I. and Walter Weiss (1951), "The Influence of Source Credibility on Communication Effectiveness," *Public Opinion Quarterly*, 15 (Winter), 635–50.

Huizinga, Johan (1949), *Homo Ludens: A Study of the Play Element in Culture*, London: Taylor & Francis.

Hunt, Shelby D. and Robert M. Morgan (1996), "The Resource-Advantage Theory of Competition: Dynamics, Path Dependencies, and Evolutionary Dimensions," *Journal of Marketing*, 107–14.

Jameson, Fredric (1991), *Postmodernism, Or, the Cultural Logic of Late Capitalism*, Raleigh, NC: Duke University Press.

Jarrett, Kylie (2003), "Labour of Love: An Archeology of Affect as Power in E-Commerce," *Journal of Sociology*, 39 (4), 335–51.

Johnston, Josee and Shyon Baumann (2010), *Foodies: Democracy and Distinction in the Gourmet Foodscape*, New York: Routledge.

Joy, Annamma and John F. Sherry, Jr. (2003), "Speaking of Art as Embodied Imagination: A Multisensory Approach to Understanding Aesthetic Experience," *Journal of Consumer Research*, 30 (September), 259–82.

Kahneman, Daniel (2011), *Thinking, Fast and Slow*, New York: Macmillan.

Kassarjian, Harold H. and Ronald C. Goodstein (2010), "The Emergence of Consumer Research," in Pauline Maclaran (ed.), *The Sage Handbook of Marketing Theory*, Los Angeles, CA: Sage, pp. 59–73.

Katriel, Tamar and Thomas Farrell (1991), "Scrapbooks as Cultural Texts: An American Art of Memory," *Text and Performance Quarterly*, 11 (1), 1–17.

Katz, Elihu (1957), "The Two-Step Flow of Communication: An Up-To-Date Report on an Hypothesis," *Public Opinion Quarterly*, 21 (1), 61–78.

Kautz, Henry, Bart Selman, and Mehul Shah (1997), "Referral Web: Combining Social Networks and Collaborative Filtering," *Communications of the ACM*, 40 (3), 63–5.

Keen, Andrew (2008), *The Cult of the Amateur*, New York: Random House.

Kingston, Paul W. (2001), "The Unfulfilled Promise of Cultural Capital Theory," *Sociology of Education*, 74, 88–99.

Kornish, Laura J. (2009), "Are User Reviews Systematically Manipulated? Evidence from the Helpfulness Ratings," Leeds School of Business Working Paper, University of Colorado.

Kossmeier, Stephan, Dan Ariely, and Anat Bracha (2009), "Doing Good or Doing Well? Image Motivation and Monetary Incentives in Behaving Prosocially," *American Economic Review*, 99 (1), 544–55.

Kozinets, Robert V. (2007), "Netnography 2.0," in Russell W. Belk (ed.), *Handbook of Qualitative Research Methods in Marketing*, Cheltenham, UK and Northampton, MA, USA: Edward Elgar Publishing, pp. 129–42.

Kozinets, Robert V. (2009), *Netnography: Doing Ethnographic Research Online*, Thousand Oaks, CA: Sage.

Kozinets, Robert V., Kristine de Valck, Andrea C. Wojnicki, and Sarah J.S. Wilner (2010), "Networked Narratives: Understanding

Word-of-Mouth Marketing in Online Communities," *Journal of Marketing*, 74 (March), 71–89.

Kretz, Gachoucha and Kristine de Valck (2010), "Pixelize Me! Creating Online Identities on Fashion Blogs through Explicit and Implicit Brand Association," *Research in Consumer Behavior*, 12, 313–29.

Krippendorf, Klaus (2004), "Reliability in Content Analysis: Some Common Misconceptions and Recommendations," *Human Communication Research*, 30 (3), 411–33.

Lakoff, George and Mark Johnson (2008), *Metaphors We Live By*, Chicago, IL: University of Chicago Press.

Lamont, Michèle (1992), *Money, Morals, and Manners: The Culture of the French and American Upper-Middle Class*, Chicago, IL: University of Chicago Press.

Lamont, Michele (2010), "Looking Back at Bourdieu," in Elizabeth Silva and Alan Warde (eds), *Cultural Analysis and Bourdieu's Legacy*, London: Routledge, pp. 128–41.

Lamont, Michele and Annette Lareau (1988), "Cultural Capital: Allusions, Gaps and Glissandos in Recent Theoretical Developments," *Sociological Theory* 6 (2), 153–68.

Lampel, Joseph and Ajay Bhalla (2007), "The Role of Status-Seeking in Online Communities: Giving the Gift of Experience," *Journal of Computer-Mediated Communication*, 12, 434–55.

Lander, Christian (2008), *Stuff White People Like*, New York: Random House.

Landes, David S. (1999), *The Wealth and Poverty of Nations*, New York: W.W. Norton.

Lanham, Richard A. (2006a), *The Economics of Attention*, Chicago, IL: University of Chicago Press.

Lanham, Richard A. (2006b), *The Longman Guide to Revising Prose*, New York: Pearson.

Levitt, Steven D. and Stephen J. Dubner (2011), *Freakonomics: A Rogue Economist Explores the Hidden Side of Everything*, New York: Harper Collins.

Lizardo, Omar (2006), "How Cultural Tastes Shape Personal Networks," *American Sociological Review*, 71 (5), 778–807.

Lovink, Geert (2008), *Zero Comments: Blogging and Critical Internet Culture*, New York: Taylor & Francis.

Luca, Michael and Georgios Zervas (2013), "Fake It Till You Make It: Reputation, Competition, and Yelp Review Fraud," Harvard Business School NOM Unit Working Paper 14-006.

Lynes, Russell (1980 [1955]), *The Tastemakers: The Shaping of American Popular Taste*, New York: Dover Publications.

Maclaran, Pauline, Margaret K. Hogg, Miriam Catterall, and Robert V. Kozinets (2004), "Gender, Technology and Computer-Mediated Communications in Consumption-Related Online Communities," in Karin M. Ekstrom and Helene Brembeck (eds), *Elusive Consumption*, Oxford: Berg, pp. 145–71.

Marchand, Roland (1985), *Advertising and the American Dream: Making Way for Modernity, 1920–1940*, Los Angeles, CA: University of California Press.

Mathwick, Charla, Caroline Wiertz, and Ko de Ruyter (2007), "Social Capital Production in a P3 Community," *Journal of Consumer Research*, 34 (April), 833–49.

Mayzlin, Dina, Yaniv Dover, and Judith Chevalier (2012), "Promotional Reviews: An Empirical Investigation of Online Review Manipulation," National Bureau of Economic Research.

McAlexander, James H., Beath Leavenworth Dufault, Diane M. Martin, and John W. Schouten (2014), "The Marketization of Religion: Field, Capital, and Consumer Identity," *Journal of Consumer Research*, 41 (October), 858–75.

McCloskey, Deidre N. (2010), *Bourgeois Dignity: Why Economics Can't Explain the Modern World*, Chicago, IL: University of Chicago Press.

McCracken, Grant (1986), "Culture and Consumption: A Theoretical Account of the Structure and Movement of the Cultural Meaning of Consumer Goods," *Journal of Consumer Research*, 13 (June), 71–84.

McGonigal, Jane (2011), *Reality Is Broken: Why Games Make Us Better and How They Can Change the World*, New York: Penguin.

McQuaid, John (2015), *Tasty: The Art and Science of What We Eat*, New York: Scribner.

McQuarrie, Edward F. (2004), "Integration of Construct and External Validity by Means of Proximal Similarity: Implications for Laboratory Experiments in Marketing," *Journal of Business Research*, 57 (2), 142–53.

McQuarrie, Edward F. (2014), "Threats to the Scientific Status of Experimental Consumer Psychology: A Darwinian Perspective," *Marketing Theory*, 14 (4), 477–94.

McQuarrie, Edward F. and David Glen Mick (1996), "Figures of Rhetoric in Advertising Language," *Journal of Consumer Research*, 22 (March), 424–38.

McQuarrie, Edward F., Jessica Miller, and Barbara J. Phillips (2013), "The Megaphone Effect: Taste and Audience in Fashion Blogging," *Journal of Consumer Research*, 40 (June), 136–58.

Mokyr, Joel (2009), *The Enlightened Economy*, New Haven, CT: Yale University Press.

Moon, Jae Yun and Lee S. Sproull (2008), "The Role of Feedback in Managing the Internet-Based Volunteer Workforce," *Information Systems Research*, 19 (4), 494–515.

Moorman, Christine, Rohit Deshpande, and Gerald Zaltman (1993), "Factors Affecting Trust in Market Research Relationships," *Journal of Marketing*, 57 (1), 81–101.

Morozov, Evgeny (2012), *The Net Delusion: The Dark Side of Internet Freedom*, New York: PublicAffairs Store.

Morris, Ian (2010), *Why the West Rules—for Now*, New York: Farrar, Straus & Giroux.

Muchnik, Lev, Sinan Aral, and Sean J. Taylor (2013), "Social Influence Bias: A Randomized Experiment," *Science*, 341 (6146), 647–51.

Muller, Jerzy C. (2007), *The Mind and the Market: Capitalism in Western Thought*, New York: Knopf Doubleday.

Muniz, Albert M., Jr and Thomas C. O'Guinn (2001), "Brand Community," *Journal of Consumer Research*, 27 (March), 412–32.

Nelson, P. (1970), 'Information and Consumer Behavior', *Journal of Political Economy*, 78 (2), 311–29.

Nicosia, Francesco M. and Robert N. Mayer (1976), "Toward a Sociology of Consumption," *Journal of Consumer Research*, 3 (September), 65–75.

Nisbet, Robert A. (1966), *The Sociological Tradition*, New York: Basic Books.

Ohanian, Roobina (1990), "Construction and Validation of a Scale to Measure Celebrity Endorsers' Perceived Expertise, Trustworthiness, and Attractiveness," *Journal of Advertising*, 19 (3), 39–52.

Pan, Yue and Jason Q. Zhang (2011), "Born Unequal: A Study of the Helpfulness of User-Generated Product Reviews," *Journal of Retailing*, 87 (4), 598–612.

Parmentier, Marie-Agnès and Eileen Fischer (2011), "You Can't Always Get What You Want: Unsustainable Identity Projects in The Fashion System," *Consumption Markets and Culture*, 14 (1), 7–27.

Pham, Minh-Ha (2011), "Blog Ambition: Fashion, Feelings, and the Political Economy of the Digital Raced Body," *Camera Obscura*, 26 (1), 1–37.

Phillips, Barbara J. and Edward F. McQuarrie (2010), "Narrative and Persuasion in Fashion Advertising," *Journal of Consumer Research*, 37 (3), 368–92.

Phillips, Barbara J., Jessica Miller, and Edward F. McQuarrie (2014), "Dreaming Out Loud on Pinterest: New Forms of Indirect Persuasion," *International Journal of Advertising*, 33 (4), 633–55.

Pinker, Steven (2014), *The Sense of Style*, New York: Viking.

Pollay, Richard W. (1985), "The Subsidizing Sizzle: A Descriptive History of Print Advertising, 1900–1980," *Journal of Marketing*, 48 (Summer), 24–37.

Powell, Walter W. and Paul J. DiMaggio (2012), *The New Institutionalism in Organizational Analysis*, Chicago, IL: University of Chicago Press.

Putnam, Robert D. (1995), "Tuning In, Tuning Out: The Strange Disappearance of Social Capital in America," *Political Science and Politics*, 28 (4), 664–84.

Ratchford, Brian T. (2001), "The Economics of Consumer Knowledge," *Journal of Consumer Research*, 27 (4), 397–411.

Reckwitz, Andreas (2002), "Toward a Theory of Social Practices: A Development in Culturalist Theorizing," *European Journal of Social Theory*, 5 (2), 243–63.

Reed, Adam (2009), "My Blog is Me: Texts and Persons in UK Online Journal Culture (and Anthropology)," *Ethnos*, 70 (2), 220–42.

Reed-Danahay, Deborah (2005), *Locating Bourdieu*, Bloomington, IN: Indiana University Press.

Rheingold, Howard (2000), *The Virtual Community: Homesteading on the Electronic Frontier*, Cambridge, MA: MIT Press.

Ritzer, George and Nathan Jurgenson (2010), "Production, Consumption, Prosumption," *Journal of Consumer Culture*, 10 (1), 13–36.

Rocamora, Agnes (2002), "Fields of Fashion: Critical Insights into Bourdieu's Sociology of Culture," *Journal of Consumer Culture*, 2 (3), 341–62.

Rose, Randall L. and Stacy L. Wood (2005), "Paradox and the Consumption of Authenticity through Reality Television," *Journal of Consumer Research*, 32 (September), 284–96.

Rosman, Katherine (2009), "Fashion's Secret Helpers," *Wall Street Journal*, September 11.

Rousseau, Denise M., Sim B. Sitkin, Ronald S. Burt, and Colin Camerer (1998), "Not So Different After All: A Cross-Discipline View of Trust," *Academy of Management Review*, 23 (3), 393–404.

Sacks, Harvey (1998), *Social Science and Conversation Analysis*, New York: Oxford University Press.

Sandel, Michael J. (2012), *What Money Can't Buy: The Moral Limits of Markets*, New York: Macmillan.

Scaraboto, Daiane and Eileen Fischer (2013), "Frustrated Fatshionistas: An Institutional Theory Perspective on Consumer Quests for Greater Choice in Mainstream Markets," *Journal of Consumer Research*, 39 (6), 1234–57.

Schatzki, Theodore R. (1996), *Social Practices: A Wittgensteinian Approach to Human Activity and the Social*, Cambridge: Cambridge University Press.

Schau, Hope Jensen and Mary Gilly (2003), "We Are What We Post? Self-Presentation in Personal Web Space," *Journal of Consumer Research*, 30 (December), 385–404.

Schau, Hope, Albert M. Muniz, Jr., and Eric J. Arnould (2009), "How Brand Community Practices Create Value," *Journal of Marketing*, 73 (September), 30–51.

Schouten, John W. and James H. McAlexander (1995), "Subcultures of Consumption: An Ethnography of the New Bikers," *Journal of Consumer Research*, 22 (June), 43–61.

Schroeder, Jonathan E. (2002), *Visual Consumption*, London: Routledge.

Scott, Linda M. (1994), "Image in Advertising: The Need for a Theory of Visual Rhetoric," *Journal of Consumer Research*, 21 (September), 252–73.

Sewell, William H. (2005), *Logics of History: Social Theory and Social Transformation*, Chicago, IL: University of Chicago Press.

Shankar, Avi, Helene Cherrier, and Robin Canniford (2006), "Consumer Empowerment: A Foucauldian Interpretation," *European Journal of Marketing*, 40 (9–10), 1013–30.

Shannon, Claude E. and Warren Weaver (1949), *The Mathematical Theory of Communication*, Urbana, IL: University of Illinois Press.

Shapin, Steven (1996), *The Scientific Revolution*, Chicago, IL: University of Chicago Press.

Silva, Elizabeth and Alan Warde (2010), *Cultural Analysis and Bourdieu's Legacy: Settling Accounts and Developing Alternatives*, London: Routledge.

Simmel, Georg (1957 [1904]), "Fashion," *American Journal of Sociology*, 62 (May), 541–58.

Simonson, Itamar and Emanuel Rosen (2014), *Absolute Value: What Really Influences Customers in the Age of (Nearly) Perfect Information*, New York: Harper Collins.

Stiglitz, Joseph E. (2002), "Information and the Change in the Paradigm in Economics," *American Economic Review*, 92 (June), 460–501.

Stove, David (2001), *Scientific Irrationalism: Origins of a Postmodern Cult*, London: Transaction Publishers.

Surowiecki, James (2004), *The Wisdom of Crowds*, Boston, MA: Little, Brown.

Swartz, David (1997), *Culture and Power: The Sociology of Pierre Bourdieu*, Chicago, IL: University of Chicago Press.

Sword, Helen (2012), *Stylish Academic Writing*, Cambridge, MA: Harvard University Press.

Tapscott, Don and Anthony D. Williams (2008), *Wikinomics: How Mass Collaboration Changes Everything*, New York: Penguin.

Thomas, Francis-Noël and Mark Turner (2011), *Clear and Simple as the Truth: Writing Classic Prose*, Princeton, NJ: Princeton University Press.

Thompson, Craig J. (2014), "The Politics of Consumer Identity Work," *Journal of Consumer Research*, 40 (5), iii–vii.

Thornton, Patricia H. (2002), "The Rise of the Corporation in a Craft Industry: Conflict and Conformity in Institutional Logics," *Academy of Management Journal*, 45 (February), 81–101.

Thornton, Sarah (1996), *Club Cultures: Music, Media, and Subcultural Capital*, Middletown, CT: Wesleyan University Press.

Tucker, Susan, Katherine Ott, and Patricia P. Buckler (2006), "An Introduction to the History of Scrapbooks," in Susan Tucker, Katherine Ott, and Patricia P. Buckler (eds), *The Scrapbook in American Life*, Philadelphia, PA: Temple University Press, pp. 1–25.

Turner, Graeme (2010), *Ordinary People and the Media: The Demotic Turn*, Los Angeles, CA: Sage.

Unger, Roberto M. and Lee Smolin (2015), *The Singular Universe and the Reality of Time*, Cambridge: Cambridge University Press.

Üstüner, Tuba and Douglas B. Holt (2010), "Toward a Theory of Status Consumption in Less Industrialized Countries," *Journal of Consumer Research*, 37 (1), 37–56.

Van Dijck, Jose (2009), "Users Like You? Theorizing Agency in User-Generated Content," *Media, Culture and Society*, 31, 41–59.

Wang, Zhongmin (2010), "Anonymity, Social Image, and the Competition for Volunteers: A Case Study of the Online Market for Reviews," *The B.E. Journal of Economic Analysis and Policy*, 10 (1), 1–33.

Warde, Alan (1997), *Consumption, Food and Taste*, London: Sage Publications.

Warde, Alan (2005), "Consumption and Theories of Practice," *Journal of Consumer Culture*, 5 (2), 131–53.

Warner, Michael (2002), "Publics and Counterpublics," *Public Culture*, 14 (1), 49–90.

Weick, Karl F. (1995), *Sensemaking in Organizations*, Thousand Oaks, CA: Sage.

Wickham, Chris (2005), *Framing the Early Middle Ages: Europe and the Mediterranean, 400–800*, New York: Oxford University Press.

Williams, Joseph M. (1990), *Style: Toward Clarity and Grace*, Chicago, IL: University of Chicago Press.

Williamson, Oliver E. (2005), *Transaction Cost Economics*, New York: Springer.

Wilson, Andrew E. and Peter R. Darke (2012), "The Optimistic Trust Effect: Use of Belief in a Just World to Cope with Decision-Generated Threat," *Journal of Consumer Research*, 39 (October), 615–29.

Zwass, Vladimir (2010), "Co-Creation: Toward a Taxonomy and an Integrated Research Perspective," *International Journal of Electronic Commerce*, 15 (1), 11–48.

Zwick, Detlev, Samuel K. Bonsu, and Aron Darmody (2008), "Putting Consumers to Work: 'Co-creation' and New Marketing Governmentality," *Journal of Consumer Culture*, 8 (2), 163–96.

Author's note

A conventional author biography spins a tale of personal history: schools attended, jobs held, honors accorded. You can find those facts by googling my name preceded by "vita." Or you can look at my profile on scholar. google.com or researchgate.net. Here, I thought it would be more useful to offer a genealogy and a sociography—information you may not get by searching the Web, but which might help you to assess my biases.

Genealogically, my father's paternal line comes from Ulva, off the island of Mull, on the west coast of Scotland; Dalriata raiders, and later, wretches driven off during the Highland Clearances, one of whom made it to Prince Edward Island, whence his grandson, my grandfather, came to Massachusetts. My father's maternal line comes from the southwest of Ireland: potato famine immigrants, Harringtons and Sullivans, who made it to Lowell.

My mother's family comes from Quebec, Three Rivers on the one side, LaPrairie on the other, with surnames like Latour and Daniau. Great-grandparents moved to New England to work in the mills, after 1870. On my mother's side, I'm ultimately from La Rochelle and Normandy in France, scion of Carignan soldiers and *filles du roi*, crossed with the occasional Huguenot.

Sociologically, I'm a first-born, an only son with three younger sisters. I grew up in Chelmsford, Massachusetts, a bedroom suburb of Lowell, that ancient mill town, and of Boston, on the next freeway ring outside of Route 128. Father served in the navy in World War II, and a brother, my namesake, was killed in France in 1945. After the war my father worked as a clerk in a General Electric wire and cable factory for three decades, starting on the factory floor; my mother was a homemaker, having first worked as a legal secretary. Both graduated from high school. Father's father was a house painter, Mother's father was a carpenter. Devout Catholics both, Father had four and Mother nine siblings. They married late for their generation, at 29 and 26. Great-grandparents owned their homes and a rental property or two, and grandparents held their homes through the Depression; my parents owned their home from before I was born, with help from their parents. I attended public schools in Chelmsford, graduating high school in 1971.

That should be enough to locate me, sociologically and historically.

Index